THE COMPLETE INSTANT POT DUO CRISP AIR FRYER COOKBOOK:

550 INCREDIBLE, DELICIOUS, HEALTHY AND FAST MOUTHWATERING RECIPES FOR SMART PEOPLE TO ROAST, BAKE, BROIL AND DEHYDRATE

Patrick C. Cooper

Table of Contents

BOOK DESCRIPTION   13

INTRODUCTION   14

CHAPTER 1: INTRODUCTION TO INSTANT POT DUO AIR FRYER CRISP   15

What is the Instant Pot Duo Crisp air fryer? 15
Benefits of Instant Pot Duo Crisp air fryer   15
- *One-pot cooking   15*
- *Ten functions in one   15*
- *Energy and Time Efficient   15*
- *Changing Lids   16*
- *User-Friendly   16*

Functions of Instant Pot Duo Crisp air fryer   16
- *Air Fry   16*
- *Bake   16*
- *Broil   16*
- *Roast   16*
- *Dehydrate   16*
- *Pressure   17*
- *Sauté   17*
- *Sous Vide   17*
- *Steam   17*
- *Keep Warm   17*

CHAPTER 2: BREAKFAST RECIPES   18

- Breakfast Tarts   18
- Baked Eggs   18
- Tomato Pepper Frittata   19
- Tropical Oatmeal   19
- Simple & Easy Breakfast Casserole   20
- Creamy Mac n Cheese   20
- Cherry Risotto   21
- Almond Coconut Risotto   21
- Mushroom Frittata   22
- Morning Churros   22
- Sweet Cherry Chocolate Oat   23
- Farro Breakfast Risotto   24
- Cajun Chicken   24
- Tasty Chicken Tenders   25
- Potato Fish Cakes   25
- Baked Cod Fillet   26
- Flavorful Chicken Skewers   26
- Air-Fried Cinnamon & Sugar Doughnuts   27
- Bok Choy And Spinach   28
- Healthy Air Fryer Granola   28
- Keto Ribs   29
- Mini Frittata   29
- Healthy Breakfast Bake   30
- Spinach Frittata   30

Tomato Mozzarella Quiche 31
Creamy Spinach Spread 32
Eggplant and Spinach Frittata 32
Zucchini and Artichokes Mix 32
Air Fryer Breakfast Frittata 33
Spinach Muffins 33
Ham Egg Muffins 34
Creamy Chicken 35
Oatmeal Cups 35
Cheesy Egg Cup 36
Healthy Apple Oatmeal Cups 36
Tarragon and Parmesan Scramble 37
Loaded Cauliflower Bake 37
Egg Frittata 38
Tuna and Spring Onions Salad 38
Cheesy Sausage Balls 39
Hard-Boiled Eggs 39
Stuffed Poblanos 39
Air-fried Shrimps with Lemon 40
Coconut Lime Breakfast Quinoa 40
Banana Buckwheat Porridge 41
Cauliflower Casserole 41
Herbed Eggs 41
Spinach and Eggs 42
Lemon Butter Brussels sprouts 42
Creamy Cauliflower Mashed 43
Spicy Cabbage 43
Bell pepper eggs 44
Banana Oatmeal 44
Quick & Easy Farro 45
Air-fried Crumbed Fish 45
Yogurt Omelet 45
Lemony Raspberries Bowls 46
Spaghetti Squash Fritters 46
Zucchini Fritters 47
Easy Lemon Garlic Chicken Breast 47
Coconut Blueberry Oatmeal 47
Pumpkin Cranberry Oatmeal 48
Cranberry Farro 48
Rice Lentil Porridge 49
Easy Cheese Bake 49
Healthy Kale Muffins 50
Breakfast Muffins 50
Zucchini Yogurt Bread 51
Saucy Eggs Bake 51

CHAPTER 3: FISH AND SEAFOOD RECIPES 53

Spicy Prawns 53
Simple & Perfect Salmon 53
Healthy Salmon Chowder 54
Pesto Shrimp 54
White Fish with Cilantro Sauce 55
Sole with Mint and Ginger 55
Creamy Parmesan Shrimp 56
Delicious Garlic Butter Salmon 56
Shrimp Mac n Cheese 57

Salmon Rice Pilaf	57
Perfect Salmon Dinner	58
Steam Clams	58
Delicious Tilapia	59
Horseradish Salmon	59
Shrimp Scampi	60
Dijon Fish Fillets	60
Bacon-Wrapped Shrimp	61
Garlic Parmesan Shrimp	61
Bang Bang Breaded Shrimp	62
Taco Fried Shrimp	62
Asparagus Shrimp Risotto	63
Parmesan Shrimp Risotto	63
Asian Pineapple Shrimp	64
Shrimp Macaroni	65
Coconut Chili Shrimp	65
Lemon Crab Patties	66
Basil Tilapia	66
Delicious Shrimp Risotto	67
Cajun shrimp	68
Quick & easy shrimp	68
Lemon Dill Tuna Patties	68
Tasty Spicy Shrimp	69
Healthy Salmon Patties	69
Lemon Garlicky Shrimp	70
Air Fried Shrimp	70
Parmesan Salmon	71
Delicious Pesto Salmon	72
Shrimp in Lemon Sauce	72
Crisp & Delicious Catfish	73
Easy Paprika Salmon	73
Healthy Catfish	74
Asian Shrimp	74
Sriracha Honey Salmon	75
Bacon Shrimps	75
Ranch Fish Fillets	76
Air Fried, Instant Pot Homemade Tuna Patties	76
Delicious Cod Nuggets	77
Balsamic Salmon	78
Garlic Shrimp	78
Tuna Noodles	79
Shrimp Scampi	79
Lemon Butter Salmon	80
Cheese Crust Salmon	80
Healthy Crab Cakes	81
Coconut Shrimp	82
Easy Garlic Lemon Shrimp	82
Cheesy Tilapia	83
Scallops Curry	83
Healthy Shrimp Boil	83
Horseradish Crusted Salmon	84
Pesto Shrimp Kebobs	84
Mahi Mahi Fillets	85
Garlic Mussels	85
Mussels with Saffron Sauce	86
Cajun Shrimp Bake	86

Shrimp with Garlic Sauce 87
Garlic Shrimp Skewers 87
Prawn Burgers 88
Old Bay Seasoned Haddock 88
Garlic Butter Shrimp 89
Crispy Crust Shrimp 89
Crispy Coconut Shrimp 90
Healthy Shrimp Pasta 91
Cajuned Salmon Meal 91
Crispy Crust Ranch Fish Fillets 92
Steam Shrimp 92
Lemon Garlic Shrimp 93
Delicious Shrimp Paella 93
Crispy Coconut Shrimp 94
Cheesy Shrimp Grits 95
Curried Salmon Patties 95
Fish Finger Sandwich in Instant Pot Air Fryer 96
Shrimp Parmesan Bake 96
Honey Mustard Salmon 97
Bacon-Wrapped Shrimp 97
Horseradish Crusted Salmon 98

CHAPTER 4: SIDES AND APPETIZER RECIPES 99

Brussels Sprouts 99
Onion Dip 99
Pineapple Bites with Yogurt Dip 100
Bok Choy And Butter Sauce 100
Chili Dip 100
Goat Cheese Cauliflower 101
Dill Red Cabbage 101
Kale and Walnuts 102
Pesto Zucchini Pasta 102
Kale and Cauliflower Mash 102
Zucchini Spaghetti 103
Jalapeno Hummus 103
Flavorful Salsa 103
Cheddar Cheese Dip 104
Creamy Eggplant Dip 104
Instant Pot Salsa 105
Tomatillo Salsa 106
Lamb Jerky 106
Buffalo Chicken Dip 107
Jalapeno Chicken Dip 107
Cauliflower Chicken Dip 108
Ranch Mushrooms 108
Teriyaki Beef Jerky 109
Zucchinis and Walnuts 110
Coriander Artichokes 110
Tasty Eggplant Slices 110
Baba Ghanoush 111
Healthy Beet Hummus 111
Chicken Jalapeno Popper Dip 112
Broccoli and Cauliflower 112
Buffalo Cauliflower 113
Roasted Eggplant 113
Spinach Dip 113

Zucchini Gratin   114
Spiced Cauliflower   114
Roasted Tomatoes   115
Roasted Red Pepper Hummus   115
Spicy Spinach Dip   116
Roasted fennel   116
Balsamic Asparagus   117
Avocado Fries   117
Radishes and Sesame Seeds   117
Herbed Radish Sauté   118
Cream Cheese Zucchini   118
Sausage Mushroom Caps   119
Minty Summer Squash   119

CHAPTER 5: POULTRY RECIPES   120

Chicken Casserole   120
Ranch Chicken Wings   121
Roasted Chicken   121
Chicken Rice   122
Yummy Hawaiian Chicken   122
Spicy Chicken Wings   123
Paprika Chicken   124
Easy Cheesy Chicken   124
Creamy Italian Chicken   125
Paprika Chicken   125
Chicken Fajitas   125
Jamaican Chicken   126
Flavorful Lemon Chicken   126
Dijon Chicken   127
Mango Chicken   127
Honey Cashew Butter Chicken   127
Sweet & Tangy Tamarind Chicken   128
Garlic Lemon Chicken   128
Flavorful Herb Chicken   129
Asian Style Chicken Meal   130
Korean chicken wings   130
Mustard Chicken   131
BBQ Chicken Wings   131
Lemon Chicken Potatoes   132
Boneless Air Fryer Turkey Breasts   133
Spicy Chicken Breast   133
Tasty Butter Chicken   134
Easy Cheesy Chicken   134
Turkey Legs   135
Asian Wings   136
Crispy Crust Whole Chicken   136
Tasty Butter Chicken   137
Chicken Pasta   137
Cheesy Chicken Wings   138
Creamy Italian Chicken   139
Air Fryer Spicy Chicken Thighs   139
Garlic Ranch Chicken Wings   140
Classic Honey Mustard Chicken   140
Parmesan Chicken Wings   141
Barbecue Air Fried Chicken   142
Balsamic Chicken   142

Italian Chicken Wings 143
Herbed Turkey Dinner 143
Garlic Lemon Chicken 144
Flavorful Herb Chicken 144
Broccoli Chicken Casserole 145
Chicken Tikka Kebab 146
Chicken Fritters 147
Chicken Kabab 147
Air Fryer Garlic Herb Turkey Breast 148
Spicy Chicken Breast 148
Zucchini Tomato Chicken 149
Garlicky Chicken 149
Spicy Chicken Wings 150
Cheesy Chicken Wings 150
Chicken Vegetable Fajitas 151
Fennel Chicken 152
Chicken Mac and Cheese 152
Broccoli Chicken Casserole 153

CHAPTER 6: SOUPS AND STEWS 155

No Bean Beef Chili 155
Vegan Cauliflower Soup 155
Flavors Squash Soup 156
Garlic Carrot Soup 157
Thyme Carrot Cauliflower Soup 158
Summer Vegetable Soup 159
Flavorful Fish Stew 159
Buffalo Chicken Soup 160
Creamy & Tasty Chicken Soup 161
Lamb Stew 162
Creamy Cauliflower Soup 162
Chicken Broccoli Soup 163
Broccoli Asparagus Soup 163
Easy Chicken Soup 164
Tasty Mexican Chicken Soup 165
Curried Chicken Soup 165
Lemon Asparagus Soup 166
Creamy Sweet Potato Soup 167
Spinach Soup 168
Creamy Corn Soup 168
Flavorful Mushroom Soup 169
Curried Squash Soup 170
Creamy Peanut Butter Carrot Soup 171
Tasty Tomato Soup 172
Lentil Carrot Soup 173

CHAPTER 7: MEAT RECIPES 174

Roast Beef 174
Steak Tips with Potatoes 174
Asian Beef Broccoli 175
Simple Steak 175
Garlic-Cumin and Orange Juice Marinated Steak 176
Bacon Wrapped Hot Dog. 176
Beef and Broccoli Stir-Fry 176
Lamb Loin and Tomato Vinaigrette 177
Beef Taco Fried Egg Rolls 177

Air Fryer Meatloaf 178
Baked Carrot Beef 179
Smoky Steak 179
Herb Garlic Lamb Chops 180
Delicious Lamb Chops 180
Garlic Roasted Pork Tenderloin 181
Crispy Breaded Pork Chops in the Air Fryer 181
Easy Air Fryer Pork Chops 182
Rogan Josh 183
Cheesy Lamb Chops 183
Garlicky Lamb 184
Pork Tenderloin in the Air Fryer 184
Air-fried Garlic-rosemary Lamb Chops 185
Rosemary Lamb Chops 185
Greek Lamb Chops 186
Herb Butter Lamb Chops 186
Asian Lamb Curry 187
Indian Lamb Curry 187
Pulled Pork 188
Swedish Meatballs 188
Air Fryer Pork Chops 189
Rice and Meatball Stuffed Bell Peppers 190
Pub Style Corned Beef Egg Rolls 190
Lamb and Pine Nuts Meatballs 191
Air Fryer Roast Beef 191
Smoked Lamb Chops 192
Spicy Beef 192
Adobo Beef 192
Pork Chop Salad 193
Fajita Flank Steak Rolls 193
Moroccan Lamb 194
Cuban Pork 194
Pork Tenderloin 195
Beef with Beans 195
Easy Pork Roast 196
Ranch Pork Chops 197
Pork Carnitas 197
Pulled Pork 198
Pork Patties 198
Herb Pork Tenderloin 199
Teriyaki Pork 199
Easy & Tasty Ribs 200
Air Fryer Steak 200
Parmesan Pork Chops 201
Crisp & Tasty Pork Chops 202
Italian Meatloaf Sliders 202
Zaatar Lamb Chops 203
Tasty Southern Pork Chops 203
Taco Meatballs 204
Tasty & Spicy Lamb 205
Lamb Shanks 205
Tasty Air Fried Pork Chops 206
Lemon Mustard Lamb Chops 206
Pork with Cabbage 207
Salsa Pork 207
Pork Fajitas 208

Beef Pork Meatballs 208
Lamb Meatballs 209
Greek Meatballs 209
Garlicky Lamb Chops 210
Mushrooms & Steak Bites 210
Air Fryer Beef with Homemade Marinade 211
Bourbon Bacon Burger in The Air Fryer 212
Crispy Air Fryer Bacon 213
Beef Pie 213
Air Fried Herb Rack of Lamb 214
Pork Chops with Asparagus 214
Tasty Lamb Chops 215
Delicious Fajitas 216
Juicy Steak 216
Mustard Pork Chops 217
Easy Pork Chops 217
Pork Roast 218
Coconut and Chili Pork 218
Herbed Lamb Rack 218
Baked Carrot Beef 219
Juicy & Crispy Meatballs 219
BBQ Meatballs 220
Lamb Roast 221
Air Fried Spicy Lamb Sirloin Steak 221
Beef & Lemon Schnitzel for One 222
Crispy Beef Schnitzel 222
Simple Burger Patties 222
Herbed Vegetable Beef 223
Russian Beef Bake 223
Beef Pie 224

CHAPTER 8: VEGETABLE RECIPES 226

Tofu with Capers 226
Hasselback Potatoes 227
Zucchini Fritters 227
Haloumi Baked Rusti 228
Roasted Broccoli 228
Garlic Lemon Green Beans 229
Spicy Beans 230
Delicious Pigeon Pea 230
Tofu in Sweet & Sour Sauce 231
Pineapple Salsa 231
Italian Seasoned Cauliflower 232
Flavorful Mushroom Rice 232
Pumpkin Lasagna 233
Haloumi Baked Rusti 234
Wheat Berry Pilaf 235
Spicy Tomato Chutney 235
Simple Green Beans 236
Kale and Mushrooms 236
Parmesan Broccoli and Asparagus 236
Beans & Veggie Burgers 237
Marinated Tofu 237
Crusted Tofu 238
Turmeric Cabbage 238
Flavors Eggplant 238

- Air-fried Avocado 239
- Mediterranean Veggies 240
- Air Fried Bell Peppers 240
- Tasty Cauliflower & Broccoli 241
- Brussels Pancetta Pizza 241
- Cheesy Brussels Sprouts 242
- Veggie Kabobs 242
- Roasted Squash 243
- Air Fried Ratatouille 244
- Asian Cauliflower 244
- Veggie Ratatouille 245
- Glazed Veggies 245
- Parmesan Mixed Veggies 246
- Roasted Beans 247
- Parmesan Zucchini & Eggplant 247
- Roasted Carrots & Potatoes 247
- Air Fried Mushrooms 248
- Indian Potato Curry 248
- Veggie Quinoa 249
- Healthy Quinoa Black Bean Chili 250
- Garlic Basil Carrots 250
- Toasted Coco Flakes 251
- Celeriac Potato Gratin 251
- Eggplant Pine Nut Roast 252
- Roasted Veggie Casserole 253

CHAPTER 9: DEHYDRATOR AND CASSEROLE RECIPES 253

- Eggplant Jerky 253
- Dehydrated Pear Slices 254
- Sausage Casserole 254
- Squash Casserole 255
- Apple Chips 256
- Apple Sweet Potato Fruit Leather 256
- Dehydrated Mango 257
- Sausage Zucchini Casserole 257
- Broccoli Rice Casserole 258
- Cheesy Mashed Potato Casserole 258
- Corn Gratin 259
- Flavors Crab Casserole 259
- Broccoli Chicken Casserole 260
- Asian Mushroom Jerky 260
- Banana Fruit Leather 261
- Cauliflower Casserole 261
- Buffalo Chicken Casserole 262
- Turkey Stroganoff 262
- Parmesan Zucchini Chips 263
- Peanut Butter Banana Chips 263
- Corn Chips 264
- Strawberry Mango Fruit Leather 264
- Noodle Ham Casserole 265
- Banana Chocolate Fruit Leather 265
- Spicy Chickpeas 266
- Delicious Nacho Zucchini Chips 266
- Banana Peanut Butter Roll 267
- Pumpkin Fruit Leather 267
- Dried Lemon Slices 268

- Banana Jerky 268
- Parsnips Chips 269
- Cauliflower Popcorn 269
- Spaghetti Casserole 270
- Tater Tot Casserole 270
- Dehydrated Okra 271
- Cucumber Chips 271

CHAPTER 10: SNACKS AND DESSERTS 273

- Cheese Zucchini Bites 273
- Potato Chips 273
- Tortilla Chips 274
- Beet chips 274
- Avocado Fries 274
- Onion Rings 275
- Chocolate Smarties Cookies 275
- Strawberry Cupcakes 276
- Lava Cakes 277
- Chocolate Strawberry Cups 277
- Sweet Potato Tots 278
- Corn Nuts 278
- Chocolate Souffle 279
- Lemon Muffins 279
- Corn on The Cob 280
- Stuffed Bell Peppers 280
- Healthy Steamed Vegetables 281
- Simple Pepper & Salt Baby Potatoes 281
- Mini Coffee Cake 282
- Strawberry Muffins 282
- Banana Muffins 283
- Peanut Butter Muffins 284
- Parmesan Carrot Fries 284
- Tater Tots 285
- Air Fried Cauliflower Bites 285
- Potato Wedges 286
- Ranch Chickpeas 286
- Crunchy Zucchini Chips 287
- Cauliflower Fritters 287
- Cinnamon Fried Bananas 288
- Cinnamon Bread Pudding 288
- Cranberry Coconut Pudding 289
- Raspberry Cake 290
- Coconutty Lemon Bars 290
- Instant Pot Duo Crisp Crisp-Fried Cheeseburgers 291
- Cream Cheese and Zucchinis Bars 291
- Air Fried Zucchini Fried 292
- Apple Chips in Instant Pot Air Fryer 292
- Beef Olive Balls 293
- Yummy Broccoli Popcorn 293
- Avocado Fries 294
- Strawberry Cupcakes 294
- Coconut bars 295
- Air-fried Kale Chips 295
- Instant Pot Duo Crisp - Crisp Air-Fried Pickles 296
- Broccoli Tots 296
- Air Fried Bananas 297

Curried Fries 297
Easy Salmon Bites 298
Blueberry Cream 298
Coconut Donuts 299
Cocoa and Nuts Bombs 299
Vanilla Pumpkin Pudding 299
Chocolate Rice Pudding 300
Choco Fudge 301
Delicious Lime Pudding 301
Buckwheat Cobbler 302
Baked Plums 302
Crispy Potatoes in Instant Pot Duo Crisp+ Crisp Air Fryer 303
Dill Pickle Fries 303
Broccoli Nuggets 304
Simple Shrimp Kabobs 304
French Fries in Instant Pot Air Fryer 305
Radish Chips 305
Lemon Cupcakes 306
Apple Crisp 306
Parmesan Truffle Fries 307
Moist Chocolate Cake 307
Raspberry Bites 308
Endives and Walnuts 308
Air-fried Toasted Sticks 309
Currant Cream 309
Plum Cake 310
Crumbly Fruit Cakes 310
Breaded Avocado Fries 311
Cinnamon Maple Chickpeas 311
Fluffy Baked Donuts 312
Healthy Eggplant Chips 313
Crispy Roasted Cashews 313
Vanilla Brownie 314
Crunchy Zucchini Chips 314
Fried Hot Dogs 315
Sweet Potato Chips 315
Cauliflower Fritters 316
Buffalo Chicken Strips 316

CONCLUSION 318

Book Description

Do you want to know how the new Instant Pot duo Air Fryer Crisp works?
Do you want to know all the foods you can prepare with the Instant Pot duo Air Fryer Crisp?
If you answered YES to these questions, then continue reading. This book contains a wide variety of recipes from breakfast, poultry, meat and seafood, vegetables, snacks and appetizer, dehydrator, casserole, soups and desserts. All the recipes written in this book are easily understandable and selected and from globally inspired dishes.
Instant Pot duo Air Fryer Crisp is a ten in one multipurpose kitchen miracle which has brought much-wanted peace and comfort to the lives of the homemakers who can now cook a healthy and delicious meal for their family, in no time.
With the Instant Pot Air Fryer Lid enhance the operation of instant pot by adding crisp benefits of the air fryer such as air frying, reheating, broil, roasting, baking, and even dehydrating. The use of Instant Pot Air Fryer Lid is super easy as well; you just have to swipe the air fryer lid with the regular instant pot lid.
This book covers the following topics:

- Breakfast

- Sides and appetizers

- Fish and Seafood

- Poultry

- Meat

- Vegetables

- Soups and stews

- Dehydrators and casserole

- Snacks and Desserts

Are you excited?
Look no more!
Download my book now!!!

Introduction

The new instant pot duo crisp air fryer is one of the versatile cooking appliances available now in the market. You never need to purchase another air fryer which will help to reduce your cost and saves your money. The instant pot air fryer lid comes with instant crisp technology. It makes your food crisp from outside and tenders from inside, also given a nice brown texture to your food. Instant pot air fryer lid air fry your food into very less oil. if you are one of those people who like fried food but also worried about extra calories then this cooking gadget is for you. It makes your French fries crisp from outside and tenders from inside within a tablespoon of oil.

Instant Pot is not a new appliance for most people. Your food is tasty to tempt you and should not be unhealthy every time. It's time for the new Instant Pot revolutions that now fries too. This marvelous appliance combines science and art to provide you with wholesome meals for your whole family. By combining the dual functions of pressure cooking and air frying, it allows you to prepare all types of pressure-cooking recipes as well as air frying recipes.

Instant Pot Air Fryer Crisp uses minimal cooking oil or fats so that you can enjoy healthy air fried foods at home. It minimizes unhealthy fats, including saturated and trans-fat, and at the same time maintains essential nutrients intact Instant Pot Air Fryer Crisp comes with multiple new cooking functions steam, pressure cook, slow cook, sous vide, dehydrate, roast, bake, sauté, air fry, and broil. Discover the secret to fast, healthy, and delicious meals with this new kitchen appliance in this particular book. This book covers a detailed introduction to know everything about this new invention.

This is a complete book that unveils a collection of recipes (appetizers, snacks, poultry, pork, beef, lamb, fish, seafood, vegetarian, and dessert) that you can cook effortlessly using the marvelous Instant Pot Air Fryer Crisp. Each recipe is tested to perfection and has been narrated in easy to follow instruction to suit beginners. Even if you are cooking for the first time, you can easily prepare all the recipes with simple Directions. Gear up for the amazing mealtime with crispy, crunchy & caramelized meals. Let's find out what this new Instant Pot can do for you. Indeed, the Instant Pot Air Fryer Lid is a big saving on money, space, time, and clean up.

Chapter 1: Introduction to Instant Pot duo Air Fryer Crisp

What is the Instant Pot Duo Crisp air fryer?

With the 11-in-1 function, the Instant Pot Duo Crisp 11-in-1 Air Fryer/Electric Pressure Cooker has made cooking and living easier for every household. It holds with the impeccable features of 'set and forget' functions. The basic function of the Instant Pot is just like any other cooking appliance. Still, in this version, it comes with both pressure cooker and air fry options, which is made possible with the help of two separate lids, the crisp lid for air frying and pressure cook lid for pressure cooking – fast and easy, all by simply changing the covers.

With such ease, you will have all the cooking methods available over the control panel of this Instant Pot. The pressure cook lid offers you the function of six wet cooking options like PRESSURE COOK, STEAM, SAUTÉ, SLOW COOK, WARM, and SOUS VIDE. Similarly, in the air fryer function, it offers you the option to AIR FRY, BAKE, ROAST, BROIL, and DEHYDRATE. Since the cookbook is all about air fry recipes, you can find exclusive features of Instant Pot Duo Crisp Air Fryer.

Instant pot air fryer crisp is a convertible cooking appliance, and with a switch of a lid, the device can be converted into an air fryer from a pressure cooker. And that's not just it; there are several other functions that you can use within this device.

Benefits of Instant Pot Duo Crisp air fryer

One-pot cooking

The good news is that the basic design of the new duo crisp air fryer is almost the same as the instant pot original series. So, it brought the same one-pot cooking formula into play, and now instead of the switch from pot to another, you can continue cooking a single meal using different cooking options. For an instant, if you want to first pressure cook the food, then broil then. You can do it just by replacing the lid on the top and selecting the desired method.

Ten functions in one

When you look at the control panel of this instant pot air fryer, there are far many options than any other ordinary fryer. A total of ten cooking modes are given in the duo crisp. The basic instant pot functions along with the additional modes of bake, air fry, broil and dehydrate.

The Instant Pot Duo Crisp is a convertible cooking appliance, and with a switch of a lid, the device can be converted into an Air fryer from a pressure cooker. And that's not just it; there are several other functions that you can use within this device.

Energy and Time Efficient

Instant Pot Duo Crisp barely takes a few minutes to get everything done. It is both time and energy efficient. Once the food is cooked, the appliance switches to this "keep warm" mode, and minimum heat are used to keep the food fresh.

Changing Lids

Forget about the days when you used to switch between different appliances. The best feature of this appliance is that it is so simple and easy to convert it from one form to another. There are two different lids that can be used to carry out a range of different functions. The pressure-cooking lid is used for pressure cooking modes, and with Air frying lid, you can bake, air fry and roast, etc.

User-Friendly

Since the design is the same and as simple as the original Instant Pot pressure cooker series, the user wouldn't find much difficulty in understanding its control panel and its use. All button is labeled with their respective functions and the LED screen guides about the on-going operations.

Functions of Instant Pot Duo Crisp air fryer

Let's get to know what different functions you can use for a comprehensive cooking experience. The following are the key functions that you can see in the display unit.

Air Fry

For all air frying recipes, it is mandatory to use Air Frying lid. You can use this function along with adjusting the temperature and time of your choice. The default temperature on the display unit is 400°F. However, you can cook meals in a temperature range of 180°F to 400°F. The minimum cooking time is 1 minute, and the maximum is 60 minutes per recipe cycle.

Bake

You can prepare all types of baking recipes using this function. The default temperature on the display unit is 365°F. However, you can cook meals in a temperature range of 180°F to 400°F. The minimum cooking time is 1 minute, and the maximum is 60 minutes per recipe cycle.

Broil

You have to use Air Frying lid to prepare all types of broiling recipes. However, one notable thing is that the temperature remains fixed at 400°F, which is not adjustable. Broiling requires high-temperature cooking, and that is why it remains fixed; the cooking time you can adjust to your preference from a minimum of 1 minute to a maximum of 40 minutes per recipe cycle.

Roast

Roast mouthwatering recipes with this setting with a default cooking time of 40 minutes and a default temperature of 380°F. However, you can cook meals in a temperature range of 180°F to 400°F. The minimum cooking time is 1 minute, and the maximum is 60 minutes per recipe cycle.

Dehydrate

Using Pressure Lid, you can dehydrate foods (dried fruits, dried veggies, etc.) in a temperature range of 105°F to 165°F. The minimum cooking time is 1 hour, and the maximum is 72 hours per recipe cycle.

Pressure

For all pressure-cooking recipes, you can effortlessly prepare meals with the customized pressure level of either HI or LOW depending on recipe type. The minimum cooking time is 0 minutes, and the maximum is 4 hours per recipe cycle.

Sauté

Replacing the traditional open lid browning, you can sauté veggies, meat cuts, bacon, sausages, etc. using this setting. You do not have to use either Pressure Lid or Crisping Lid for sautéing. You can also simmer until you get the desired result. The default cooking time is 30 minutes; the minimum cooking time is 1 minute, and the maximum is 30 minutes per recipe cycle.

Sous Vide

This setting is for all non-frying recipes using vacuum-sealed cooking techniques. Sous Vide is a unique cooking technique for an extended cooking time lasting for hours.
The default cooking time is 3 hours with minimum cooking time is 30 minutes, and the maximum is 99 hours per recipe cycle—default temperature of 56°F.

Steam

If you wish just to steam veggies and other foods, you can cook them quickly with either HI or Low-pressure level and time duration of your choice. You have to use Pressure Lid to build pressure for steam generation.

Keep Warm

To keep warm prepared recipe after cooking is over.

Chapter 2: Breakfast Recipes

Breakfast Tarts

Preparation time:10 minutes
Cooking Time: 12 minutes
Serving: 4
Ingredients:
1 sheet frozen puff pastry
4 tablespoons Cheddar cheese, shredded
4 tablespoons cooked ham, diced
4 eggs
fresh chives, chopped
Directions:
Spread the pastry sheet on a flat surface and slice into 4 equal squares.
Place 2 pastry squares in the Air Fryer Basket.
Set the Air Fryer Basket in the Instant Pot Duo.
Put on the Air Fryer lid and seal it.
Hit the "Air fry Button" and select 6 minutes of cooking time, then press "Start."
Once the Instant Pot Duo beeps, remove its lid.
Press the center of each pastry square with the back of a spoon.
Add 1 tablespoon cheddar cheese, 1 tablespoon ham, and 1 egg to each of the square groove.
Return the basket to the Air fryer.
Put on the Air Fryer lid and seal it.
Hit the "Air fry Button" and select 6 minutes of cooking time, then press "Start."
Once the Instant Pot Duo beeps, remove its lid.
Cook the remaining pastry squares in a similar manner.
Garnish with chives.
Serve.
Nutrition:
Calories 161
Total Fat 11.3g
Saturated Fat 3.7g
Cholesterol 176mg
Sodium 241mg
Total Carbohydrate 5.3g
Dietary Fiber 0.3g
Total Sugars 0.5g
Protein 9.4g

Baked Eggs

Preparation Time: 10 minutes
Cooking Time: 8 minutes
Serving: 2
Ingredients:
2 eggs
1/4 cup spinach, chopped

1/4 onion, diced
1/4 tsp parsley
1/4 tsp garlic powder
Pepper
Salt
Directions:
Spray two ramekins with cooking spray.
In a small bowl, whisk together eggs, parsley, garlic powder, pepper, and salt.
Add onion and spinach and stir well.
Pour egg mixture into the prepared ramekins.
Place the dehydrating tray in a multi-level air fryer basket and place basket in the instant pot.
Place ramekins on dehydrating tray.
Seal pot with air fryer lid and select air fry mode then set the temperature to 350 F and timer for 8 minutes.
Serve and enjoy.
Nutrition:
Calories 71
Fat 4.4 g
Carbohydrates 2.1 g
Sugar 1 g
Protein 5.9 g
Cholesterol 164 mg

Tomato Pepper Frittata

Preparation Time: 10 minutes
Cooking Time: 15 minutes
Serving: 2
Ingredients:
1 cup egg whites
1/4 cup tomato, sliced
1/4 cup pepper, sliced
2 tbsp milk
Pepper
Salt
Directions:
Add all ingredients into the large bowl and whisk until well combined.
Pour bowl mixture into the baking dish.
Place steam rack into the instant pot then place baking dish on top of the rack.
Seal pot with air fryer lid and select air fry mode and set the temperature to 320 F and timer for 15 minutes.
Serve and enjoy.
Nutrition:
Calories 87
Fat 0.7 g
Carbohydrates 5.6 g
Sugar 2.2 g
Protein 14.5 g
Cholesterol 1 mg

Tropical Oatmeal

Preparation time: 10 minutes

Cooking time: 4 minutes
Servings: 4
Ingredients:
1 cup steel-cut oats
3 tbsp hemp seeds
1/2 papaya, chopped
1/2 cup coconut cream
2 cups of water
Directions:
Add oats, coconut cream, and water into the instant pot and stir well.
Seal pot with lid and cook on manual high pressure for 4 minutes.
Once done then allow to release pressure naturally for 10 minutes then release using the quick-release method.
Open the lid.
Stir in hemp seeds and papaya.
Serve and enjoy.
Nutrition: Calories 195 Fat 11.2 g Carbohydrates 20.1 g Sugar 4.3 g Protein 5.5 g Cholesterol 0 mg

Simple & Easy Breakfast Casserole

Preparation time: 10 minutes
Cooking time: 20 minutes
Servings: 4
Ingredients:
2 1/2 cups egg whites
1/2 cup Mexican blend cheese
1/4 cup cream cheese
1/2 cup onion, chopped
1 cup bell pepper, chopped
1/2 tsp onion powder
1/4 tsp garlic powder
1/4 tsp pepper
1/4 tsp salt
Directions:
Spray instant pot from inside with cooking spray.
Add onion and bell pepper to the pot and cook until softened, about 5 minutes.
Transfer onion and bell pepper to the baking dish.
Add egg whites, seasonings, and cream cheese and stir well. Top with mexican blend cheese.
Pour 1 cup of water into the instant pot then place the trivet in the pot.
Place baking dish on top of the trivet.
Seal pot with lid and cook on manual mode for 15 minutes.
Once done then release pressure using the quick-release method than open the lid.
Slice and serve.
Nutrition: Calories 208 Fat 10.4 g Carbohydrates 6.3 g Sugar 4.1 g Protein 21.7 g Cholesterol 33 mg

Creamy Mac n Cheese

Preparation time: 10 minutes
Cooking time: 5 minutes
Servings: 8
Ingredients:
15 oz elbow macaroni
1 cup milk
1/2 cup parmesan cheese, shredded

1 cup mozzarella cheese, shredded
2 cups cheddar cheese, shredded
1 tsp garlic powder
1 tsp hot pepper sauce
2 tbsp butter
4 cups vegetable broth
1/4 tsp pepper
1/2 tsp salt
Directions:
Add macaroni, garlic powder, hot sauce, butter, broth, pepper, and salt into the instant pot and stir well.
Seal pot with lid and cook on manual high pressure for 5 minutes.
Once done then release pressure using the quick-release method than open the lid.
Add cheese and milk and stir until cheese is melted.
Serve and enjoy.
Nutrition: Calories 388 Fat 15.3 g Carbohydrates 42.5 g Sugar 3.4 g Protein 19 g Cholesterol 43 mg

Cherry Risotto

Preparation time: 10 minutes
Cooking time: 10 minutes
Servings: 4
Ingredients:
1 1/2 cups arborio rice
1/2 cup dried cherries
3 cups of milk
1 cup apple juice
1/3 cup brown sugar
1 1/2 tsp cinnamon
2 apples, cored and diced
2 tbsp butter
1/4 tsp salt
Directions:
Add butter into the instant pot and set the pot on sauté mode.
Add rice and cook for 3-4 minutes.
Add brown sugar, spices, apples, milk, and apple juice and stir well.
Seal pot with lid and cook on manual high pressure for 6 minutes.
Once done then release pressure using the quick-release method than open the lid.
Stir in dried cherries and serve.
Nutrition: Calories 544 Fat 10.2 g Carbohydrates 103.2 g Sugar 37.6 g Protein 11.2 g Cholesterol 30 mg

Almond Coconut Risotto

Preparation time: 10 minutes
Cooking time: 5 minutes
Servings: 4
Ingredients:
1 cup arborio rice
1 cup of coconut milk
3 tbsp almonds, sliced and toasted
2 tbsp shredded coconut
2 cups almond milk
1/2 tsp vanilla
1/3 cup coconut sugar

Directions:
Add coconut and almond milk in instant pot and set the pot on sauté mode.
Once the milk begins to boil then add rice and stir well.
Seal pot with lid and cook on manual high pressure for 5 minutes.
Once done then allow to release pressure naturally then open the lid.
Add remaining ingredients and stir well.
Serve and enjoy.
Nutrition: Calories 425 Fat 20.6 g Carbohydrates 53.7 g Sugar 9.6 g Protein 6.8 g Cholesterol 0 mg

---

Mushroom Frittata

Preparation Time: 10 minutes
Cooking Time: 15 minutes
Serving: 2
Ingredients:
4 eggs
1 1/2 cups water
1/4 tsp garlic powder
4 oz mushrooms, sliced
1/8 tsp white pepper
1/8 tsp onion powder
2 tsp heavy cream
2 Swiss cheese slices, cut each slice into 4 pieces
1/4 tsp salt
Directions:
In a bowl, whisk eggs with spices and heavy cream.
Spray a 7-inch baking dish with cooking spray.
Add sliced mushrooms to the dish then pour egg mixture over the mushrooms.
Arrange cheese slices on top of the mushroom and egg mixture. Cover dish with foil.
Pour 1 1/2 cups of water to the instant pot then place steamer rack in the pot.
Place dish on top of the steamer rack.
Seal the pot with pressure cooking lid and cook on high for 15 minutes.
Once done, release pressure using a quick release. Remove lid.
Serve and enjoy.
Nutrition:
Calories 264
Fat 18.5 g
Carbohydrates 4.6 g
Sugar 2.2 g
Protein 20.6 g
Cholesterol 360 mg

Morning Churros

Preparation time:10 minutes
Cooking Time: 5 minutes
Serving: 4
Ingredients:
1/4 cup butter
1/2 cup milk
1 pinch salt
1/2 cup all-purpose flour

2 eggs
1/4 cup white sugar
1/2 teaspoon ground cinnamon
Directions:
Melt butter in a 1-quart saucepan and add salt and milk.
Stir cook the butter mixture to a boil then stir in flour. Mix it quickly.
Remove the butter-flour mixture from the heat and allow the flour mixture to cool down.
Stir in egg and mix to get choux pastry and transfer the dough to a pastry bag.
Put a star tip on the pastry bag and pine the dough into straight strips in the Air Fryer Basket.
Set the Air Fryer Basket in the Instant Pot Duo.
Put on the Air Fryer lid and seal it.
Hit the "Air fry Button" and select 5 minutes of cooking time, then press "Start."
Once the Instant Pot Duo beeps, remove its lid.
Mix sugar with cinnamon in a mini bowl and drizzle over the churros.
Serve.
Nutrition:
Calories 253
Total Fat 14.5g
Saturated Fat 8.4g
Cholesterol 115mg
Sodium 166mg
Total Carbohydrate 26.3g
Dietary Fiber 0.6g
Total Sugars 14.1g
Protein 5.5g

Creamy Polenta
Preparation time: 10 minutes
Cooking time: 5 minutes
Servings: 3
Ingredients:
1/2 cup polenta
1 cup of coconut milk
1 cup of water
1/2 tbsp butter
1/4 tsp salt
Directions:
Set instant pot on sauté mode.
Add milk, water, and salt in a pot and stir well.
Once milk mixture begins to boil then add polenta and stir to combine.
Seal pot with lid and cook on high pressure for 5 minutes.
Once done then allow to release pressure naturally then open the lid.
Stir and serve.
Nutrition: Calories 293 Fat 21.2 g Carbohydrates 24.7 g Sugar 2.9 g Protein 3.8 g Cholesterol 5 mg

Sweet Cherry Chocolate Oat

Preparation time: 10 minutes
Cooking time: 15 minutes
Servings: 4
Ingredients:
2 cups steel cuts oats
3 tbsp honey
2 cups of water
2 cups of milk
3 tbsp chocolate chips

1 1/2 cups cherries
1/4 tsp cinnamon
Pinch of salt
Directions:
Spray instant pot from inside with cooking spray.
Add all ingredients into the pot and stir everything well.
Seal pot with lid and cook on high pressure for 15 minutes.
Once done then allow to release pressure naturally then open the lid.
Stir well and serve.
Nutrition: Calories 503 Fat 10.9 g Carbohydrates 85.5 g Sugar 22.5 g Protein 16.8 g Cholesterol 12 mg

Farro Breakfast Risotto

Preparation time: 10 minutes
Cooking time: 12 minutes
Servings: 4
Ingredients:
1 cup farro
1 tsp Italian seasoning
1/2 cup parmesan cheese, grated
1/2 cup mozzarella cheese, grated
2 tbsp heavy whipping cream
2 cups vegetable stock
1 tbsp butter
Directions:
Add butter into the instant pot and set the pot on sauté mode.
Add farro and cook for 2 minutes. Add stock and stir everything well.
Seal pot with lid and cook on manual high pressure for 10 minutes.
Once done then allow to release pressure naturally for 10 minutes then release using the quick-release method. Open the lid.
Add remaining ingredients and stir well.
Serve and enjoy.
Nutrition: Calories 206 Fat 13.7 g Carbohydrates 13.4 g Sugar 1.8 g Protein 9.9 g Cholesterol 37 mg

Cajun Chicken

Preparation Time: 10 minutes
Cooking Time: 15 minutes
Serving: 2
Ingredients:
2 chicken breasts, boneless & skinless
3 tbsp Cajun spice
Directions:
Season chicken breasts with Cajun spice from both the sides.
Place the dehydrating tray in a multi-level air fryer basket and place basket in the instant pot.
Place chicken breasts on dehydrating tray.
Seal pot with air fryer lid and select air fry mode then set the temperature to 350 F and timer for 15 minutes.
Serve and enjoy.
Nutrition:
Calories 277
Fat 10.8 g
Carbohydrates 0 g
Sugar 0 g

Protein 42.4 g
Cholesterol 130 mg

Tasty Chicken Tenders

Preparation Time: 10 minutes
Cooking Time: 18 minutes
Serving: 4
Ingredients:
1 lb chicken tenders
2 tbsp sesame oil
6 tbsp pineapple juice
2 tbsp soy sauce
1 tsp ginger, minced
4 garlic cloves, minced
Directions:
Add all ingredients except chicken in a bowl and mix well.
Add chicken and coat well. Cover and place in the refrigerator for 2 hours.
Place the dehydrating tray in a multi-level air fryer basket and place basket in the instant pot.
Place marinated chicken tenders on dehydrating tray.
Seal pot with air fryer lid and select air fry mode then set the temperature to 350 F and timer for 18 minutes. Turn chicken halfway through.
Serve and enjoy.
Nutrition:
Calories 298
Fat 15.3 g
Carbohydrates 4.9 g
Sugar 2.5 g
Protein 33.6 g
Cholesterol 101 mg

Potato Fish Cakes

Preparation Time: 10 minutes
Cooking Time: 15 minutes
Serving: 4
Ingredients:
2 cups white fish
1 tsp coriander
1 tsp Worcestershire sauce
2 tsp chili powder
1 cup potatoes, mashed
1 tsp mix herbs
1 tsp mix spice
1 tsp milk
1 tsp butter
1 small onion, diced
1/4 cup breadcrumbs
Pepper
Salt
Directions:

Add all ingredients into the bowl and mix well to combine.
Make small patties from mixture and place in the refrigerator for 2 hours.
Place the dehydrating tray in a multi-level air fryer basket and place basket in the instant pot.
Place patties on dehydrating tray.
Seal pot with air fryer lid and select air fry mode then set the temperature to 400 F and timer for 15 minutes. Turn patties halfway through.
Serve and enjoy.
Nutrition:
Calories 290
Fat 21.5 g
Carbohydrates 13.8 g
Sugar 2.1 g
Protein 11.2 g
Cholesterol 3 mg

Baked Cod Fillet

Preparation Time: 10 minutes
Cooking Time: 20 minutes
Serving: 4
Ingredients:
1 lbs cod fillet
1 tbsp olive oil
1 tsp Italian seasoning
1/4 cup olives, sliced
1 cup cherry tomatoes, halved
Pepper
Salt
Directions:
Line instant pot multi-level air fryer basket with foil.
Coat fish fillet with oil and season with Italian seasoning, pepper, and salt.
Place fish fillet into the air fryer basket and place basket into the instant pot.
Add cherry tomatoes and olives on top fo fish fillet.
Seal pot with air fryer lid and select air fry mode then set the temperature to 400 F and timer for 20 minutes.
Serve and enjoy.
Nutrition:
Calories 143
Fat 5.9 g
Carbohydrates 2.4 g
Sugar 1.3 g
Protein 20.7 g
Cholesterol 57 mg

Flavorful Chicken Skewers

Preparation Time: 10 minutes
Cooking Time: 20 minutes
Serving: 4
Ingredients:
1 1/2 lbs chicken breast, cut into 1-inch cubes
For marinade:

1/4 cup fresh mint leaves
5 garlic cloves
1/2 cup lemon juice
1/4 tsp cayenne
1 cup olive oil
1 tbsp vinegar
1/2 cup yogurt
2 tbsp fresh rosemary, chopped
2 tbsp dried oregano
Pepper
Salt
Directions:
Add all marinade ingredients into the blender and blend until smooth.
Pour marinade in a mixing bowl.
Add chicken to the bowl and coat well and place it in the refrigerator for 1 hour.
Thread marinated chicken onto the soaked wooden skewers.
Spray instant pot multi-level air fryer basket with cooking spray.
Place chicken skewers into the air fryer basket and place basket into the instant pot.
Seal pot with air fryer lid and select air fry mode then set the temperature to 400 F and timer for 20 minutes. Turn halfway through.
Serve and enjoy.
Nutrition:
Calories 677
Fat 55.8 g
Carbohydrates 7.1 g
Sugar 3 g
Protein 38.8 g
Cholesterol 111 mg

Air-Fried Cinnamon & Sugar Doughnuts

Preparation: 25 minutes
Cooking: 8 minutes
Servings: 9
Ingredients:
2¼ + ¼ cup all-purpose flour
¾ + ⅓ cup white sugar
2 egg yolks, large
2½ tablespoons butter kept in room temperature
1½ teaspoons baking powder
½ cup sour cream
2 tablespoons butter, melted
1 teaspoon cinnamon
1 teaspoon salt
Directions:
In a bowl combine, 2½ tablespoon butter kept in room temperature with ¾ cup white sugar, until it takes a crumbly shape.
Now add the egg yolk and mix thoroughly.
Put the all-purpose flour, salt, and baking powder in a medium bowl and combine.
Put one-third of the flour mixture into the egg-sugar mix and combine thoroughly.
Add the remaining flour and sour cream and mix well.
Refrigerate the mixture for 3-4 hours.
Mix cinnamon and ⅓ cup of white sugar in another medium bowl.
Keep ready your kitchen working table and spread some flour on it.

Take out the refrigerated dough and spread it into ½" thick sheet.
Cut it into 9 large dough using a dough dye cutter and make a small circle in the center of each dough, to make it look like a dough.
Place the air fryer basket in the inner pot of the Instant Pot Air Fryer.
Close the crisp cover of your Instant Pot Air Fryer and preheat at 340°F for 3 minutes in the AIR FRYER mode.
Press START to begin preheating.
Apply melted butter on both sides of the doughnut before placing it in the air fryer.
Place the doughs in the basket without overlapping.
If space is not enough, use the separator and place the remaining dough on it.
Close the crisp lid.
Set the timer to 8 minutes and temperature at 340°F.
Press START for cooking.
Brush the melted butter on the cooked doughnuts and dredge it into the cinnamon-sugar mixture.
Your doughnuts are ready to serve.
Nutrition: Calories: 276, Total fat: 9.7g, Saturated fat: 6g, Cholesterol: 66mg, Sodium: 390mg, Protein: 4.3g, Potassium: 59mg, Total carbs: 43.5g, Dietary fiber: 1g, Sugars: 19g.

Bok Choy And Spinach

Preparation time: 20 minutes
Cooking Time: 30 minutes
Servings: 4
Ingredients:
3 oz. Mozzarella; shredded
7oz. Baby spinach; torn
7 oz. Bok choy; torn
2 eggs; whisked
2 tbsp. Olive oil
2 tbsp. Coconut cream
Salt and black pepper to taste.
Directions:
In your air fryer, combine all the ingredients except the mozzarella and toss them gently.
Sprinkle the mozzarella on top, cook at 360°f for 15 minutes.
Divide between plates and serve
Nutrition: Calories: 200; Fat: 12g; Fiber: 2g; Carbs: 3g; Protein: 8g

Healthy Air Fryer Granola

Preparation time:5 minutes
Cooking time: 15 minutes
Serving 8
18 Ingredients
2 cup Rolled Oats
1/2 cup Toasted Wheat Germ
1/4 cup Dried Cherries
1/8 cup Dried Cranberries
1/4 cup Dried Blueberries
1/8 cup Pepitas
1/8 cup Sunflower Seeds
1 Tbsp Flaxseed
1/8 cup Chopped pecans
1/8 cup Chopped Almonds

1/8 cup Chopped Walnuts
1/8 cup Chopped Hazelnuts.
2 tbsp Honey or Agave Extract
1/2 tsp Vanilla extract
1/4 cup Maple Syrup
6 tbsp Olive Oil
1/2 tsp Ground Cinnamon
1/8 tsp Ground Cloves

Directions

Combine all the dry ingredients in a large or a medium bowl.
Mix the agave or honey with the oil and maple syrup.
Thoroughly mix the syrup mix with the dry ingredients, stirring well to fully coat all of the ingredients.
Choose the Air Fry option from the Instant Pot Duo Crisp Air Fryer and set the temperature to 350°F. Press start and let it preheat.
Add the food to the Air Fryer and Air Fry at 350°F for 15 minutes, stirring every 5 minutes until the granola is golden brown.
Let it cool and store for up to three weeks in an airtight container
Nutrition: Calories 351, Total Fat 19g, Total Carbs 38g, Protein 7g

Keto Ribs

Preparation time:10 minutes
Cooking time: 35 minutes
Serving 6
4 Ingredients
3.5 lbs pork baby back ribs about 2 racks of ribs
1/3 cup spicy dry rub
1/2 cup Keto BBQ sauce
1 cup Zevia Cola or Chicken Broth

Directions
Season the pork ribs on the both sides with the dry rub.
Marinate the ribs for at least 4 hours.
Set the ribs in the Instant Pot Duo Crisp Air Fryer.
Pour the chicken broth or keto-friendly Cola soda at the bottom of the pot.
Close the Air Fryer lid and cook the ribs for 25-30 minutes at 390°F.
Place them into the Instant Pot Duo Crisp Air Fryer Basket.
Top the ribs with BBQ sauce.
Select the option Air Fryer.
Close the Air Fryer lid and cook for about 5 minutes.
Nutrition: Calories 379, Total Fat 27g, Total Carbs 3g, Protein 31g

Mini Frittata

Preparation Time: 10 minutes
Cooking Time: 15 minutes
Serving: 4
Ingredients:
6 eggs
1/2 small onion, chopped
1/2 bell pepper, chopped
3 bacon slices, chopped
1/4 cup cheddar cheese, shredded

1/4 cup coconut milk
1/4 tsp black pepper
1/2 tsp sea salt
Directions:
Add bacon slices on the bottom of each silicone muffin mold. Add chopped vegetables on top of the bacon.
In a bowl, whisk eggs with pepper and salt.
Pour egg mixture over vegetables.
Sprinkle shredded cheddar cheese on top.
Place silicone muffin molds into the instant pot air fryer basket and place basket in the pot.
Seal the pot with pressure cooking lid and select bake mode and cook at 350 F for 10-15 minutes.
Serve and enjoy.
Nutrition:
Calories 243
Fat 18.5 g
Carbohydrates 3.7 g
Sugar 2.2 g
Protein 15.9 g
Cholesterol 269 mg

Healthy Breakfast Bake

Preparation: 6 minutes
Cooking: 25 minutes
Servings: 2
Ingredients
1 slice whole grain bread, torn into pieces
4 eggs
1½ cups baby spinach
¼ cup + 2 tbsps. shredded cheddar cheese, divided
½ cup bell pepper, diced
2 tbsps. 1% low-fat milk
1 tsp. hot sauce
½ tsp. Kosher salt
Directions
Preheat your air fryer to 250 degrees F. Spritz a 6-inch soufflé dish with nonstick spray and set aside.
In a medium bowl, add the beaten eggs, hot sauce, milk and salt.
Gently fold in the spinach, ¼ cup cheddar, bread pieces and bell peppers.
Pour the egg mixture into the prepared soufflé dish and place the dish into the air fryer basket.
Set up the trivet to the inner pot of the cooker and place the basket on top.
Cook at 250 degrees F for 20 minutes. Sprinkle the top with the remaining cheese and cook for another 5 minutes or until the eggs are set and the edges are golden brown.
Remove from the air fryer basket and set aside for about 10 minutes before serving.
Nutrition: Calories – 173; Carbohydrates – 14g; Fat – 9g; Fiber – 3g; Protein – 9g; Sodium – 524mg; Sugar – 2g

Spinach Frittata

Preparation Time: 10 minutes
Cooking Time: 15 minutes
Serving: 4
Ingredients:

6 eggs
1/4 cup bacon, cooked and chopped
1 tomato, chopped
1/4 tsp garlic powder
3/4 cup fresh spinach
1 tsp Italian seasoning
1 tbsp heavy cream
1/4 tsp pepper
1/4 tsp salt
Directions:
In a bowl, whisk eggs with spices and heavy cream.
Spray a 7-inch baking dish with cooking spray.
Add bacon, tomato, and spinach to the prepared dish.
Pour egg mixture over the bacon mixture. Cover dish with foil.
Pour 1 1/2 cups of water into the inner pot of instant pot then place steamer rack in the pot.
Place baking dish on top of the steamer rack.
Seal the pot with pressure cooking lid and cook on high for 15 minutes.
Once done, release pressure using a quick release. Remove lid.
Serve and enjoy.
Nutrition:
Calories 122
Fat 8.9 g
Carbohydrates 1.8 g
Sugar 1.1 g
Protein 9.2 g
Cholesterol 253 mg

Tomato Mozzarella Quiche

Preparation Time: 10 minutes
Cooking Time: 30 minutes
Serving: 6
Ingredients:
8 eggs
1 red pepper, chopped
1/2 cup almond flour
1/2 cup almond milk
1 1/2 cup mozzarella cheese, shredded
2 tbsp green onions, chopped
1 cup tomatoes, chopped
1/4 tsp pepper
1/4 tsp salt
Directions:
Pour 1 1/2 cups of water to the instant pot then place steamer rack in the pot.
In a large bowl, whisk eggs, almond flour, milk, pepper, and salt.
Add vegetables and cheese and stir to combine.
Pour egg mixture into the baking dish. Cover dish with foil and place on top of the steamer rack.
Seal the pot with pressure cooking lid and cook on high for 30 minutes.
Once done, allow to release pressure naturally for 10 minutes then release remaining pressure using a quick release.
Remove lid.
Serve and enjoy.
Nutrition:
Calories 219

Fat 16.4 g
Carbohydrates 6.7 g
Sugar 3 g
Protein 12.4
Cholesterol 222 mg

Creamy Spinach Spread

Preparation time: 15 minutes
Cooking Time: 30 minutes
Servings: 4
Ingredients:
3 cups spinach leaves
2 tbsp. Bacon, cooked and crumbled
2 tbsp. Coconut cream
2 tbsp. Cilantro
Salt and black pepper to taste.
Directions:
In a pan that fits the air fryer, combine all the ingredients except the bacon, put the pan in the machine and cook at 360°f for 10 minutes
Transfer to a blender, pulse well, divide into bowls and serve with bacon sprinkled on top.
Nutrition: Calories: 200; Fat: 4g; Fiber: 2g; Carbs: 4g; Protein: 4g

Eggplant and Spinach Frittata

Preparation time: 25 minutes
Cooking Time: 30 minutes
Servings: 4
Ingredients:
6 eggs; whisked
8 oz. Spinach; torn
1 eggplant; cubed
1 tbsp. Chives; chopped.
Cooking spray
Salt and black pepper to taste.
Directions:
Take a bowl and mix the eggs with the rest of the ingredients except the cooking spray and whisk well.
Grease a pan that fits your air fryer with the cooking spray, pour the frittata mix, spread and put the pan in the machine
Cook at 380°f for 20 minutes, divide between plates and serve for breakfast.
Nutrition: Calories: 240; Fat: 8g; Fiber: 3g; Carbs: 6g; Protein: 12g

Zucchini and Artichokes Mix

Preparation time: 25 minutes
Cooking Time: 30 minutes
Servings: 4
Ingredients:
8 oz. Canned artichokes drained and chopped.
2 tomatoes; cut into quarters
4 eggs; whisked
4 spring onions; chopped.

2 zucchinis; sliced
Cooking spray
Salt and black pepper to taste.
Directions:
Grease a pan with cooking spray and mix all the other ingredients inside.
Put the pan in the air fryer and cook at 350°f for 20 minutes.
Divide between plates and serve
Nutrition: Calories: 210; Fat: 11g; Fiber: 3g; Carbs: 4g; Protein: 6g

---

Air Fryer Breakfast Frittata

Preparation: 15 minutes
Cooking: 18 minutes
Servings: 2

Ingredients:
4 eggs
¼ pound breakfast sausage, cooked.
2 tablespoons, red bell pepper, chopped
½ cup cheddar cheese, grated
1 green onion, finely chopped
¼ teaspoon ground cayenne pepper
¼ teaspoon salt
Cooking spray

Directions:
Beat the eggs in a large bowl.
Crumble the sausages.
In bowl, combine beaten egg, crumbled sausages, grated cheddar cheese, onion, salt, and cayenne pepper thoroughly.
Take an Instant Pot Air Fryer compatible non-stick pan and spritz some cooking spray.
Pour the egg mix into the tray and place it in the air fryer basket in the inner pot.
Close the crisp lid.
Set the temperature 350°C and timer for 18 minutes in the AIR FRYER mode.
Press START to begin the cooking.
Remove the Frittata when the cooking stops.
Serve hot.
Nutrition: Calories: 380, Total fat: 27.4g, Saturated fat: 12g, Cholesterol: 443mg, Sodium: 694mg, Potassium: 328mg, Total carbs: 2.9g, Dietary fiber: 0.4g, Protein: 31.2g, Sugars: 1g, Calcium: 69mg, Iron: 3mg.

Spinach Muffins

Preparation Time: 10 minutes
Cooking Time: 15 minutes
Serving: 6
Ingredients:
5 eggs
1 cup spinach, chopped
1/4 tsp garlic powder
1/4 tsp onion powder
1 bacon slice, cooked and crumbled

1/2 cup mushrooms, chopped
Pepper
Salt
Directions:
In a bowl, whisk eggs with garlic powder, onion powder, pepper, and salt.
Add spinach, mushrooms, and bacon and stir well.
Pour egg mixture into the 6 silicone muffin molds.
Place the dehydrating tray in a multi-level air fryer basket and place basket in the instant pot.
Place muffin molds on dehydrating tray.
Seal pot with air fryer lid and select bake mode then set the temperature to 400 F and timer for 15 minutes.
Serve and enjoy.
Nutrition:
Calories 73
Fat 5 g
Carbohydrates 0.9 g
Sugar 0.5 g
Protein 6.1 g
Cholesterol 140 mg

Ham Egg Muffins

Preparation Time: 10 minutes
Cooking Time: 25 minutes
Serving: 6
Ingredients:
6 eggs
6 tbsp cheddar cheese, shredded
1/4 tsp garlic powder
1/2 cup milk
1 green onion, sliced
4 oz ham, cubed
Pepper
Salt
Directions:
In a large bowl, whisk eggs with milk, garlic powder, pepper, and salt.
Add green onion, ham, and cheese and stir well.
Place the dehydrating tray in a multi-level air fryer basket and place basket in the instant pot.
Place muffin molds on dehydrating tray.
Seal pot with air fryer lid and select bake mode then set the temperature to 350 F and timer for 25 minutes.
Serve and enjoy.
Nutrition:
Calories 134
Fat 8.8 g
Carbohydrates 2.4 g
Sugar 1.4 g
Protein 11.2 g
Cholesterol 184 mg

Creamy Chicken

Preparation Time: 10 minutes
Cooking Time: 4 hours
Serving: 4
Ingredients:
1 lb chicken breasts, skinless and boneless
1 tbsp garlic, minced
2 tbsp olive oil
1 tsp chicken bouillon
1/2 cup water
1/2 cup ricotta cheese
4 oz cream cheese
1/2 tsp ground pepper
1 tsp oregano, dried
1 tsp thyme, dried
1 tsp rosemary, dried
Directions:
Place chicken into the inner pot of instant pot.
Top with cream cheese and ricotta cheese.
Pour water, oregano, thyme, basil, thyme, rosemary, garlic, oil, bouillon, and pepper over the chicken.
Seal the pot with pressure cooking lid and select slow cook mode and cook on high for 4 hours.
Serve and enjoy.
Nutrition:
Calories 425
Fat 26 g
Carbohydrates 3 g
Sugar 0.2 g
Protein 38 g
Cholesterol 142 mg

Oatmeal Cups

Preparation Time: 10 minutes
Cooking Time: 20 minutes
Serving: 4
Ingredients:
1 egg
1/2 cup milk
1/2 tsp baking powder
3 tbsp brown sugar
1 1/4 cup rolled oats
2 tbsp olive oil
1/3 cup raisin
1/4 tsp ground cinnamon
Pinch of salt
Directions:
Spray 4 ramekins with cooking spray and set aside.
Add all ingredients into the large bowl and mix until well combined.
Pour oatmeal mixture into the prepared ramekins.
Place the dehydrating tray in a multi-level air fryer basket and place basket in the instant pot.
Place ramekins on dehydrating tray.
Seal pot with air fryer lid and select bake mode then set the temperature to 350 F and timer for 20 minutes.

Serve and enjoy.
Nutrition:
Calories 251
Fat 10.4 g
Carbohydrates 35.5 g
Sugar 15.4 g
Protein 6.1 g
Cholesterol 43 mg

Cheesy Egg Cup

Preparation Time: 10 minutes
Cooking Time: 15 minutes
Serving: 1
Ingredients:
2 eggs
2 tbsp half and half
1 tbsp parmesan cheese, grated
2 tbsp cheddar cheese, shredded
Pepper
Salt
Directions:
Spray a ramekin with cooking spray and set aside.
In a small bowl, whisk eggs and a half and half.
Stir in cheddar cheese, parmesan cheese, pepper, and salt.
Pour egg mixture into the prepared ramekin.
Place the dehydrating tray in a multi-level air fryer basket and place basket in the instant pot.
Place ramekin on dehydrating tray.
Seal pot with air fryer lid and select bake mode then set the temperature to 380 F and timer for 15 minutes.
Serve and enjoy.
Nutrition:
Calories 241
Fat 18.2 g
Carbohydrates 2.4 g
Sugar 0.8 g
Protein 17.4 g
Cholesterol 358 mg

Healthy Apple Oatmeal Cups

Preparation Time: 10 minutes
Cooking Time: 20 minutes
Serving: 6
Ingredients:
1 egg
1/2 cup milk
1 tsp cinnamon
3/4 tsp baking powder
1 1/2 cups quick oats
1/2 apple, diced
2 tbsp honey

1/2 cup applesauce
Directions:
Add oats into the mixing bowl.
Add remaining ingredients and mix until well combined.
Pour oat mixture into the 6 silicone muffin molds
Place the dehydrating tray in a multi-level air fryer basket and place basket in the instant pot.
Place muffin molds on dehydrating tray.
Seal pot with air fryer lid and select bake mode then set the temperature to 375 F and timer for 20 minutes.
Serve and enjoy.
Nutrition:
Calories 139
Fat 2.5 g
Carbohydrates 26.2 g
Sugar 10.9 g
Protein 4.4 g
Cholesterol 29 mg

Tarragon and Parmesan Scramble

Preparation time: 25 minutes
Cooking Time: 30 minutes
Servings: 4
Ingredients:
8 eggs; whisked
¼ cup coconut cream
2 tbsp. Parmesan; grated
2 tbsp. Tarragon; chopped.
Salt and black pepper to taste.
Directions:
Take a bowl and mix the eggs with all the ingredients and whisk.
Pour this into a pan that fits your air fryer, introduce it in the preheated fryer and cook at 350°f for 20 minutes, stirring often
Divide the scramble between plates and serve for breakfast.
Nutrition: Calories: 221; Fat: 12g; Fiber: 4g; Carbs: 5g; Protein: 9g

Loaded Cauliflower Bake

Preparation time: 35 minutes
Cooking Time: 30 minutes
Servings: 4
Ingredients:
2 scallions, sliced on the bias
12 slices sugar-free bacon; cooked and crumbled
1 cup shredded medium cheddar cheese.
1 medium avocado; peeled and pitted
¼ cup heavy whipping cream.
1 ½ cups chopped cauliflower
6 large eggs.
8 tbsp. Full-fat sour cream.
Directions:
Take a medium bowl, whisk eggs and cream together. Pour into a 4-cup round baking dish.
Add cauliflower and mix, then top with cheddar

Place dish into the air fryer basket. Adjust the temperature to 320 degrees f and set the timer for 20 minutes. When completely cooked, eggs will be firm and cheese will be browned. Slice into four pieces

Slice avocado and divide evenly among pieces. Top each piece with 2 tbsp. Sour cream, sliced scallions and crumbled bacon.

Nutrition: Calories: 512; Protein: 27.1g; Fiber: 3.2g; Fat: 38.3g; Carbs: 7.5g

---

Egg Frittata

Preparation time:10 minutes
Cooking time: 15 minutes
Serving 2
10 Ingredients
4 eggs
½ cup milk
2 green onions chopped
¼ cup baby Bella mushrooms chopped
¼ cup spinach chopped
¼ cup red bell pepper chopped
¼ cup cheddar cheese
½ tsp salt
½ tsp black pepper
Dash of hot sauce

Directions
Grease a 6x3 inch round or square pan with butter and set it aside.
Whisk the eggs and milk in a large bowl until they are thoroughly blended. Stir in green onions, mushrooms, salt, black pepper, spinach, red bell pepper, cheddar cheese, and hot sauce.
Pour the egg mixture into a greased pan.
Place in the Instant Pot Duo Crisp Air Fryer and close the lid. Cook on 360°F for 15-18 minutes, or until a toothpick comes out clean.
Nutrition: Calories 227, Total Fat 15g, Total Carbs 6g, Protein 17g

---

Tuna and Spring Onions Salad

Preparation time: 20 minutes
Cooking time: 15 minutes
Servings: 4
Ingredients:
14 oz. Canned tuna, drained and flaked
2 spring onions; chopped.
1 cup arugula
1 tbsp. Olive oil
A pinch of salt and black pepper
Directions:
In a bowl, all the ingredients except the oil and the arugula and whisk.
Preheat the air fryer over 360°f, add the oil and grease it.
Pour the tuna mix, stir well and cook for 15 minutes
In a salad bowl, combine the arugula with the tuna mix, toss and serve.
Nutrition: Calories: 212; Fat: 8g; Fiber: 3g; Carbs: 5g; Protein: 8g

Cheesy Sausage Balls

Preparation time: 22 minutes
Cooking time: 15 minutes
Servings: 16 balls
Ingredients:
1 lb. Pork breakfast sausage
1 large egg.
1 oz. Full-fat cream cheese; softened.
½ cup shredded cheddar cheese
Directions:
Mix all ingredients in a large bowl. Form into sixteen (1-inchballs).
Place the balls into the air fryer basket.
Adjust the temperature to 400 degrees f and set the timer for 12 minutes.
Shake the basket two-or three-times during cooking
Sausage balls will be browned on the outside and have an internal temperature of at least 145 degrees f when completely cooked.
Nutrition: Calories: 424; Protein: 22.8g; Fiber: 0.0g; Fat: 32.2g; Carbs: 1.6g

Hard-Boiled Eggs

Preparation time: 20 minutes
Cooking time: 15 minutes
Servings: 4
Ingredients:
1 cup water
4 large eggs.
Directions:
Place eggs into a 4-cup round baking-safe dish and pour water over eggs.
Place dish into the air fryer basket.
Adjust the temperature to 300 degrees f and set the timer for 18 minutes.
Store cooked eggs in the refrigerator until ready to use or peel and eat warm.
Nutrition: Calories: 77; Protein: 6.3g; Fiber: 0.0g; Fat: 4.4g; Carbs: 0.6g

Stuffed Poblanos

Preparation time: 30 minutes
Cooking time: 15 minutes
Servings: 4
Ingredients:
½ lb. Spicy ground pork breakfast sausage
4 large poblano peppers
4 large eggs.
½ cup full-fat sour cream.
4 oz. Full-fat cream cheese; softened.
¼ cup canned diced tomatoes and green chiles, drained
8 tbsp. Shredded pepper jack cheese
Directions:
In a medium skillet over medium heat, crumble and brown the ground sausage until no pink remains. Remove sausage and drain the fat from the pan.
Crack eggs into the pan, scramble and cook until no longer runny
Place cooked sausage in a large bowl and fold in cream cheese.
Mix in diced tomatoes and chiles. Gently fold in eggs

Cut a 4"–5" slit in the top of each poblano, removing the seeds and white membrane with a small knife.
Separate the filling into four serving and spoon carefully into each pepper.
Top each with 2 tbsp. Pepper jack cheese
Place each pepper into the air fryer basket.
Adjust the temperature to 350 degrees f and set the timer for 15 minutes.
Peppers will be soft and cheese will be browned when ready.
Serve immediately with sour cream on top.
Nutrition: Calories: 489; Protein: 22.8g; Fiber: 3.8g; Fat: 35.6g; Carbs: 12.6g

---

Air-fried Shrimps with Lemon

Preparation Time: 10 minutes
Cooking Time: 15 minutes
Servings: 2-4
Ingredients
¼ tsp. garlic powder
1 pound raw shrimps, peeled and deveined
A dash of vegetable oil or cooking spray, for coating
A pinch of parsley or chili flakes, optional
Black pepper and salt to taste
2 lemon wedges, juiced
Directions
In a bowl, combine shrimps with oil and add salt, pepper and garlic. Toss thoroughly to mix well.
Place shrimps in the air fryer basket and insert the basket inside the instant pot. Attach the air fryer lid and set to air-fry at 400 degrees F for 10-14 minutes. Gently shake the air fryer basket to flip halfway through cooking.
Once done, transfer the shrimp dish to a bowl and drizzle lemon juice over it.
Sprinkle parsley or chili flakes on top and serve hot.
Nutrition: Calories - 117 kcal; Fat – 1.66 g; Carbohydrates – 2.07 g; Protein – 23.46 g; Sugar – 0.88 g; Sodium – 988 mg

---

Coconut Lime Breakfast Quinoa

Preparation time: 10 minutes
Cooking time: 1 minute
Servings: 5
Ingredients:
1 cup quinoa, rinsed
1/2 tsp coconut extract
1 lime juice
1 lime zest
2 cups of coconut milk
1 cup of water
Directions:
Add all ingredients into the instant pot and stir well.
Seal pot with lid and cook on manual high pressure for 1 minute.
Once done then allow to release pressure naturally for 10 minutes then release using the quick-release method.
Open the lid.
Stir well and serve.
Nutrition: Calories 350 Fat 25 g Carbohydrates 28.1 g Sugar 3.5 g Protein 7.1 g Cholesterol 0 mg

Banana Buckwheat Porridge

Preparation Time: 10 minutes
Cooking Time: 6 minutes
Serving: 4
Ingredients:
1 cup raw buckwheat grouts, rinsed
1/4 cup raisins
1 banana, sliced
3 cups almond milk
1/2 tsp vanilla
1 tsp cinnamon
Directions:
Add all ingredients into the inner pot of instant pot duo crisp and stir well.
Seal the pot with pressure cooking lid and cook on high for 6 minutes.
Once done, allow to release pressure naturally. Remove lid.
Serve and enjoy.
Nutrition:
Calories 571
Fat 44 g
Carbohydrates 45.6 g
Sugar 15.8 g
Protein 8.5 g
Cholesterol 0 mg

Cauliflower Casserole

Preparation time: 25 minutes
Cooking Time: 30 minutes
Servings: 4
Ingredients:
4 eggs; whisked
2 cups cauliflower florets, separated
2 tbsp. Butter; melted
1 tsp. Sweet paprika
A pinch of salt and black pepper
Directions:
Heat up your air fryer at 320°f, grease with the butter, add cauliflower florets on the bottom.
Add eggs whisked with paprika, salt and pepper, toss and cook for 20 minutes.
Divide between plates and serve
Nutrition: Calories: 240; Fat: 9g; Fiber: 2g; Carbs: 4g; Protein: 8g

Herbed Eggs

Preparation time: 25 minutes
Cooking Time: 30 minutes
Servings: 4
Ingredients:
½ cup cheddar; shredded
10 eggs; whisked
2 tbsp. Chives; chopped.
2 tbsp. Basil; chopped.

2 tbsp. Parsley; chopped.
Cooking spray
Salt and black pepper to taste.
Directions:
Take a bowl and mix the eggs with all the ingredients except the cheese and the cooking spray and whisk well
Preheat the air fryer at 350°f, grease it with the cooking spray and pour the eggs mixture inside
Sprinkle the cheese on top and cook for 20 minutes.
Divide everything between plates and serve.
Nutrition: Calories: 232; Fat: 12g; Fiber: 4g; Carbs: 5g; Protein: 7g

Spinach and Eggs

Preparation time: 25 minutes
Cooking Time: 30 minutes
Servings: 4
Ingredients:
3 cups baby spinach
12 eggs; whisked
1 tbsp. Olive oil
½ tsp. Smoked paprika
Salt and black pepper to taste.
Directions:
Take a bowl and mix all the ingredients except the oil and whisk them well.
Heat up your air fryer at 360°f, add the oil, heat it up, add the eggs and spinach mix, cover, cook for 20 minutes.
Divide between plates and serve
Nutrition: Calories: 220; Fat: 11g; Fiber: 3g; Carbs: 4g; Protein: 6g

Lemon Butter Brussels sprouts

Preparation Time: 10 minutes
Cooking Time: 5 minutes
Serving: 4
Ingredients:
1 lb Brussels sprouts, trimmed and washed
1 fresh lemon juice
1/4 cup parmesan cheese, grated
1/4 tsp garlic powder
2 tbsp butter
1 cup of water
Directions:
Pour water into the inner pot of instant pot duo crisp.
Add Brussels sprouts into the steamer basket and place basket in the pot.
Seal the pot with pressure cooking lid and cook on high for 2 minutes.
Once done, release pressure using a quick release. Remove lid.
Drain Brussels sprouts well and place in mixing bowl.
Clean the pot. Add butter into the pot and set the pot on sauté mode.
Add cooked Brussels sprouts, garlic powder, and lemon juice and sauté for 2-3 minutes.
Top with cheese and serve.
Nutrition:
Calories 123
Fat 7.6 g
Carbohydrates 10.9 g
Sugar 2.7 g

Protein 6.1 g
Cholesterol 20 mg

Creamy Cauliflower Mashed

Preparation Time: 10 minutes
Cooking Time: 15 minutes
Serving: 4
Ingredients:
1 medium cauliflower head, cut into florets
2 tbsp heavy cream
1/4 tsp garlic powder
1/4 tsp onion powder
4 tbsp butter
1 1/2 tbsp ranch seasoning
1 cup of water
Directions:
Pour water into the instant pot.
Add cauliflower florets into the steamer basket and place basket in the pot.
Seal the pot with pressure cooking lid and cook on high for 15 minutes.
Once done, release pressure using a quick release. Remove lid.
Transfer cauliflower florets into the mixing bowl.
Add remaining ingredients and mash cauliflower mixture until smooth.
Serve and enjoy.
Nutrition:
Calories 176
Fat 14.4 g
Carbohydrates 8.1 g
Sugar 3.6 g
Protein 3.2 g
Cholesterol 41 mg

Spicy Cabbage

Preparation Time: 10 minutes
Cooking Time: 5 minutes
Serving: 6
Ingredients:
1 cabbage head, chopped
2 tbsp olive oil
1 tsp chili powder
3 tbsp soy sauce
1/2 onion, diced
1 tsp paprika
1/2 tsp garlic salt
1 cup vegetable stock
1/2 tsp salt
Directions:
Add oil into the inner pot of instant pot duo crisp and set pot on sauté mode.
Add cabbage and sauté for 1-2 minutes.
Add remaining ingredients and stir everything well.

Seal the pot with pressure cooking lid and cook on high for 3 minutes.
Once done, release pressure using a quick release. Remove lid.
Stir and serve.
Nutrition:
Calories 82
Fat 4.9 g
Carbohydrates 9.1 g
Sugar 4.6 g
Protein 2.3 g
Cholesterol 0 mg

Bell pepper eggs

Preparation time: 25 minutes
Cooking Time: 30 minutes
Servings: 4
Ingredients:
4 medium green bell peppers
¼ medium onion; peeled and chopped
3 oz. Cooked ham; chopped
8 large eggs.
1 cup mild cheddar cheese
Directions:
Cut the tops off each bell pepper. Remove the seeds and the white membranes with a small knife.
Place ham and onion into each pepper
Crack 2 eggs into each pepper. Top with ¼ cup cheese per pepper.
Place into the air fryer basket
Adjust the temperature to 390 degrees f and set the timer for 15 minutes.
When fully cooked, peppers will be tender and eggs will be firm. Serve immediately.
Nutrition: Calories: 314; Protein: 24.9g; Fiber: 1.7g; Fat: 18.6g; Carbs: 6.3g

Banana Oatmeal

Preparation Time: 10 minutes
Cooking Time: 5 minutes
Serving: 2
Ingredients:
1 cup oatmeal
1 banana, sliced
1 cup of water
1 cup almond milk
1 tbsp maple syrup
1 1/2 tsp cinnamon
Directions:
Spray instant pot inner pot with cooking spray.
Add water, oatmeal, and almond milk and stir well.
Add maple syrup, cinnamon, and banana and stir well.
Seal the pot with pressure cooking lid and cook on high for 5 minutes.
Once done, allow to release pressure naturally. Remove lid.
Stir and serve.
Nutrition:
Calories 514
Fat 31.5 g

Carbohydrates 55.9 g
Sugar 17.6 g
Protein 8.8 g
Cholesterol 0 mg

Quick & Easy Farro

Preparation time: 5 minutes
Cooking time: 10 minutes
Servings: 4
Ingredients:
1 cup pearl farro
1 tsp olive oil
2 cups vegetable broth
1/4 tsp salt
Directions:
Add all ingredients into the instant pot and stir well.
Seal pot with lid and cook on manual mode for 10 minutes.
Once done then allow to release pressure naturally for 5 minutes then release using the quick-release method. Open the lid.
Stir well and serve.
Nutrition: Calories 169 Fat 1.9 g Carbohydrates 30.5 g Sugar 0.4 g Protein 8.4 g Cholesterol 0 mg

Air-fried Crumbed Fish

Preparation Time: 10 minutes
Cooking Time: 12 minutes
Servings: 4
Ingredients:
¼ cup vegetable oil
1 egg, beaten
4 flounder fillets
1 cup dry breadcrumbs
1 lemon, sliced
Directions
In a mixing bowl, mix oil and breadcrumbs. Stir to combine.
Dredge fillets into the egg, shaking off excess liquid.
Dip fillets into the breadcrumbs to coat evenly on all sides.
Lay coated fillets on the air fryer basket and place inside the instant pot. Attach the air fryer lid and cook at 350 degrees F for about 12 minutes. Flip halfway through cooking.
Garnish with lemon slices and serve.
Nutrition: Calories – 357 kcal; Carbohydrates – 22.5g; Fat – 17.7g; Protein – 26.9g; Sugar – 2g; Sodium – 309mg

Yogurt Omelet

Preparation time: 25 minutes
Cooking Time: 12 minutes
Servings: 4
Ingredients:
1 ½ cups greek yogurt

4 eggs; whisked
1 tbsp. Cilantro; chopped.
1 tbsp. Chives; chopped.
Cooking spray
Salt and black pepper to taste.
Directions:
Take a bowl and mix all the ingredients except the cooking spray and whisk well.
Now, take a pan that fits in your air fryer and grease it with the cooking spray, pour the eggs mix, spread well, put the pan into the machine and cook the omelet at 360°f for 20 minutes.
Divide between plates and serve for breakfast
Nutrition: Calories: 221; Fat: 14g; Fiber: 4g; Carbs: 6g; Protein: 11g

Lemony Raspberries Bowls

Preparation time: 17 minutes
Cooking Time: 12 minutes
Servings: 2
Ingredients:
1 cup raspberries
2 tbsp. Butter
2 tbsp. Lemon juice
1 tsp. Cinnamon powder
Directions:
In your air fryer, mix all the ingredients, toss, cover, cook at 350°f for 12 minutes
Divide into bowls and serve for breakfast
Nutrition: Calories: 208; Fat: 6g; Fiber: 9g; Carbs: 14g; Protein: 3g

Spaghetti Squash Fritters

Preparation time: 23 minutes
Cooking Time: 12 minutes
Servings: 4
Ingredients:
2 cups cooked spaghetti squash
2 stalks green onion, sliced
1 large egg.
¼ cup blanched finely ground almond flour.
2 tbsp. Unsalted butter; softened.
½ tsp. Garlic powder.
1 tsp. Dried parsley.
Directions:
Remove excess moisture from the squash using a cheesecloth or kitchen towel.
Mix all ingredients in a large bowl. Form into four patties
Cut a piece of parchment to fit your air fryer basket. Place each patty on the parchment and place into the air fryer basket
Adjust the temperature to 400 degrees f and set the timer for 8 minutes.
Flip the patties halfway through the cooking time.
Serve warm.
Nutrition: Calories: 131; Protein: 3.8g; Fiber: 2.0g; Fat: 10.1g; Carbs: 7.1g

Zucchini Fritters

Preparation time: 13 minutes
Cooking Time: 12 minutes
Servings: 4
Ingredients:
2 eggs; whisked
8 oz. Zucchinis; chopped.
2 spring onions; chopped.
¼ tsp. Sweet paprika; chopped.
Cooking spray
Salt and black pepper to taste.
Directions:
Take a bowl and mix all the ingredients except the cooking spray, stir well and shape medium fritters out of this mix
Put the basket in the air fryer, add the fritters inside, grease them with cooking spray and cook at 400°f for 8 minutes.
Divide the fritters between plates and serve for breakfast.
Nutrition: Calories: 202; Fat: 10g; Fiber: 2g; Carbs: 4g; Protein: 5g

Easy Lemon Garlic Chicken Breast

Preparation Time: 10 minutes
Cooking Time: 15 minutes
Serving: 1
Ingredients:
1 chicken breast, boneless and skinless
1 lemon juice
1 tsp garlic, minced
1 tbsp chicken seasoning
Pepper
Salt
Directions:
Season chicken with pepper and salt.
Mix together lemon juice, garlic, and chicken seasoning and rub all over chicken breast.
Place the dehydrating tray in a multi-level air fryer basket and place basket in the instant pot.
Place chicken on the dehydrating tray.
Seal pot with air fryer lid and select air fry mode then set the temperature to 350 F and timer for 15 minutes. Turn chicken halfway through.
Serve and enjoy.
Nutrition:
Calories 143
Fat 3.2 g
Carbohydrates 2 g
Sugar 1 g
Protein 24.3 g
Cholesterol 72 mg

Coconut Blueberry Oatmeal

Preparation time: 10 minutes
Cooking time: 30 minutes

Servings: 6
Ingredients:
2 1/4 cups oats
1 cup blueberries
1/4 cup gluten-free flour
1/2 tsp vanilla
3 cups of water
14 oz coconut milk
6 tbsp brown sugar
1/8 tsp salt
Directions:
Add all ingredients into the instant pot and stir well.
Seal pot with lid and cook on manual mode for 30 minutes.
Once done then release pressure using the quick-release method than open the lid.
Stir well and serve.
Nutrition: Calories 337 Fat 18.1 g Carbohydrates 40.3 g Sugar 13.7 g Protein 6.4 g Cholesterol 0 mg

Pumpkin Cranberry Oatmeal

Preparation time: 10 minutes
Cooking time: 3 minutes
Servings: 4
Ingredients:
1 cup steel-cut oats
2 tbsp honey
1/2 cup dried cranberries
3/4 cup pumpkin puree
1 cup milk
2 cups of water
1 1/2 tsp pumpkin pie spice
Pinch of salt
Directions:
Add oats, cranberries, pumpkin puree, milk, water, pumpkin pie spice, and salt and stir well.
Seal pot with lid and cook on manual high pressure for 3 minutes.
Once done then release pressure using the quick-release method than open the lid.
Add honey and stir well.
Serve and enjoy.
Nutrition: Calories 165 Fat 2.8 g Carbohydrates 30.9 g Sugar 13.6 g Protein 5.3 g Cholesterol 5 mg

Cranberry Farro

Preparation time: 10 minutes
Cooking time: 20 minutes
Servings: 8
Ingredients:
15 oz farro
1/2 cup dried cranberries
1 tsp lemon extract
1/2 cup brown sugar
4 1/2 cups water
1/4 tsp salt
Directions:
Add farro, lemon extract, brown sugar, water, and salt into the instant pot and stir well.

Seal pot with lid and cook on high pressure for 20 minutes.
Once done then allow to release pressure naturally for 10 minutes then release using the quick-release method.
Open the lid.
Add cranberries and stir well.
Serve and enjoy.
Nutrition: Calories 130 Fat 3.9 g Carbohydrates 21.2 g Sugar 10.4 g Protein 3.9 g Cholesterol 6 mg

Rice Lentil Porridge

Preparation time: 10 minutes
Cooking time: 21 minutes
Servings: 4
Ingredients:
1/2 cup yellow lentils, soaked for 15 minutes and drained
1 cup rice, soaked for 15 minutes and drained
6 cups vegetable stock
1 bay leaf
1 tsp turmeric
1 1/2 tsp cumin seeds
2 tbsp olive oil
1 1/2 tsp salt
Directions:
Add oil into the inner pot of instant pot duo crisp and set pot on sauté mode.
Add cumin seeds and bay leaf and sauté for 30 seconds.
Add lentils, turmeric, rice, salt, and stock. Stir well.
Seal the pot with pressure cooking lid and cook on high for minutes.
Once done, allow to release pressure naturally for 10 minutes then release remaining pressure using a quick release.
Remove lid.
Stir and serve.
Nutrition: Calories 320 Fat 7.9 g Carbohydrates 51.9 g Sugar 1.2 g Protein 10.1 g Cholesterol 0 mg

Easy Cheese Bake

Preparation Time: 10 minutes
Cooking Time: 25 minutes
Serving: 3
Ingredients:
6 eggs
1/4 tsp dry mustard
2 tbsp butter, melted
1/4 lb cheddar cheese, grated
1/2 cup milk
Pepper
Salt
Directions:
Spray a baking dish with cooking spray and set aside.
In a bowl, whisk eggs with milk, mustard, pepper, and salt. Stir in grated cheese.
Pour egg mixture into the prepared baking dish.
Place steam rack into the instant pot then place baking dish on top of the rack.
Seal pot with air fryer lid and select bake mode then set the temperature to 350 F and timer for 25 minutes.
Serve and enjoy.
Nutrition:
Calories 368

Fat 29.9 g
Carbohydrates 3.3 g
Sugar 2.7 g
Protein 22 g
Cholesterol 391 mg

Healthy Kale Muffins

Preparation Time: 10 minutes
Cooking Time: 30 minutes
Serving: 8
Ingredients:
6 large eggs
1/2 cup almond milk
1 cup kale, chopped
1/4 cup chives, chopped
Pepper
Salt
Directions:
Add all ingredients into the bowl and whisk well.
Pour egg mixture into the 8 silicone muffin molds.
Place the dehydrating tray in a multi-level air fryer basket and place basket in the instant pot.
Place 6 muffin molds on dehydrating tray.
Seal pot with air fryer lid and select bake mode then set the temperature to 350 F and timer for 30 minutes.
Bake remaining muffins using the same method.
Serve and enjoy.
Nutrition:
Calories 93
Fat 7.3 g
Carbohydrates 2.1 g
Sugar 0.8 g
Protein 5.4 g
Cholesterol 140 mg

Breakfast Muffins

Preparation Time: 10 minutes
Cooking Time: 25 minutes
Serving: 6
Ingredients:
4 large eggs
2 tbsp butter
4 oz cream cheese
1 scoop whey protein
Directions:
In a bowl, melt cream cheese and butter.
Add eggs and whey protein in a bowl and beat until well combined.
Pour batter into the 6 silicone muffin molds.
Place the dehydrating tray in a multi-level air fryer basket and place basket in the instant pot.
Place muffin molds on dehydrating tray.
Seal pot with air fryer lid and select air fry mode then set the temperature to 350 F and timer for 25 minutes.

Serve and enjoy.
Nutrition:
Calories 168
Fat 14.1 g
Carbohydrates 1.4 g
Sugar 0.5 g
Protein 9.4 g
Cholesterol 166 mg

Zucchini Yogurt Bread

Preparation time:10 minutes
Cooking Time: 45 minutes
Serving: 6
Ingredients:
1 cup walnut halves
2 cups all-purpose flour
1/2 teaspoon baking powder
1/2 teaspoon baking soda
1/2 teaspoon salt
3/4 cup 2 tablespoons sugar
2 large eggs
1/2 cup vegetable oil
1/2 cup plain Greek yogurt
1 cup zucchini, grated
Directions:
Whisk baking powder, flour, salt, and baking soda in a medium bowl.
Stir in eggs, vegetable oil, yogurt, and sugar, then mix well.
Add flour mixture and mix well until smooth.
Fold in walnuts and zucchini, then spread this batter in a greased baking pan.
Place this pan in the Instant Pot Duo.
Put on the Air Fryer lid and seal it.
Hit the "Bake Button" and select 45 minutes of cooking time, then press "Start."
Once the Instant Pot Duo beeps, remove its lid.
Slice and serve.
Nutrition:
Calories 575
Total Fat 32.8g
Saturated Fat 5g
Cholesterol 64mg
Sodium 333mg
Total Carbohydrate 60.6g
Dietary Fiber 2.8g
Total Sugars 26.4g

Saucy Eggs Bake

Preparation time:10 minutes
Cooking Time: 35 minutes
Serving: 4
Ingredients:
1 1/2 pounds plum tomatoes
2 garlic cloves, smashed

2 tablespoons olive oil
Salt and ground pepper
1 teaspoon oregano, chopped
8 large eggs
2 tablespoons Parmigiano-Reggiano cheese, grated

Directions:

Place the tomatoes in the Instant Pot Duo and add garlic, olive oil, salt, and black pepper on top.
Put on the Air Fryer lid and seal it.
Hit the "Roast Button" and select 20 minutes of cooking time, then press "Start."
Once the Instant Pot Duo beeps, remove its lid.
Transfer the tomatoes to a blender and puree them with oregano.
Take a suitable baking pan and spread the sauce in it.
Whisk eggs with salt and black pepper then pour over the sauce.
Top it with shredded cheese.
Place the egg pan in the Instant Pot Duo.
Put on the Air Fryer lid and seal it.
Hit the "Bake Button" and select 15 minutes of cooking time, then press "Start."
Once the Instant Pot Duo beeps, remove its lid.
 Serve.

Nutrition:
Calories 291
Total Fat 20.3g
Saturated Fat 6.2g
Cholesterol 382mg
Sodium 292mg
Total Carbohydrate 10.7g
Dietary Fiber 2.1g
Total Sugars 7.6g
Protein 19.3g

Chapter 3: Fish and seafood Recipes

Spicy Prawns

Preparation Time: 10 minutes
Cooking Time: 6 minutes
Serving: 4
Ingredients:
12 king prawns
1/4 tsp black pepper
1 tsp chili powder
1 tsp red chili flakes
1 tbsp vinegar
1 tbsp ketchup
3 tbsp mayonnaise
1/2 tsp sea salt
Directions:
Add prawns, chili flakes, chili powder, black pepper, and salt to the bowl and toss well.
Spray instant pot multi-level air fryer basket with cooking spray.
Add shrimp into the air fryer basket and place basket into the instant pot.
Seal pot with air fryer lid and select air fry mode then set the temperature to 350 F and timer for 6 minutes. Stir halfway through.
In a small bowl, mix together mayonnaise, ketchup, and vinegar.
Serve shrimp with mayo mixture.
Nutrition:
Calories 254
Fat 5.9 g
Carbohydrates 6.5 g
Sugar 1.6 g
Protein 43.2 g
Cholesterol 636 mg

Simple & Perfect Salmon

Preparation Time: 10 minutes
Cooking Time: 7 minutes
Serving: 2
Ingredients:
2 salmon fillets, remove any bones
2 tsp olive oil
2 tsp paprika
Pepper
Salt
Directions:
Coat salmon with oil and season with paprika, pepper, and salt.
Place the dehydrating tray in a multi-level air fryer basket and place basket in the instant pot.
Place salmon fillets on dehydrating tray.
Seal pot with air fryer lid and select air fry mode then set the temperature to 390 F and timer for 7 minutes.

Serve and enjoy.
Nutrition:
Calories 282
Fat 15.9 g
Carbohydrates 1.2 g
Sugar 0.2 g
Protein 34.9 g
Cholesterol 78 mg

Healthy Salmon Chowder

Preparation time: 10 minutes
Cooking time: 8 minutes
Servings: 4
Ingredients:
1 lb frozen salmon
2 garlic cloves, minced
2 tbsp butter
2 celery stalks, chopped
1 onion, chopped
1 cup corn
1 medium potato, cubed
2 cups half and half
4 cups chicken broth
Directions:
Add butter into the instant pot and select sauté.
Add onion and garlic into the pot and sauté for 3-4 minutes.
Add remaining ingredients except for the half and a half and stir well.
Seal pot with lid and cook on manual high pressure for 5 minutes.
Once done then allow to release pressure naturally then open the lid.
Add half and half and stir well.
Serve and enjoy.
Nutrition: Calories 571 Fat 35.1 g Carbohydrates 26 g Sugar 3.9 g Protein 36.9 g Cholesterol 133 mg

Pesto Shrimp

Preparation Time: 10 minutes
Cooking Time: 5 minutes
Serving: 6
Ingredients:
1 lb shrimp, defrosted
14 oz basil pesto
Directions:
Add shrimp and pesto into the mixing bowl and toss well.
Spray instant pot multi-level air fryer basket with cooking spray.
Add shrimp into the air fryer basket and place basket into the instant pot.
Seal pot with air fryer lid and select air fry mode then set the temperature to 400 F and timer for 5 minutes.
Serve and enjoy.
Nutrition:
Calories 105
Fat 1.7 g
Carbohydrates 2.9 g

Sugar 0.2 g
Protein 19.3 g

White Fish with Cilantro Sauce

Preparation time:10 minutes
Cooking Time: 30 minutes
Serving: 4
Ingredients:
1 large bunch of cilantros, chopped
1 small onion, chopped
3 cloves of fresh garlic, peeled and chopped
3 tablespoons butter
2 cups sour cream
2 teaspoons salt
4 tablespoons lime juice
2 1/2 pounds white fish fillets
Directions:
Add butter to a suitably sized skillet to melt over medium heat.
Stir in garlic and onion, then sauté for 5 minutes, then transfer to a blender.
Add cream, cilantro, salt, and lime juice, then puree this sauce until smooth.
Place the fish fillets in the Instant Pot Duo basket.
Put on the Air Fryer lid and seal it.
Hit the "Bake Button" and select 25 minutes of cooking time, then press "Start."
Once the Instant Pot Duo beeps, do a quick release and remove its lid.
Serve.
Nutrition:
Calories 462
Total Fat 33.8g
Saturated Fat 20.7g
Cholesterol 135mg
Sodium 1375mg
Total Carbohydrate 11g
Dietary Fiber 0.6g
Total Sugars 1.7g
Protein 29.9g

Sole with Mint and Ginger

Preparation time:10 minutes
Cooking Time: 15 minutes
Serving: 4
Ingredients:
2 pounds sole fillets
1 bunch mint
1 2-inch piece ginger, peeled and chopped
1 tablespoon vegetable or canola oil
1/2 teaspoon salt
1/4 teaspoon freshly ground black pepper
Directions:
Add mint, salt, black pepper, ginger, and oil to a blender and blend until smooth.
Stir in 2 teaspoon water if the sauce is too thick then mix well.

Rub the fish with the mint sauce to coat it liberally.
Place the coated fish in the Instant Pot Duo.
Put on the Air Fryer lid and seal it.
Hit the "Air fry Button" and select 15 minutes of cooking time, then press "Start."
Once the Instant Pot Duo beeps, remove its lid.
Serve warm.
Nutrition:
Calories 302
Total Fat 7.6g
Saturated Fat 0.3g
Cholesterol 147mg
Sodium 559mg
Total Carbohydrate 1g
Dietary Fiber 0.3g
Total Sugars 0g
Protein 50.9g

Creamy Parmesan Shrimp

Preparation Time: 10 minutes
Cooking Time: 5 minutes
Serving: 4
Ingredients:
1 lb shrimp, deveined and cleaned
1 oz parmesan cheese, grated
1 tbsp garlic, minced
1 tbsp lemon juice
1/4 cup salad dressing
Directions:
Spray instant pot multi-level air fryer basket with cooking spray.
Add shrimp into the air fryer basket and place basket into the instant pot.
Seal pot with air fryer lid and select air fry mode then set the temperature to 400 F and timer for 5 minutes.
Transfer shrimp into the mixing bowl. Add remaining ingredients over shrimp and stir for 1 minute.
Serve and enjoy.
Nutrition:
Calories 219
Fat 8.4 g
Carbohydrates 6.3 g
Sugar 1 g
Protein 28.4 g
Cholesterol 248 mg

Delicious Garlic Butter Salmon

Preparation Time: 10 minutes
Cooking Time: 7 minutes
Serving: 4
Ingredients:
1 lb salmon fillets
2 tbsp parsley, chopped
2 tbsp garlic, minced

1/4 cup parmesan cheese, grated
1/4 cup butter, melted
Pepper
Salt
Directions:
Season salmon with pepper and salt.
In a small bowl, mix together butter, cheese, garlic, and parsley and brush over salmon fillets.
Place the dehydrating tray in a multi-level air fryer basket and place basket in the instant pot.
Place salmon fillets on dehydrating tray.
Seal pot with air fryer lid and select air fry mode then set the temperature to 400 F and timer for 7 minutes.
Serve and enjoy.
Nutrition:
Calories 277
Fat 19.8 g
Carbohydrates 1.7 g
Sugar 0.1 g
Protein 24.3 g
Cholesterol 85 mg

Shrimp Mac n Cheese

Preparation time: 10 minutes
Cooking time: 10 minutes
Servings: 2
Ingredients:
1 1/4 cups elbow macaroni
1 tbsp butter
2/3 cup milk
1 bell pepper, chopped
15 shrimp
1 tbsp cajun spice
1/2 cup flour
1 cup cheddar cheese, shredded
Directions:
Add butter in instant pot and set the pot on sauté mode.
Add bell pepper and sauté for minutes.
Add water and pasta and stir well.
Seal pot with lid and cook on manual high pressure for 3 minutes.
Once done then release pressure using the quick-release method than open the lid.
Add cajun spices and flour and stir well.
Set pot on sauté mode. Add shrimp and cook for 2 minutes.
Add cheese and milk and stir well.
Serve and enjoy.
Nutrition: Calories 843 Fat 30.2 g Carbohydrates 74.8 g Sugar 8.4 g Protein 65.1 g Cholesterol 429 mg

Salmon Rice Pilaf

Preparation time: 10 minutes
Cooking time: 5 minutes
Servings: 2
Ingredients:
2 salmon fillets

1 cup chicken stock
1 tbsp butter
1/2 cup of rice
1/4 cup vegetable soup mix
1/4 tsp sea salt

Directions:
Add all ingredients except fish fillets into the instant pot and stir well.
Place steamer rack on top of rice mixture.
Place fish fillets on top of rack and season with pepper and salt.
Seal pot with lid and cook on manual high pressure for 5 minutes.
Once done then release pressure using the quick-release method than open the lid.
Serve and enjoy.

Nutrition: Calories 474 Fat 17.4 g Carbohydrates 40 g Sugar 0.8 g Protein 39 g Cholesterol 94 mg

---

Perfect Salmon Dinner

Preparation time: 10 minutes
Cooking time: 2 minutes
Servings: 3

Ingredients:
1 lb. salmon fillet, cut into three pieces
2 garlic cloves, minced
1/2 tsp ground cumin
1 tsp red chili powder
Pepper
Salt

Directions:
Pour 1 1/2 cups water into the instant pot then place trivet into the pot.
In a small bowl, mix together garlic, cumin, chili powder, pepper, and salt.
Rub salmon with spice mixture and place on top of the trivet.
Seal pot with lid and cook on steam mode for 2 minutes.
Once done then release pressure using the quick-release method than open the lid.
Serve and enjoy.

Nutrition: Calories 207 Fat 9.6 g Carbohydrates 1.3 g Sugar 0.1 g Protein 29.6 g Cholesterol 67 mg

---

Steam Clams

Preparation time: 10 minutes
Cooking time: 3 minutes
Servings: 3

Ingredients:
1 lb mushy shell clams
2 tbsp butter, melted
1/4 cup white wine
1/2 tsp garlic powder
1/4 cup fresh lemon juice

Directions:
Add white wine, lemon juice, garlic powder, and butter into the instant pot.
Place trivet into the pot.
Arrange clams on top of the trivet.
Seal pot with lid and cook on manual high pressure for 3 minutes.
Once done then allow to release pressure naturally then open the lid.
Serve and enjoy.

Nutrition: Calories 336 Fat 18.5 g Carbohydrates 24.8 g Sugar 2.8 g Protein 13.1 g Cholesterol 20 mg

---

Delicious Tilapia

Preparation Time: 10 minutes
Cooking Time: 8 minutes
Serving: 4
Ingredients:
2 tilapia fillets
1/4 tsp cayenne
1/2 tsp cumin
1 tsp garlic powder
1 tsp dried oregano
2 tsp brown sugar
2 tbsp paprika
Salt
Directions:
In a small bowl, mix together cayenne, cumin, garlic powder, oregano, sugar, paprika, and salt and rub over tilapia fillets.
Place the dehydrating tray in a multi-level air fryer basket and place basket in the instant pot.
Place tilapia fillets on dehydrating tray.
Seal pot with air fryer lid and select air fry mode then set the temperature to 400 F and timer for 8 minutes. Turn tilapia fillets halfway through.
Serve and enjoy.
Nutrition:
Calories 67
Fat 1.1 g
Carbohydrates 4.3 g
Sugar 2 g
Protein 11.2 g
Cholesterol 28 mg

Horseradish Salmon

Preparation Time: 10 minutes
Cooking Time: 7 minutes
Serving: 2
Ingredients:
2 salmon fillets
1/4 cup breadcrumbs
2 tbsp olive oil
1 tbsp horseradish
Pepper
Salt
Directions:
Place the dehydrating tray in a multi-level air fryer basket and place basket in the instant pot.
Place salmon fillets on dehydrating tray.
In a small bowl, mix together breadcrumbs, oil, horseradish, pepper, and salt and spread over salmon fillets.
Seal pot with air fryer lid and select air fry mode then set the temperature to 400 F and timer for 7 minutes.
Serve and enjoy.
Nutrition:
Calories 413

Fat 25.8 g
Carbohydrates 10.6 g
Sugar 1.4 g
Protein 36.4 g
Cholesterol 78 mg

Shrimp Scampi

Preparation time: 10 minutes
Cooking time: 2 minutes
Servings: 2
Ingredients:
1 lb shrimp, peeled and deveined
1 cup of water
1/4 tsp red chili flakes
3 garlic cloves, minced
2 tbsp butter
2 tbsp lemon juice
Pepper
Salt
Directions:
Add butter into the instant pot and set the pot on sauté mode.
Add garlic, pepper, red chili flakes, and salt to the pot and sauté for 2 minutes.
Add shrimp and water. Stir well.
Seal pot with lid and cook on manual high pressure for 2 minutes.
Once done then release pressure using the quick-release method than open the lid.
Stir in lemon juice and serve.
Nutrition: Calories 382 Fat 15.5 g Carbohydrates 5.3 g Sugar 0.4 g Protein 52.2 g Cholesterol 508 mg

---

Dijon Fish Fillets

Preparation time: 10 minutes
Cooking time: 3 minutes
Servings: 2
Ingredients:
2 halibut fillets
1 tbsp dijon mustard
1 1/2 cups water
Pepper
Salt
Directions:
Pour water into the instant pot then place steamer basket in the pot.
Season fish fillets with pepper and salt and brush with dijon mustard.
Place fish fillets in the steamer basket.
Seal pot with lid and cook on manual high pressure for 3 minutes.
Once done then release pressure using the quick-release method than open the lid.
Serve and enjoy.
Nutrition: Calories 323 Fat 7 g Carbohydrates 0.5 g Sugar 0.1 g Protein 60.9 g Cholesterol 93 mg

Bacon-Wrapped Shrimp

Preparation time: 10 minutes
Cooking Time: 10 minutes
Serving: 6
Ingredients:
1-pound shrimp
1 package bacon
1/2 teaspoon cayenne pepper
1/2 teaspoon ground cumin
1/2 teaspoon onion powder
1/2 teaspoon lemon zest
1 teaspoon garlic powder
1 tablespoon Worcestershire sauce
1 tablespoon lemon juice
Directions:
Whisk Worcestershire sauce with cayenne pepper, onion powder, cumin, lemon zest, and garlic powder in a large bowl.
Toss in shrimp and mix well to coat then cover them to refrigerate for 1 hour.
Cut the bacon in half and wrap each half around each shrimp.
Place the wrapped shrimp in the Air Fryer Basket and set it in the Instant Pot Duo.
Put on the Air Fryer lid and seal it.
Hit the "Air fry Button" and select 10 minutes of cooking time, then press "Start."
Once the Instant Pot Duo beeps, remove its lid.
Serve.
Nutrition:
Calories 114
Total Fat 2.7g
Saturated Fat 0.9g
Cholesterol 163mg
Sodium 286mg
Total Carbohydrate 2.4g
Dietary Fiber 0.1g
Total Sugars 0.8g
Protein 18.6g

Garlic Parmesan Shrimp

Preparation time: 10 minutes
Cooking time: 10 minutes
Servings: 4
Ingredients:
1lb shrimp, deveined and peeled
1 tablespoon olive oil
1 teaspoon salt
1 teaspoon fresh cracked pepper
1 tablespoon lemon juice
6 cloves garlic, diced
1/2 cup grated parmesan cheese
1/4 cup diced cilantro
Directions:
Toss the shrimp with oil and all other ingredients in a bowl.
Spread the seasoned shrimp in the air fryer basket.
Press "power button" of air fry oven and turn the dial to select the "air roast" mode.

Press the time button and again turn the dial to set the cooking time to 10 minutes.
Now push the temp button and rotate the dial to set the temperature at 350 degrees f.
Once preheated, place the air fryer basket in the oven and close its lid.
Toss and flip the shrimp when cooked halfway through.
Serve warm.
Nutrition: Calories 184 Total fat 6.2g Saturated fat 1.6g Cholesterol 241mg Sodium 893mg Total carbohydrate 3.5g Dietary fiber 0.1g Total sugars 0.1g Protein 27.3g

Bang Bang Breaded Shrimp

Preparation time: 10 minutes
Cooking time: 14 minutes
Servings: 4
Ingredients:
1 lb. Raw shrimp peeled and deveined
1 egg white
1/2 cup flour
3/4 cup panko bread crumbs
1 teaspoon paprika
Montreal seasoning to taste
Salt and pepper to taste
Cooking spray
Bang bang sauce
1/3 cup greek yogurt
2 tablespoon sriracha
1/4 cup sweet chili sauce
Directions:
Mix flour with salt, black pepper, paprika, and Montreal seasoning in a bowl.
Dredge the shrimp the flour then dips in the egg.
Coat the shrimp with the breadcrumbs and place them in an air fryer basket.
Press "power button" of air fry oven and turn the dial to select the "air roast" mode.
Press the time button and again turn the dial to set the cooking time to 14 minutes.
Now push the temp button and rotate the dial to set the temperature at 400 degrees f.
Once preheated, place the air fryer basket in the oven and close its lid.
Toss and flip the shrimp when cooked halfway through.
Serve warm.
Nutrition: Calories 200 Total fat 2.7g Saturated fat 0.5g Cholesterol 100mg Sodium 663mg Total carbohydrate 25.1g Dietary fiber 1g Total sugars 6.1g Protein 17.4g

Taco Fried Shrimp

Preparation time: 10 minutes
Cooking time: 5 minutes
Servings: 6
Ingredients:
17 shrimp, defrosted, peeled, and deveined
1 cup breadcrumbs Italian
1 tablespoon taco seasoning
1 tablespoon garlic salt
4 tablespoon butter melted
Olive oil spray
Directions:
Toss the shrimp with oil and all other ingredients in a bowl.

Spread the seasoned shrimp in the air fryer basket.
Press "power button" of air fry oven and turn the dial to select the "air roast" mode.
Press the time button and again turn the dial to set the cooking time to 5 minutes.
Now push the temp button and rotate the dial to set the temperature at 400 degrees f.
Once preheated, place the air fryer basket in the oven and close its lid.
Toss and flip the shrimp when cooked halfway through.
Serve warm.
Nutrition: Calories 350 Total fat 17.6g Saturated fat 10.1g Cholesterol 235mg Sodium 760mg Total carbohydrate 21.4g Dietary fiber 1g Total sugars 2g Protein 25.4g

---

Asparagus Shrimp Risotto

Preparation time: 10 minutes
Cooking time: 16 minutes
Servings: 6
Ingredients:
1 1/2 cups arborio rice
1 tbsp butter
3 1/2 cups chicken stock
1/2 cup white wine
1 cup mushrooms, sliced
1/4 cup parmesan cheese, grated
1 lb shrimp, cooked
1 cup asparagus, chopped
1/2 onion, diced
2 tsp olive oil
1/2 tsp pepper
Salt
Directions:
Add oil into the instant pot and set the pot on sauté mode.
Add onion to the pot and sauté for 2-3 minutes.
Add mushrooms and cook for 5 minutes.
Add rice and cook until lightly brown.
Add stock and wine and stir well.
Seal pot with lid and cook on manual high pressure for 6 minutes,
Once done then release pressure using the quick-release method than open the lid.
Add asparagus and butter and cook on sauté mode for 1 minute.
Add shrimp and cook for 1 minute.
Stir in cheese and serve.
Nutrition: Calories 339 Fat 6.4 g Carbohydrates 42.3 g Sugar 1.6 g Protein 23.3 g Cholesterol 168 mg

---

Parmesan Shrimp Risotto

Preparation Time: 10 minutes
Cooking Time: 6 minutes
Serving: 6
Ingredients:
1 lb jumbo shrimp, deveined and uncooked
1 lb Arborio rice
1 tbsp butter
1 tbsp olive oil
1/2 onion, diced
1 tbsp garlic, minced

1/2 cup peas
1 3/4 cups parmesan cheese, grated
8 cups chicken broth

Directions:

Add butter and oil into the inner pot of instant pot duo crisp and set pot on sauté mode.
Add onion and garlic and cook for 2-3 minutes.
Add shrimp and cook until just opaque. Remove shrimp from pot and set aside.
Add broth and rice. Stir well.
Seal the pot with pressure cooking lid and cook on high for 6 minutes.
Once done, allow to release pressure naturally. Remove lid.
Stir in parmesan cheese, peas, and shrimp.
Serve and enjoy.

Nutrition:
Calories 464
Fat 8.3 g
Carbohydrates 66.3 g
Sugar 3.4 g
Protein 28.6 g
Cholesterol 166 mg

Asian Pineapple Shrimp

Preparation Time: 10 minutes
Cooking Time: 2 minutes
Serving: 4

Ingredients:
1 1/2 cups pineapple chunks
2 tbsp soy sauce
1/4 cup dry white wine
1/2 cup pineapple juice
12 oz quinoa, rinsed and drained
1 bell pepper, sliced
2 scallions, chopped
1 lb shrimp, frozen
3/4 tbsp chili paste
2 tbsp Thai sweet chili paste

Directions:

Add all ingredients except scallion and pineapple chunks into the inner pot of instant pot duo crisp and stir well.
Seal the pot with pressure cooking lid and cook on high for 2 minutes.
Once done, allow to release pressure naturally. Remove lid.
Add pineapple chunks and scallion and stir well.
Serve and enjoy.

Nutrition:
Calories 548
Fat 7.7 g
Carbohydrates 76.9 g
Sugar 14.9 g
Protein 39.4 g
Cholesterol 240 mg

Shrimp Macaroni

Preparation Time: 10 minutes
Cooking Time: 8 minutes
Serving: 6
Ingredients:
1 lb frozen shrimp, cooked
1 cup shredded gouda cheese
2 cups cheddar cheese, shredded
1 1/2 cups elbow macaroni, uncooked
1/4 tsp ground nutmeg
1/4 tsp white pepper
2 tbsp parsley, chopped
2 tbsp chives, minced
1 1/2 tbsp hot sauce
1 cup blue cheese, crumbled
1/2 tsp onion powder
1 tsp ground mustard
1 tbsp butter
1 cup half and half
2 cups of milk
Directions:
Add milk, butter, mustard, onion powder, white pepper, half and half, and ground nutmeg into the inner pot of instant pot duo crisp and stir well.
Seal the pot with pressure cooking lid and cook on high for 3 minutes.
Once done, allow to release pressure naturally. Remove lid.
Add remaining ingredients and stir well and cook on sauté mode for 5 minutes.
Serve and enjoy.
Nutrition:
Calories 590
Fat 38.1 g
Carbohydrates 17.7 g
Sugar 5.2 g
Protein 43.7 g

Coconut Chili Shrimp

Preparation time:5-10 Minutes
Cooking Time: 6 Minutes
Servings: 5-6
Ingredients:
3 cups panko breadcrumbs
½ cup all-purpose flour
2 large eggs
½ teaspoon ground black pepper
¼ cup honey
1 serrano chili, thinly sliced
½ teaspoon kosher salt
2 teaspoon fresh cilantro, chopped
3 cups flaked coconut, unsweetened
12 ounce medium-size raw shrimps, peeled, and deveined) ¼ cup lime juice
Directions:
In a mixing bowl, combine honey, Serrano chili with lime juice.
In a mixing bowl, combine the pepper and flour. In a mixing bowl, beat the eggs.

In another bowl, combine the coconut and breadcrumbs. Coat the shrimps with the eggs, then with the flour, and then with the crumbs. Coat with some cooking spray.

Place Instant Pot Air Fryer Crisp over kitchen platform. Press Air Fry, set the temperature to 400°F and set the timer to 5 minutes to preheat. Press "Start" and allow it to preheat for 5 minutes.

In the inner pot, place the Air Fryer basket. Line with a parchment paper, add the shrimps.

Close the Crisp Lid and press the "Air Fry" setting. Set temperature to 200°F and set the timer to 6 minutes. Press "Start."

Halfway down, open the Crisp Lid, shake the basket and close the lid to continue cooking for the remaining time. Open the Crisp Lid after cooking time is over. Serve the shrimps warm with the chili sauce.

Nutrition: **Calories: 233**
Fat: 8.5g
Saturated Fat: 1g
Trans Fat: 0g
Carbohydrates: 28g
Fiber: 6g
Sodium: 349mg
Protein: 13g

Lemon Crab Patties

Preparation Time: 10 minutes
Cooking Time: 10 minutes
Serving: 4
Ingredients:
1 egg
12 oz crabmeat
2 green onion, chopped
1/4 cup mayonnaise
1 cup almond flour
1 tsp old bay seasoning
1 tsp red pepper flakes
1 tbsp fresh lemon juice
Directions:
Add half almond flour into the shallow bowl.
Add remaining ingredients and mix until well combined.
Place the dehydrating tray in a multi-level air fryer basket and place basket in the instant pot.
Make patties and coat with remaining almond flour and place on dehydrating tray.
Seal pot with air fryer lid and select air fry mode then set the temperature to 400 F and timer for 10 minutes. Turn patties halfway through.
Serve and enjoy.
Nutrition:
Calories 327
Fat 19.8 g
Carbohydrates 23.2 g
Sugar 6.6 g
Protein 14.2 g
Cholesterol 62 mg

Basil Tilapia

Preparation time: 10 minutes

Cooking time: 4 minutes
Servings: 4
Ingredients:
4 tilapia fillets
3 garlic cloves, minced
2 tomatoes, chopped
2 tbsp olive oil
1/2 cup basil, chopped
1/8 tsp pepper
1/4 tsp salt
Directions:
Pour half cup of water into the instant pot.
Add fish fillets into the steamer basket and season with pepper and salt.
Place a steamer basket into the pot.
Seal pot with lid and cook on manual high pressure for 2 minutes.
Once done then release pressure using the quick-release method than open the lid.
In a bowl, mix together tomatoes, basil, oil, garlic, pepper, and salt.
Place cooked fish fillets on serving plate and top with tomato mixture.
Serve and enjoy.
Nutrition: Calories 168 Fat 8.2 g Carbohydrates 3.3 g Sugar 1.7 g Protein 21.8 g Cholesterol 55 mg

Delicious Shrimp Risotto

Preparation time: 10 minutes
Cooking time: 17 minutes
Servings: 4
Ingredients:
1 lb. shrimp, peeled, deveined, and chopped
1 1/2 cups arborio rice
1/2 tbsp paprika
1/2 tbsp oregano, minced
1 red pepper, chopped
1 onion, chopped
1/2 cup parmesan cheese, grated
1 cup clam juice
3 cups chicken stock
1/4 cup dry sherry
2 tbsp butter
1/4 tsp pepper
1/2 tsp salt
Directions:
Add butter into the instant pot and set the pot on sauté mode.
Add onion and pepper and sauté until onion is softened.
Add paprika, oregano, pepper, and salt. Stir for minute.
Add rice and stir for a minute.
Add sherry, clam juice, and stock. Stir well.
Seal pot with lid and cook on manual high pressure for 10 minutes.
Once done then release pressure using the quick-release method than open the lid.
Add shrimp and cook on sauté mode for 2 minutes.
Stir in cheese and serve.
Nutrition: Calories 530 Fat 10.4 g Carbohydrates 71.6 g Sugar 5.3 g Protein 34.5 g Cholesterol 259 mg

Cajun shrimp

Preparation time: 10 minutes
Cooking time: 2 minutes
Servings: 4
Ingredients:
1 lb. shrimp, peeled and deveined
15 asparagus spears
1 tbsp cajun seasoning
1 tsp olive oil
Directions:
Pour 1 cup of water in instant pot then place the steam rack inside the pot.
Arrange asparagus on a steam rack in a layer.
Place shrimp on the top of asparagus.
Sprinkle cajun seasoning over shrimp and drizzle with olive oil.
Seal pot with lid and cook on steam mode for 2 minutes.
Once done then release pressure using the quick-release method than open the lid.
Serve and enjoy.
Nutrition: Calories 163 Fat 3.2 g Carbohydrates 5.2 g Sugar 1.7 g Protein 27.8 g Cholesterol 239 mg

Quick & easy shrimp

Preparation time: 10 minutes
Cooking time: 1 minute
Servings: 6
Ingredients:
30 oz frozen shrimp, deveined
1/2 cup chicken stock
1/2 cup apple cider vinegar
Directions:
Add all ingredients into the instant pot and stir well.
Seal pot with lid and cook on manual high pressure for 1 minute.
Once done then release pressure using the quick-release method than open the lid.
Serve and enjoy.
Nutrition: Calories 156 Fat 2.6 g Carbohydrates 1.5 g Sugar 0.1 g Protein 29 g Cholesterol 213 mg

Lemon Dill Tuna Patties

Preparation Time: 10 minutes
Cooking Time: 10 minutes
Serving: 2
Ingredients:
2 cans of tuna
1 1/2 tbsp mayonnaise
1 1/2 tbsp almond flour
1/4 tsp pepper
1/2 lemon juice
1/2 tsp onion powder
1 tsp garlic powder
1/2 tsp dried dill
1/4 tsp salt
Directions:

Add all ingredients in a mixing bowl and mix until well combined.
Place the dehydrating tray in a multi-level air fryer basket and place basket in the instant pot.
Make four patties from mixture and place on dehydrating tray.
Seal pot with air fryer lid and select air fry mode then set the temperature to 400 F and timer for 10 minutes.
Serve and enjoy.
Nutrition:
Calories 416
Fat 20.7 g
Carbohydrates 5.8 g
Sugar 1.5 g
Protein 48.9 g
Cholesterol 58 mg

Tasty Spicy Shrimp

Preparation Time: 10 minutes
Cooking Time: 6 minutes
Serving: 2
Ingredients:
1/2 lb shrimp, peeled and deveined
1/2 tsp old bay seasoning
1/4 tsp cayenne pepper
1 tbsp olive oil
1/4 tsp paprika
1/8 tsp salt
Directions:
Add all ingredients into the mixing bowl and toss well.
Spray instant pot multi-level air fryer basket with cooking spray.
Add shrimp into the air fryer basket and place basket into the instant pot.
Seal pot with air fryer lid and select air fry mode then set the temperature to 390 F and timer for 6 minutes.
Serve and enjoy.
Nutrition:
Calories 196
Fat 9 g
Carbohydrates 2 g
Sugar 0.1 g
Protein 25.9 g
Cholesterol 239 mg

Healthy Salmon Patties

Preparation Time: 10 minutes
Cooking Time: 10 minutes
Serving: 4
Ingredients:
14 oz can salmon, drained and remove bones
2 eggs, lightly beaten
1/2 cup almond flour
1/2 onion, minced
1/4 cup butter
1/2 tsp pepper

1 avocado, diced
1 tsp salt
Directions:
Add all ingredients into the mixing bowl and mix until well combined.
Place the dehydrating tray in a multi-level air fryer basket and place basket in the instant pot.
Make patties from mixture and place on dehydrating tray.
Seal pot with air fryer lid and select air fry mode then set the temperature to 400 F and timer for 10 minutes. Turn patties halfway through.
Serve and enjoy.
Nutrition:
Calories 464
Fat 36.2 g
Carbohydrates 9 g
Sugar 1 g
Protein 26.7 g
Cholesterol 167 mg

Lemon Garlicky Shrimp

Preparation Time: 10 minutes
Cooking Time: 5 minutes
Serving: 4
Ingredients:
1 lb shrimp, peeled
1 tbsp olive oil
1 lemon juice
1 lemon zest
1/4 cup fresh parsley, chopped
4 garlic cloves, minced
1/4 tsp red pepper flakes
1/4 tsp sea salt
Directions:
Add all ingredients except parsley and lemon juice into the mixing bowl and toss well.
Spray instant pot multi-level air fryer basket with cooking spray.
Add shrimp into the air fryer basket and place basket into the instant pot.
Seal pot with air fryer lid and select air fry mode then set the temperature to 400 F and timer for 5 minutes.
Garnish shrimp with parsley and drizzle with lemon juice.
Serve and enjoy.
Nutrition:
Calories 174
Fat 5.6 g
Carbohydrates 3.4 g
Sugar 0.4 g
Protein 26.3 g
Cholesterol 239 mg

Air Fried Shrimp

Preparation Time: 10 minutes
Cooking Time: 5 minutes
Serving: 4

Ingredients:
1 1/4 lbs shrimp, peeled and deveined
1 tbsp olive oil
1/2 tsp paprika
1/2 tsp old bay seasoning
1/4 tsp cayenne pepper
1/4 tsp salt

Directions:
Add all ingredients into the mixing bowl and toss well.
Place seasoned shrimp in instant pot air fryer basket and place basket in the pot.
Seal the pot with air fryer lid and select air fry mode and cook at 400 F for 5 minutes.
Serve and enjoy.

Nutrition:
Calories 200
Fat 6 g
Carbohydrates 2.4 g
Sugar 0 g
Protein 32.3 g
Cholesterol 299 mg

Parmesan Salmon

Preparation Time: 10 minutes
Cooking Time: 15 minutes
Serving: 4

Ingredients:
4 salmon fillets
1/4 cup parmesan cheese, grated
1/2 cup walnuts
1 tsp olive oil
1 tbsp lemon rind

Directions:
Line instant pot air fryer basket with parchment paper.
Place salmon fillets on parchment paper in air fryer basket.
Add walnuts into the food processor and process until finely ground.
Mix together ground walnuts, cheese, oil, and lemon rind.
Spoon walnut mixture over the salmon fillets and press gently.
Place air fryer basket in the pot.
Seal the pot with air fryer lid and select bake mode and cook at 400 F for 15 minutes.
Serve and enjoy.

Nutrition:
Calories 349
Fat 21.8 g
Carbohydrates 1.9 g
Sugar 0.3 g
Protein 38.9 g
Cholesterol 80 mg

Delicious Pesto Salmon

Preparation Time: 10 minutes
Cooking Time: 20 minutes
Serving: 2
Ingredients:
2 salmon fillets
1/4 cup parmesan cheese, grated
For pesto:
1/4 cup olive oil
1 1/2 cups fresh basil leaves
3 garlic cloves, peeled and chopped
1/4 cup parmesan cheese, grated
1/4 cup pine nuts
1/4 tsp black pepper
1/2 tsp salt
Directions:
Add all pesto ingredients into the blender and blend until smooth.
Line instant pot air fryer basket with parchment paper.
Place salmon fillet on parchment paper in the air fryer basket. Spread 2 tablespoons of the pesto on each salmon fillet.
Sprinkle cheese on top of the pesto.
Place basket in the pot.
Seal the pot with air fryer lid and select bake mode and cook at 400 F for 20 minutes.
Serve and enjoy.
Nutrition:
Calories 589
Fat 48.7 g
Carbohydrates 4.5 g
Sugar 0.7 g
Protein 38.9 g
Cholesterol 81 mg

Shrimp in Lemon Sauce

Preparation time: 10 minutes
Cooking time: 8 minutes
Servings: 4
Ingredients:
1 1/4 lbs. Large shrimp, peeled and deveined
Cooking spray
1/4 cup fresh lemon juice
2 tablespoons light butter, melted
3 garlic cloves, minced
1 teaspoon worcestershire sauce
3/4 teaspoon lemon-pepper seasoning
1/4 teaspoon ground red pepper
2 tablespoons chopped fresh parsley
Directions:
Toss the shrimp with oil and all other ingredients in a bowl.
Spread the seasoned shrimp in the baking tray.
Press "power button" of air fry oven and turn the dial to select the "air roast" mode.
Press the time button and again turn the dial to set the cooking time to 8 minutes.
Now push the temp button and rotate the dial to set the temperature at 425 degrees f.

Once preheated, place the shrimp's baking tray in the oven and close its lid.
Serve warm.
Nutrition: Calories 176 Total fat 6.1g Saturated fat 3.8g Cholesterol 218mg Sodium 237mg Total carbohydrate 4.3g Dietary fiber 0.3g Total sugars 0.6g Protein 27g

---

Crisp & Delicious Catfish

Preparation Time: 10 minutes
Cooking Time: 20 minutes
Serving: 2
Ingredients:
2 catfish fillets
1/4 cup cornmeal
1/2 tsp garlic powder
1/2 tsp onion powder
1/2 tsp salt
Directions:
Add cornmeal, garlic powder, onion powder, and salt into a zip-lock bag.
Add fish fillets to the zip-lock bag. Seal bag and shake gently to coat fish fillet.
Line instant pot air fryer basket with parchment paper.
Place coated fish fillets on parchment paper in the air fryer basket. Place basket in the pot.
Seal the pot with air fryer lid and select air fry mode and cook at 400 F for 20 minutes. Turn fish fillets halfway through.
Serve and enjoy.
Nutrition:
Calories 276
Fat 12.7 g
Carbohydrates 12.7 g
Sugar 0.5 g
Protein 26.3 g
Cholesterol 75 mg

Easy Paprika Salmon

Preparation Time: 10 minutes
Cooking Time: 7 minutes
Serving: 2
Ingredients:
2 salmon fillets, remove any bones
2 tsp paprika
2 tsp olive oil
Pepper
Salt
Directions:
Brush each salmon fillet with oil, paprika, pepper, and salt.
Line instant pot air fryer basket with parchment paper.
Place salmon fillets on parchment paper in the air fryer basket. Place basket in the pot.
Seal the pot with air fryer lid and select air fry mode and cook at 390 F for 7 minutes.
Serve and enjoy.
Nutrition:
Calories 282
Fat 15.9 g

Carbohydrates 1.2 g
Sugar 0.2 g
Protein 34.9 g
Cholesterol 78 mg

Healthy Catfish

Preparation Time: 10 minutes
Cooking Time: 20 minutes
Serving: 3
Ingredients:
3 catfish fillets
1/4 cup fish seasoning
1 tbsp fresh parsley, chopped
1 tbsp olive oil
Directions:
Place the dehydrating tray in a multi-level air fryer basket and place basket in the instant pot.
Seasoned fish with seasoning and place on dehydrating tray. Brush with olive oil.
Seal pot with air fryer lid and select air fry mode then set the temperature to 400 F and timer for 20 minutes. Turn fish fillets halfway through.
Garnish with parsley and serve.
Nutrition:
Calories 286
Fat 16.8 g
Carbohydrates 6.1 g
Sugar 0 g
Protein 24.9 g
Cholesterol 75 mg

Asian Shrimp

Preparation Time: 10 minutes
Cooking Time: 10 minutes
Serving: 4
Ingredients:
1 lb shrimp, peeled and deveined
1 tbsp cornstarch
1/8 tsp ginger, minced
2 garlic cloves, minced
2 tbsp soy sauce
1 tsp sesame seeds
1 tbsp green onion, sliced
2 tbsp Thai chili sauce
Directions:
Spray instant pot multi-level air fryer basket with cooking spray.
Toss shrimp with cornstarch and place into the air fryer basket and place basket into the instant pot.
Seal pot with air fryer lid and select air fry mode then set the temperature to 400 F and timer for 10 minutes. Turn shrimp halfway through.
Meanwhile, in a bowl, mix together soy sauce, ginger, garlic, and chili sauce.
Add shrimp to the bowl and mix well.
Sprinkle with green onions and sesame seeds.

Nutrition:
Calories 164
Fat 2.3 g
Carbohydrates 7.5 g
Sugar 2.2 g
Protein 26.6 g
Cholesterol 239 mg

Sriracha Honey Salmon

Preparation Time: 10 minutes
Cooking Time: 12 minutes
Serving: 2
Ingredients:
2 salmon fillets, skin on
3 tbsp sriracha
1 tbsp soy sauce
6 tbsp honey
Directions:
In a bowl, mix together soy sauce, sriracha, and honey.
Add salmon fillets to the bowl and coat well with the sauce and let marinate for 60 minutes.
Spray instant pot multi-level air fryer basket with cooking spray.
Place marinated salmon fillets into the air fryer basket and place basket into the instant pot.
Seal pot with air fryer lid and select air fry mode then set the temperature to 400 F and timer for 12 minutes. Turn salmon fillets halfway through.
Serve and enjoy.
Nutrition:
Calories 454
Fat 11 g
Carbohydrates 57 g
Sugar 51.9 g
Protein 35.2 g
Cholesterol 78 mg

Bacon Shrimps

Preparation time:5-10 Minutes
Cooking Time: 10 Minutes
Serving: 5-6
Ingredients:
1/2 teaspoon cayenne pepper
1/2 teaspoon ground cumin
1/2 teaspoon onion powder
1 pound shrimp
1 package bacon
1 teaspoon garlic powder
1/2 teaspoon lemon zest
1 tablespoon lemon juice
1 tablespoon Worcestershire sauce
Directions:

In a mixing bowl, whisk the Worcestershire sauce, cayenne pepper, onion powder, cumin, lemon zest, and garlic powder. Add and combine the shrimp. Refrigerate for 1-2 hours to marinate.
Take the bacon, slice into two parts, and wrap each shrimp with them.
Place Instant Pot Air Fryer Crisp over kitchen platform. Press Air Fry, set the temperature to 400°F and set the timer to 5 minutes to preheat. Press "Start" and allow it to preheat for 5 minutes.
In the inner pot, place the Air Fryer basket. In the basket, add the wrapped shrimps.
Close the Crisp Lid and press the "Air Fry" setting. Set temperature to 380°F and set the timer to 10 minutes. Press "Start."
Halfway down, open the Crisp Lid, shake the basket and close the lid to continue cooking for the remaining time.
Open the Crisp Lid after cooking time is over. Serve warm.
Nutrition: Calories: 138
Fat: 3g
Saturated Fat: 1g
Trans Fat: 0.5g
Carbohydrates: 6g
Fiber: 0.5g
Sodium: 301mg
Protein: 17g

Ranch Fish Fillets

Preparation Time: 10 minutes
Cooking Time: 12 minutes
Serving: 2
Ingredients:
2 fish fillets
1 egg, lightly beaten
1 1/4 tbsp olive oil
1/4 cup breadcrumbs
1/2 packet ranch dressing mix
Directions:
In a shallow dish, mix together breadcrumbs, ranch dressing mix, and oil.
Dip fish fillet in egg then coats with breadcrumb mixture and place on parchment paper in the air fryer basket.
Place basket in the pot.
Seal the pot with air fryer lid and select air fry mode and cook at 400 F for 12 minutes.
Serve and enjoy.
Nutrition:
Calories 373
Fat 22.9 g
Carbohydrates 25.7 g
Sugar 1.2 g
Protein 18 g
Cholesterol 113 mg

Air Fried, Instant Pot Homemade Tuna Patties

Preparation: 5 minutes
Cooking Time: 6 minutes
Servings: 4
Ingredients:
7 ounces of canned tuna

1 egg, large
¼ cup breadcrumbs
1 tablespoon mustard
½ teaspoon ground black pepper
¼ teaspoon salt
Cooking oil spray
Directions:
In a medium bowl, combine egg, tuna, breadcrumbs, pepper, salt, and mustard with your hand.
Spray some cooking oil in the inner pot of the Instant Pot Air Fryer.
Make the tuna egg mix into four patties and place it in the inner pot.
Close the crisp cover.
In the AIR FRYER mode, select BROIL, which comes with a default temperature of 400°F
Set the timer for 6 minutes and press START to air fry.
After 3 minutes, open the crisp cover, flip the patties.
Close the crisp cover to resume cooking for the remaining period.
Serve along with ketchup.
Nutrition: Calories: 67, Total fat: 1.8g, Saturated fat: 0.5g, Trans fat: 0g, Cholesterol: 64mg, Sodium: 324mg, Total carbs: 2g, Dietary fiber: 0g, Sugars: 0g, Protein: 11g

Delicious Cod Nuggets

Preparation Time: 10 minutes
Cooking Time: 15 minutes
Serving: 4
Ingredients:
1 lb cod fillet, cut into chunks
1/2 cup all-purpose flour
1 tbsp olive oil
1 cup cracker crumbs
1 egg, lightly beaten
Pepper
Salt
Directions:
Line instant pot air fryer basket with parchment paper.
Add crackers crumb and oil in food processor and process until it forms crumbly.
Season fish chunks with pepper and salt.
Coat fish chunks with flour then dip in egg and coat with cracker crumbs.
Place coated fish chunks on parchment paper in the air fryer basket. Place basket in the pot.
Seal the pot with air fryer lid and select air fry mode and cook at 350 F for 15 minutes.
Serve and enjoy.
Nutrition:
Calories 272
Fat 9.7 g
Carbohydrates 21.5 g
Sugar 0.4 g
Protein 24.4 g
Cholesterol 97 mg

Balsamic Salmon

Preparation Time: 10 minutes
Cooking Time: 8 minutes
Serving: 2
Ingredients:
2 salmon fillets
2 tbsp balsamic vinegar
2 tbsp honey
1 cup of water
Pepper
Salt
Directions:
Season salmon with pepper and salt.
In a small bowl, mix together vinegar and honey.
Brush salmon with vinegar and honey mixture.
Pour water into the inner pot of instant pot duo crisp then place steamer rack into the pot.
Place salmon skin-side down on the steamer rack.
Seal the pot with pressure cooking lid and cook on high for 3 minutes.
Once done, release pressure using a quick release. Remove lid.
Seal the pot with air fryer lid and select air fry mode and cook at 400 F for 5 minutes.
Serve and enjoy.
Nutrition:
Calories 303
Fat 11 g
Carbohydrates 17.5 g
Sugar 17.3 g
Protein 34.6 g
Cholesterol 78 mg

Garlic Shrimp

Preparation Time: 10 minutes
Cooking Time: 8 minutes
Serving: 4
Ingredients:
1 lb shrimp, peeled and deveined
2 tsp olive oil
For sauce:
1/4 cup honey
1/4 cup soy sauce
1 tbsp ginger, minced
1 tbsp garlic, minced
Directions:
In a mixing bowl, mix together all sauce ingredients. Add shrimp into the bowl and toss well.
Add oil, shrimp with sauce mixture into the inner pot of instant pot duo crisp and cook on sauté mode for 3 minutes.
Seal the pot with pressure cooking lid and cook on high for 5 minutes.
Once done, release pressure using a quick release. Remove lid.
Stir well and serve.
Nutrition:
Calories 235
Fat 4.4 g
Carbohydrates 22 g

Sugar 17.7 g
Protein 27.1 g
Cholesterol 239 mg

Tuna Noodles

Preparation Time: 10 minutes
Cooking Time: 4 minutes
Serving: 4
Ingredients:
1 can tuna, drained
15 oz egg noodles
3 cups of water
3/4 cup frozen peas
4 oz cheddar cheese, shredded
28 oz can cream of mushroom soup
Directions:
Add noodles and water into the inner pot of instant pot duo crisp and stir well.
Add cream of mushroom soup, peas, and tuna on top of noodles.
Seal the pot with pressure cooking lid and cook on high for 4 minutes.
Once done, release pressure using a quick release. Remove lid.
Add cheese and stir well and serve.
Nutrition:
Calories 470
Fat 18.6 g
Carbohydrates 47.5 g
Sugar 6.2 g
Protein 27.7 g
Cholesterol 80 mg

Shrimp Scampi

Preparation Time: 10 minutes
Cooking Time: 4 minutes
Serving: 6
Ingredients:
1 lb frozen shrimp
2 cups pasta, uncooked
1/2 tsp paprika
1/2 tsp red pepper flakes
1 tbsp garlic, minced
1/2 cup parmesan cheese
1/2 cup half and half
1 cup chicken broth
2 tbsp butter, melted
Pepper
Salt
Directions:
Add butter into the inner pot of instant pot duo crisp and set pot on sauté mode.
Add garlic, and red pepper flakes and cook for 2 minutes.
Add shrimp, pepper, noodles, paprika, broth, and salt. Stir well.
Seal the pot with pressure cooking lid and cook on high for 2 minutes.

Once done, release pressure using a quick release. Remove lid.
Add cheese and half and half and stir until cheese is melted.
Serve and enjoy.
Nutrition:
Calories 280
Fat 9.3 g
Carbohydrates 25.8 g
Sugar 0.2 g
Protein 22.6 g
Cholesterol 164 mg

Lemon Butter Salmon

Preparation Time: 10 minutes
Cooking Time: 11 minutes
Serving: 2
Ingredients:
2 salmon fillets
1 tsp olive oil
2 tsp garlic, minced
2 tbsp butter
2 tbsp fresh lemon juice
1/4 cup white wine
Pepper
Salt
Directions:
Place the dehydrating tray in a multi-level air fryer basket and place basket in the instant pot.
Season salmon with pepper and salt and place on dehydrating tray.
Seal pot with air fryer lid and select air fry mode then set the temperature to 350 F and timer for 6 minutes.
Meanwhile, in a saucepan, add remaining ingredients and cook over low heat for 5 minutes.
Place cooked salmon fillets on serving dish and pour prepared sauce over salmon.
Serve and enjoy.
Nutrition:
Calories 390
Fat 25 g
Carbohydrates 2.1 g
Sugar 0.6 g
Protein 35 g
Cholesterol 109 mg

Cheese Crust Salmon

Preparation Time: 10 minutes
Cooking Time: 10 minutes
Serving: 2
Ingredients:
2 salmon fillets
2 tbsp fresh parsley, chopped
1 garlic clove, minced
1/4 cup parmesan cheese, shredded
1/2 tsp McCormick's BBQ seasoning

1/2 tsp paprika
1 tbsp olive oil
Pepper
Salt

Directions:
Add salmon, seasoning, and olive oil to the bowl and mix well.
Mix together cheese, garlic, and parsley.
Sprinkle cheese mixture on top of salmon.
Place the dehydrating tray in a multi-level air fryer basket and place basket in the instant pot.
Place salmon fillets on dehydrating tray.
Seal pot with air fryer lid and select air fry mode then set the temperature to 400 F and timer for 10 minutes.
Serve and enjoy.

Nutrition:
Calories 341
Fat 20.5 g
Carbohydrates 2.2 g
Sugar 0.6 g
Protein 38.5 g
Cholesterol 87 mg

Healthy Crab Cakes

Preparation Time: 10 minutes
Cooking Time: 10 minutes
Serving: 2

Ingredients:
3/4 cup crabmeat, drained
1 large egg whites
2 green onions, chopped
1/2 celery rib, chopped
1/2 sweet red pepper, chopped
1/4 cup breadcrumbs
1/8 tsp wasabi
1 1/2 tbsp mayonnaise
1/8 tsp salt

Directions:
Place breadcrumbs in a shallow bowl.
In a bowl, add remaining ingredients except for crab and mix well. Fold in crabmeat.
Drop a tablespoon of crabmeat mixture to the breadcrumbs and slowly coat and shape into patties.
Place the dehydrating tray in a multi-level air fryer basket and place basket in the instant pot.
Place crab patties on dehydrating tray.
Seal pot with air fryer lid and select air fry mode then set the temperature to 375 F and timer for 10 minutes. Turn patties halfway through.
Serve and enjoy.

Nutrition:
Calories 151
Fat 4.7 g
Carbohydrates 21 g
Sugar 5.6 g
Protein 6.8 g
Cholesterol 9 mg

Coconut Shrimp

Preparation time: 10 minutes
Cooking time: 12 minutes
Servings: 4
Ingredients:
Shrimp
1/2 cup flour
Salt
Black pepper
1 cup panko bread crumbs
1/2 cup sweetened coconut shredded
2 large eggs, beaten
1 lb. Large shrimp, peeled and deveined
Dipping sauce
1/2 cup mayonnaise
1 tablespoon sriracha
1 tablespoon Thai sweet chili sauce
Directions:
Mix flour with black pepper and salt in a bowl and dredge the shrimp through it.
Dip the shrimp in the egg and coat well with the breadcrumbs.
Place the crusted shrimp in the air fryer basket.
Press "power button" of air fry oven and turn the dial to select the "air roast" mode.
Press the time button and again turn the dial to set the cooking time to 12 minutes.
Now push the temp button and rotate the dial to set the temperature at 400 degrees f.
Once preheated, place the air fryer basket in the oven and close its lid.
Toss and flip the shrimp when cooked halfway through.
Whisk mayonnaise with sriracha and chili sauce in a bowl.
Serve shrimp with mayo sauce.
Nutrition: Calories 301 Total fat 11.5g Saturated fat 3.7g Cholesterol 175mg Sodium 452mg Total carbohydrate 29.8g Dietary fiber 1.7g Total sugars 3.9g Protein 20.2g

Easy Garlic Lemon Shrimp

Preparation time: 10 minutes
Cooking time: 5 minutes
Servings: 3
Ingredients:
1 lb large shrimp
2 garlic cloves, minced
3 tbsp butter
1/2 tsp paprika
2 lemons, sliced
Directions:
Add butter into the pot and set the pot on sauté mode.
Add garlic and sauté for 1 minute.
Add shrimp, paprika, and lemon slices, and stirs well.
Seal pot with lid and cook on manual high pressure for 4 minutes.
Once done then allow to release pressure naturally then open the lid.
Serve and enjoy.
Nutrition: Calories 229 Fat 11.6 g Carbohydrates 4 g Sugar 0.2 g Protein 28.7 g Cholesterol 247 mg

Cheesy Tilapia

Preparation time: 10 minutes
Cooking time: 10 minutes
Servings: 2
Ingredients:
2 tilapia fillets
3/4 cup parmesan cheese, grated
2 tbsp fresh lemon juice
2 tbsp mayonnaise
Pepper
Salt
Directions:
In a bowl, mix together mayo, lemon juice, pepper, and salt and marinate fish fillets in this mixture.
Place marinated tilapia fillets into the instant pot.
Seal pot with lid and cook on manual high pressure for 7 minutes.
Once done then allow to release pressure naturally then open the lid.
Top with cheese and cook on sauté mode for 3 minutes.
Serve and enjoy.
Nutrition: Calories 244 Fat 12.1 g Carbohydrates 4.9 g Sugar 1.3 g Protein 30.3 g Cholesterol 485 mg

Scallops Curry

Preparation time: 10 minutes
Cooking time: 9 minutes
Servings: 4
Ingredients:
1 lb. scallops
1 cup of coconut milk
1/2 tsp soy sauce
1/4 tsp nutmeg powder
1/2 cup red curry paste
1 1/2 cup chicken broth
1/2 tsp curry powder
1 tsp vinegar
1 tbsp olive oil
1/2 tsp salt
Directions:
Add oil into the instant pot and set the pot on sauté mode.
Add scallops and sauté for 3 minutes.
Add remaining ingredients and stir well.
Seal pot with lid and cook on manual high pressure for 6 minutes.
Once done then release pressure using the quick-release method than open the lid.
Serve and enjoy.
Nutrition: Calories 404 Fat 28.3 g Carbohydrates 12.6 g Sugar 2.3 g Protein 22.3 g Cholesterol 37 mg

Healthy Shrimp Boil

Preparation time: 10 minutes
Cooking time: 1 minute
Servings: 6
Ingredients:
2 lbs. frozen shrimp, deveined

1 onion, chopped
1/2 tsp red pepper flakes
1 tbsp old bay seasoning
10 oz sausage, sliced
5 frozen half corn on the cobs
3 garlic cloves, crushed
1 cup chicken stock
1/2 tsp salt
Directions:
Add all ingredients into the instant pot and stir well.
Seal pot with lid and cook on manual high pressure for 1 minute.
Once done then release pressure using the quick-release method than open the lid.
Stir and serve.
Nutrition: Calories 407 Fat 17.1 g Carbohydrates 19.6 g Sugar 5.1 g Protein 43 g Cholesterol 267 mg

Horseradish Crusted Salmon

Preparation time:10 minutes
Cooking Time: 5 minutes
Serving: 2
Ingredients:
2 pieces of salmon fillet
1 teaspoon salt
1 teaspoon black pepper
1 tablespoon horseradish
2 tablespoons olive oil
1/4 cup bread crumbs
Directions:
Whisk bread crumbs with salt, olive oil, horseradish and black pepper in a bowl.
Coat the salmon with this crumbly mixture liberally.
Place the breaded salmon in the Air Fryer Basket and set it inside the Instant Pot Duo.
Put on the Air Fryer lid and seal it.
Hit the "Air fry Button" and select 5 minutes of cooking time, then press "Start."
Once the Instant Pot Duo beeps, remove its lid.
Serve.
Nutrition:
Calories 415
Total Fat 25.8g
Saturated Fat 3.8g
Cholesterol 78mg
Sodium 1364mg
Total Carbohydrate 11.3g
Dietary Fiber 1.1g
Total Sugars 1.5g
Protein 36.5g

Pesto Shrimp Kebobs

Preparation time:10 minutes
Cooking Time: 5 minutes
Serving: 12
Ingredients:

1-pound shrimp
16 oz. basil pesto
Directions:
Toss the shrimp with pesto and coat them well.
Thread these pesto shrimp on the skewers.
Place the skewers in the Air Fryer Basket and set it in the Instant Pot Duo.
Put on the Air Fryer lid and seal it.
Hit the "Air fry Button" and select 5 minutes of cooking time, then press "Start."
Once the Instant Pot Duo beeps, remove its lid.
Serve.
Nutrition:
Calories 92
Total Fat 1.3g
Saturated Fat 0.3g
Cholesterol 147mg
Sodium 172mg
Total Carbohydrate 2g
Dietary Fiber 1.2g
Total Sugars 0.2g
Protein 18.2g

Mahi Mahi Fillets

Preparation time: 10 minutes
Cooking time: 13 minutes
Servings: 4
Ingredients:
6 mahi-mahi fillets
29 oz can tomato, diced
1/2 onion, sliced
2 tbsp lemon juice
1/2 tsp dried oregano
3 tbsp butter
Pepper
Salt
Directions:
Add butter into the instant pot and set the pot on sauté mode.
Add onion and sauté for 2 minutes.
Add remaining ingredients except for fish fillets and sauté for 3 minutes.
Place fish fillets into the pot.
Seal pot with lid and cook on manual high pressure for 8 minutes.
Once done then release pressure using the quick-release method than open the lid.
Serve and enjoy.
Nutrition: Calories 263 Fat 8.7 g Carbohydrates 12.1 g Sugar 7.8 g Protein 33.7 g Cholesterol 83 mg

Garlic Mussels

Preparation time: 10 minutes
Cooking time: 6 minutes
Servings: 4
Ingredients:
1 lb. Mussels

1 tablespoon butter
1 cup of water
2 teaspoons minced garlic
1 teaspoon chives
1 teaspoon basil
1 teaspoon parsley
Directions:
Toss the mussels with oil and all other ingredients in a bowl.
Spread the seasoned shrimp in the oven baking tray.
Press "power button" of air fry oven and turn the dial to select the "air roast" mode.
Press the time button and again turn the dial to set the cooking time to 6 minutes.
Now push the temp button and rotate the dial to set the temperature at 390 degrees f.
Once preheated, place the mussel's tray in the oven and close its lid.
Serve warm.
Nutrition: Calories 125 Total fat 5.4g Saturated fat 2.3g Cholesterol 39mg Sodium 347mg Total carbohydrate 4.7g Dietary fiber 0.1g Total sugars 0g Protein 13.6g

Mussels with Saffron Sauce

Preparation time: 10 minutes
Cooking time: 8 minutes
Servings: 4
Ingredients:
1 tablespoon unsalted butter
1 tablespoon minced garlic
1 tablespoon minced shallot
1/4 cup dry white wine
3 tablespoons heavy cream
4 threads saffron
1 lb. Fresh mussels
Directions:
Whisk cream with saffron, shallots, white wine, and butter in a bowl.
Place the mussels in the oven baking tray and pour the cream sauce on top.
Press "power button" of air fry oven and turn the dial to select the "bake" mode.
Press the time button and again turn the dial to set the cooking time to 8 minutes.
Now push the temp button and rotate the dial to set the temperature at 370 degrees f.
Once preheated, place the mussel's baking tray in the oven and close its lid.
Serve warm.
Nutrition: Calories 374 Total fat 14.7g Saturated fat 5.9g Cholesterol 118mg Sodium 999mg Total carbohydrate 14.4g Dietary fiber 0g Total sugars 0.2g Protein 40.9g

Cajun Shrimp Bake

Preparation time: 10 minutes
Cooking time: 40 minutes
Servings: 8
Ingredients:
4 andouille sausages, chopped
1 lb. Shrimp, peeled and deveined
4 red potatoes, quartered
2 pieces corn, quartered
2 tablespoons oil, divided
1 tablespoon butter, cubed

4 cloves garlic, minced
Cajun spice mix
2 teaspoons garlic powder
2 ½ teaspoons paprika
1 ¼ teaspoons dried oregano
1 teaspoon onion powder
1 ¼ teaspoons dried thyme
½ teaspoon red pepper flakes
1 teaspoon cayenne pepper
2 teaspoons salt
1 teaspoon pepper
Directions:
Mix cajun mix spices in a bowl and then toss in all the veggies and seafood.
Stir in sausage, corn, oil, and butter then mix well.
Spread potatoes, corn, and garlic in the oven baking tray.
Press "power button" of air fry oven and turn the dial to select the "bake" mode.
Press the time button and again turn the dial to set the cooking time to 25 minutes.
Now push the temp button and rotate the dial to set the temperature at 375 degrees f.
Once preheated, place the potato's baking tray in the oven and close its lid.
When potatoes are done, add shrimp and sausage to the potatoes.
Return the baking tray to the oven and bake for 15 minutes.
Serve warm.
Nutrition: Calories 363 Total fat 17.7g Saturated fat 5.7g Cholesterol 147mg Sodium 662mg Total carbohydrate 27.3g Dietary fiber 2.9g Total sugars 2.7g Protein 24.2g

Shrimp with Garlic Sauce

Preparation time: 10 minutes
Cooking time: 13 minutes
Servings: 4
Ingredients:
1 1/4 lbs. Shrimp, peeled and deveined
1/4 cup butter
1 tablespoon minced garlic
2 tablespoon fresh lemon juice
Salt and pepper
1/8 teaspoon red pepper flakes
2 tablespoon minced fresh parsley
Directions:
Toss the shrimp with oil and all other ingredients in a bowl.
Spread the seasoned shrimp in the baking pan.
Press "power button" of air fry oven and turn the dial to select the "bake" mode.
Press the time button and again turn the dial to set the cooking time to 13 minutes.
Now push the temp button and rotate the dial to set the temperature at 350 degrees f.
Once preheated, place the baking pan in the oven and close its lid.
Serve warm.
Nutrition: Calories 207 Total fat 14.1g Saturated fat 7.4g Cholesterol 212mg Sodium 885mg Total carbohydrate 2.3g Dietary fiber 0.1g Total sugars 0.2g Protein 19.1g

Garlic Shrimp Skewers

Preparation time: 10 minutes
Cooking time: 8 minutes

Servings: 8
Ingredients:
1 lb. Prawns, peeled and deveined
2 tablespoons olive oil
Salt, to taste
3 tablespoons butter
3 garlic cloves, minced
1/4 teaspoon salt
1 teaspoon minced chives for garnish
Directions:
Toss the shrimp with oil and all other ingredients in a bowl.
Spread the seasoned shrimp in the baking tray.
Press "power button" of air fry oven and turn the dial to select the "air roast" mode.
Press the time button and again turn the dial to set the cooking time to 8 minutes.
Now push the temp button and rotate the dial to set the temperature at 425 degrees f.
Once preheated, place the shrimp's baking tray in the oven and close its lid.
Serve warm.
Nutrition: Calories 105 Total fat 6.1g Saturated fat 3g Cholesterol 116mg Sodium 520mg Total carbohydrate 0.4g Dietary fiber 0g Total sugars 0g Protein 12.1g

Prawn Burgers

Preparation time: 15 minutes
Cooking time: 6 minutes
Servings: 2
Ingredients:
½ cup prawns, peeled, deveined and chopped very finely
½ cup breadcrumbs
2-3 tablespoons onion, chopped finely
½ teaspoon ginger, minced
½ teaspoon garlic, minced
½ teaspoon red chili powder
½ teaspoon ground cumin
¼ teaspoon ground turmeric
Salt and ground black pepper, as required
Directions:
In a bowl, add all ingredients and mix until well combined.
Make small sized patties from mixture.
Press "power button" of air fry oven and turn the dial to select the "air fry" mode.
Press the time button and again turn the dial to set the cooking time to 6 minutes.
Now push the temp button and rotate the dial to set the temperature at 355 degrees f.
Press "start/pause" button to start.
When the unit beeps to show that it is preheated, open the lid.
Arrange the patties in greased "air fry basket" and insert in the oven.
Serve hot.
Nutrition: Calories 186 Total fat 2.7 g Saturated fat 0.7 g Cholesterol 119 mg Sodium 422 mg Total carbs 22.5 g Fiber 1.8 g Sugar 2.2 g Protein 16.9 g

Old Bay Seasoned Haddock

Preparation time: 10 minutes
Cooking time: 7 minutes
Servings: 2

Ingredients:
1/2 lb haddock
1 tbsp fresh lemon juice
1/4 cup water
1 tbsp mayonnaise
1/4 tsp old bay seasoning
1/2 tsp olive oil
1/4 tsp dill, chopped

Directions:
Add water, mayonnaise, seasoning, olive oil, dill, and lemon juice in instant pot and stir well.
Place fish fillets in the pot.
Seal pot with lid and cook on manual high pressure for 7 minutes.
Once done then release pressure using the quick-release method than open the lid.
Serve and enjoy.

Nutrition: Calories 168 Fat 4.7 g Carbohydrates 2 g Sugar 0.6 g Protein 27.7 g Cholesterol 86 mg

Garlic Butter Shrimp

Preparation Time: 10 minutes
Cooking Time: 10 minutes
Serving: 4

Ingredients:
1 lb shrimp, peeled and deveined
2 tbsp olive oil
1/4 cup butter, melted
4 tbsp garlic, minced
Pepper
Salt

Directions:
Add shrimp into the mixing bowl. Add remaining ingredients and toss well.
Line instant pot multi-level air fryer basket with aluminum foil.
Add shrimp into the air fryer basket and place basket into the instant pot.
Seal pot with air fryer lid and select air fry mode then set the temperature to 400 F and timer for 10 minutes. Mix halfway through.
Serve and enjoy.

Nutrition:
Calories 309
Fat 20.5 g
Carbohydrates 4.5 g
Sugar 0.1 g
Protein 26.5 g
Cholesterol 269 mg

Crispy Crust Shrimp

Preparation Time: 10 minutes
Cooking Time: 20 minutes
Serving: 4

Ingredients:
1 lb shrimp, peeled and deveined
1 tsp garlic powder
1 tsp onion powder

1/2 cup breadcrumbs
2 eggs, lightly beaten
Pepper
Salt
Directions:
In a shallow bowl, whisk eggs with pepper and salt.
In a shallow dish, mix together breadcrumbs, onion powder, and garlic powder.
Place the dehydrating tray in a multi-level air fryer basket and place basket in the instant pot.
Dip shrimp in egg mixture then coat with breadcrumb and place on dehydrating tray.
Seal pot with air fryer lid and select air fry mode then set the temperature to 350 F and timer for 20 minutes. Turn shrimp halfway through.
Serve and enjoy.
Nutrition:
Calories 224
Fat 4.9 g
Carbohydrates 12.6 g
Sugar 1.4 g
Protein 30.6 g
Cholesterol 321 mg

Crispy Coconut Shrimp

Preparation Time: 10 minutes
Cooking Time: 10 minutes
Serving: 2
Ingredients:
1 cup egg white, lightly beaten
12 large shrimp
1 tbsp cornstarch
1 cup shredded coconut
1 cup flour
1 cup breadcrumbs
Directions:
Line instant pot air fryer basket with parchment paper.
In a shallow dish, mix together coconut and breadcrumbs.
In another dish, mix together flour and cornstarch.
Add egg white in a small bowl.
Dip shrimp in egg white then roll in flour mixture and coat with breadcrumb mixture.
Place coated shrimp in instant pot air fryer basket. Place basket in the pot.
Seal the pot with air fryer lid and select air fry mode and cook at 350 F for 10 minutes.
Serve and enjoy.
Nutrition:
Calories 700
Fat 17.6 g
Carbohydrates 97.7 g
Sugar 6.9 g
Protein 35.8 g
Cholesterol 69 mg

Healthy Shrimp Pasta

Preparation Time: 10 minutes
Cooking Time: 4 minutes
Serving: 6
Ingredients:
1 lb jumbo shrimp, peeled and deveined
1/2 cup green onion, chopped
1 tbsp sriracha sauce
1 1/2 cups yogurt
1 tbsp vinegar
1 lime juice
1/4 cup Fresno pepper, diced
1/4 cup honey
1 tsp coconut oil
1 tsp garlic, minced
4 cups of water
13 oz spaghetti noodles, break in half
1/4 tsp pepper
Directions:
Add oil into the inner pot of instant pot duo crisp and set pot on sauté mode.
Add Fresno peppers and garlic and sauté for 30 seconds.
Add noodles then pour water over noodles.
Add shrimp, lime juice, honey, vinegar, and pepper on top of noodles.
Seal the pot with pressure cooking lid and cook on high for 3 minutes.
Once done, release pressure using a quick release. Remove lid.
Add sriracha, yogurt, and green onions and stir well.
Serve and enjoy.
Nutrition:
Calories 348
Fat 4.6 g
Carbohydrates 51.5 g
Sugar 17.9 g
Protein 24.2 g
Cholesterol 205 mg

Cajuned Salmon Meal

Preparation time:5-10 Minutes
Cooking Time: 8 Minutes
Serving: 2
Ingredients: 1 tablespoon Cajun seasoning
2 salmon fillets (6 ounce each and with skin)
1 teaspoon brown sugar
Directions:
In a mixing bowl, combine Cajun seasoning and brown sugar. Add the fillets and coat well.
Place Instant Pot Air Fryer Crisp over kitchen platform. Press Air Fry, set the temperature to 400°F and set the timer to 5 minutes to preheat. Press "Start" and allow it to preheat for 5 minutes.
In the inner pot, place the Air Fryer basket. Spray it with some cooking oil, and in the basket, add the fillets.
Close the Crisp Lid and press the "Air Fry" setting. Set temperature to 390°F and set the timer to 8 minutes. Press "Start."
Halfway down, open the Crisp Lid, flip the fillets, and close the lid to continue cooking for the remaining time.
Open the Crisp Lid after cooking time is over. Serve warm.
Nutrition: Calories: 145

Fat: 5g
Saturated Fat: 1g
Trans Fat: 0g
Carbohydrates: 2g
Fiber: 0g
Sodium: 359mg
Protein: 19g

Crispy Crust Ranch Fish Fillets

Preparation Time: 10 minutes
Cooking Time: 12 minutes
Serving: 2
Ingredients:
2 fish fillets
1/2 packet ranch dressing mix
1/4 cup breadcrumbs
1 egg, lightly beaten
1 1/4 tbsp olive oil
Directions:
In a shallow dish mix together ranch dressing mix and breadcrumbs.
Add oil and mix until the mixture becomes crumbly.
Place the dehydrating tray in a multi-level air fryer basket and place basket in the instant pot.
Dip fish fillet in egg then coats with breadcrumb and place on dehydrating tray.
Seal pot with air fryer lid and select air fry mode then set the temperature to 350 F and timer for 12 minutes. Turn fish fillets halfway through.
Serve and enjoy.
Nutrition:
Calories 373
Fat 22.9 g
Carbohydrates 25.7 g
Sugar 1.2 g
Protein 18 g
Cholesterol 113 mg

Steam Shrimp

Preparation Time: 10 minutes
Cooking Time: 6 minutes
Serving: 4
Ingredients:
2 lbs shrimp, cleaned
1 1/2 tsp old bay seasoning
1 tsp Cajun seasoning
Pepper
Salt
Directions:
Add all ingredients into the inner pot of instant pot duo crisp and stir well.
Seal the pot with pressure cooking lid and select steam mode and cook for 6 minutes.
Once done, release pressure using a quick release. Remove lid.
Stir well and serve.

Nutrition:
Calories 270
Fat 3.8 g
Carbohydrates 3.5 g
Sugar 0 g
Protein 51.7 g
Cholesterol 478 mg

Lemon Garlic Shrimp

Preparation Time: 10 minutes
Cooking Time: 5 minutes
Serving: 4
Ingredients:
20 jumbo shrimp
1 fresh lemon juice
1/4 tsp red pepper flakes
1/4 cup fresh parsley, chopped
1/4 cup butter
1 tbsp garlic, minced
1 1/2 cups fish broth
1 cup white rice
Pepper
Salt
Directions:
Add all ingredients into the inner pot of instant pot duo crisp and stir well.
Seal the pot with pressure cooking lid and cook on high for 5 minutes.
Once done, release pressure using a quick release. Remove lid.
Stir and serve.
Nutrition:
Calories 505
Fat 13.1 g
Carbohydrates 39.4 g
Sugar 5.8 g
Protein 56.4 g
Cholesterol 611 mg

Delicious Shrimp Paella

Preparation Time: 10 minutes
Cooking Time: 5 minutes
Serving: 4
Ingredients:
1 lb jumbo shrimp, frozen
1/2 cup white wine
1 cup fish broth
1 red pepper, chopped
4 garlic cloves, chopped
1 onion, chopped
1/4 butter
1 cup of rice

1/4 cup cilantro, chopped
1/4 tsp red pepper flakes
1 tsp turmeric
1 tsp paprika
1/4 tsp pepper
1/2 tsp salt

Directions:
Add butter into the inner pot of instant pot duo crisp and set pot on sauté mode.
Add garlic and onion and cook for a minute.
Add remaining ingredients and stir well.
Seal the pot with pressure cooking lid and cook on high for 5 minutes.
Once done, release pressure using a quick release. Remove lid.
Serve and enjoy.

Nutrition:
Calories 310
Fat 1.3 g
Carbohydrates 44.4 g
Sugar 5.1 g
Protein 24.6 g
Cholesterol 235 mg

Crispy Coconut Shrimp

Preparation Time: 10 minutes
Cooking Time: 10 minutes
Serving: 2

Ingredients:
12 large shrimp
1 cup coconut, dried
1 cup flour
1 cup breadcrumbs
1 cup egg white
1 tbsp cornstarch

Directions:
In a shallow dish, mix together coconut and breadcrumbs and set aside.
In another dish, mix together flour and cornstarch and set aside.
Add egg white in a small bowl.
Line instant pot multi-level air fryer basket with aluminum foil.
Dip shrimp in egg white then roll in flour and coat with breadcrumb.
Place coated shrimp into the air fryer basket and place basket into the instant pot.
Seal pot with air fryer lid and select air fry mode then set the temperature to 350 F and timer for 10 minutes. Turn shrimp halfway through.
Serve and enjoy.

Nutrition:
Calories 700
Fat 17.6 g
Carbohydrates 97.7 g
Sugar 6.9 g
Protein 35.8 g
Cholesterol 69 mg

Cheesy Shrimp Grits

Preparation time: 10 minutes
Cooking time: 7 minutes
Servings: 6

Ingredients:
1 lb shrimp, thawed
1/2 cup cheddar cheese, shredded
1/2 cup quick grits
1 tbsp butter
1 1/2 cups chicken broth
1/4 tsp red pepper flakes
1/2 tsp paprika
2 tbsp cilantro, chopped
1 tbsp coconut oil
1/2 tsp kosher salt

Directions:
Add oil into the instant pot and set the pot on sauté mode.
Add shrimp and cook until shrimp is no longer pink. Season with red pepper flakes and salt.
Remove shrimp from the pot and set aside.
Add remaining ingredients into the pot and stir well.
Seal pot with lid and cook on manual high pressure for 7 minutes.
Once done then allow to release pressure naturally then open the lid.
Stir in cheese and top with shrimp.
Nutrition: Calories 221 Fat 9.1 g Carbohydrates 12 g Sugar 0.3 g Protein 21.9 g Cholesterol 174 mg

Curried Salmon Patties

Preparation Time: 10 minutes
Cooking Time: 8 minutes
Serving: 6

Ingredients:
14 oz can salmon, drained & remove bones
1/2 lime zest
1 tbsp brown sugar
2 eggs, lightly beaten
2 tbsp red curry paste
1/2 cup breadcrumbs
1/4 tsp salt

Directions:
Add all ingredients into the bowl and mix until well combined.
Place the dehydrating tray in a multi-level air fryer basket and place basket in the instant pot.
Make patties from mixture and place on dehydrating tray.
Seal pot with air fryer lid and select air fry mode then set the temperature to 400 F and timer for 8 minutes. Turn patties halfway through.
Serve and enjoy.

Nutrition:
Calories 174
Fat 7.4 g
Carbohydrates 9.1 g
Sugar 2.2 g
Protein 16.1 g
Cholesterol 91 mg

Fish Finger Sandwich in Instant Pot Air Fryer

Preparation: 5 minutes
Cooking: 15 minutes
Servings: 4
Ingredients:
13 ounces (4 Nos.) cod fillet, skin removed
2 tablespoons flour
1½ ounce breadcrumbs
12 capers
10 ounces of frozen peas
1 tablespoon Greek yogurt
1 tablespoon lemon juice
8 small slices of bread
¼ teaspoon salt
½ teaspoon ground black pepper
Cooking oil spray
Directions:
Wash the fillets and pat dry.
Close the crisp cover of the Instant Pot Air Fryer and set the temperature to 390°F.
Set the timer 5 minutes and press start for preheating in AIR FRY mode.
Rub salt and pepper on all sides of the fillets.
Place the flour in a medium shallow bowl.
Similarly, place the breadcrumbs in a shallow bowl.
Now dredge the cod fillets in the flour and then dredge in the breadcrumbs.
Spray some cooking in the instant fryer basket and place the cod fillets in it.
Place the basket in the inner pot of the Instant Pot.
Close the crisp cover and keep the temperature at 390°F in AIR FRY mode.
Set the timer to 15 minutes and press START for air frying.
When the cooking is under process, boil the peas for 5 minutes until it becomes tender.
Once it becomes tender, drain it and put it in a blender.
Add capers, Greek yogurt, and lemon juice.
Blitz the ingredients until it blends thoroughly.
After finish cooking, remove the fillets from the Instant Pot Air Fryer and layer it for making the sandwich.
Over the bread slice, layer fish fillet and spread the pea puree.
Serve warm.

Nutrition: Calories: 458, Total Fat: 18.8g, Saturated fat: 3.2g, Trans fat: 0g, Cholesterol: 0mg, Sodium: 1516mg, Total carbs: 44g, Dietary fiber: 10g, Sugars: 7g, Protein: 29g

Shrimp Parmesan Bake

Preparation time: 10 minutes
Cooking time: 8 minutes
Servings: 4
Ingredients:
1 1/2 lb. Large raw shrimp, peeled and deveined
1/4 cup melted butter
1 teaspoon coarse salt
1/4 teaspoon black pepper
1 teaspoon garlic powder
1/2 teaspoon crushed red pepper
1/4 cup parmesan cheese, grated
Directions:
Toss the shrimp with oil and all other ingredients in a bowl.

Spread the seasoned shrimp in the baking tray.
Press "power button" of air fry oven and turn the dial to select the "bake" mode.
Press the time button and again turn the dial to set the cooking time to 8 minutes.
Now push the temp button and rotate the dial to set the temperature at 400 degrees f.
Once preheated, place the lobster's baking tray in the oven and close its lid.
Switch the air fryer oven to broil mode and cook for 1 minute.
Serve warm.
Nutrition: Calories 231 Total fat 14.9g Saturated fat 7.6g Cholesterol 249mg Sodium 1058mg Total carbohydrate 2.3g Dietary fiber 0.2g Total sugars 0.2g Protein 23.3g

Honey Mustard Salmon

Preparation Time: 10 minutes
Cooking Time: 9 minutes
Serving: 2
Ingredients:
2 salmon fillets
2 tbsp Dijon mustard
2 tbsp honey
1/4 cup mayonnaise
Pepper
Salt
Directions:
In a small bowl, mix together mustard, honey, mayonnaise, pepper, and salt and brush over salmon.
Place the dehydrating tray in a multi-level air fryer basket and place basket in the instant pot.
Place salmon fillets on dehydrating tray.
Seal pot with air fryer lid and select air fry mode then set the temperature to 350 F and timer for 9 minutes.
Serve and enjoy.
Nutrition:
Calories 424
Fat 21.4 g
Carbohydrates 25.2 g
Sugar 19.3 g
Protein 35.5 g
Cholesterol 86 mg

Bacon-Wrapped Shrimp

Preparation time:10 minutes
Cooking Time: 10 minutes
Serving: 6
Ingredients:
1-pound shrimp
1 package bacon
1/2 teaspoon cayenne pepper
1/2 teaspoon ground cumin
1/2 teaspoon onion powder
1/2 teaspoon lemon zest
1 teaspoon garlic powder
1 tablespoon Worcestershire sauce
1 tablespoon lemon juice
Directions:

Whisk Worcestershire sauce with cayenne pepper, onion powder, cumin, lemon zest, and garlic powder in a large bowl.
Toss in shrimp and mix well to coat then cover them to refrigerate for 1 hour.
Cut the bacon in half and wrap each half around each shrimp.
Place the wrapped shrimp in the Air Fryer Basket and set it in the Instant Pot Duo.
Put on the Air Fryer lid and seal it.
Hit the "Air fry Button" and select 10 minutes of cooking time, then press "Start."
Once the Instant Pot Duo beeps, remove its lid.
Serve.
Nutrition:
Calories 114
Total Fat 2.7g
Saturated Fat 0.9g
Cholesterol 163mg
Sodium 286mg
Total Carbohydrate 2.4g
Dietary Fiber 0.1g
Total Sugars 0.8g
Protein 18.6g

Horseradish Crusted Salmon

Preparation time:10 minutes
Cooking Time: 5 minutes
Serving: 2
Ingredients:
2 pieces of salmon fillet
1 teaspoon salt
1 teaspoon black pepper
1 tablespoon horseradish
2 tablespoons olive oil
1/4 cup bread crumbs
Directions:
Whisk bread crumbs with salt, olive oil, horseradish and black pepper in a bowl.
Coat the salmon with this crumbly mixture liberally.
Place the breaded salmon in the Air Fryer Basket and set it inside the Instant Pot Duo.
Put on the Air Fryer lid and seal it.
Hit the "Air fry Button" and select 5 minutes of cooking time, then press "Start."
Once the Instant Pot Duo beeps, remove its lid.
Serve.
Nutrition:
Calories 415
Total Fat 25.8g
Saturated Fat 3.8g
Cholesterol 78mg
Sodium 1364mg
Total Carbohydrate 11.3g
Dietary Fiber 1.1g
Total Sugars 1.5g
Protein 36.5g

Chapter 4: Sides and Appetizer Recipes

Brussels Sprouts

Preparation time: 15 minutes
Cooking Time: 10 minutes
Servings: 4
Ingredients:
1 lb. Brussels sprouts
1 tbsp. Unsalted butter; melted.
1 tbsp. Coconut oil
Directions:
Remove all loose leaves from brussels sprouts and cut each in half.
Drizzle sprouts with coconut oil and place into the air fryer basket
Adjust the temperature to 400 degrees f and set the timer for 10 minutes.
You may want to gently stir halfway through the cooking time, depending on how they are beginning to brown
When completely cooked, they should be tender with darker caramelized spots.
Remove from fryer basket and drizzle with melted butter.
Serve immediately.
Nutrition: Calories: 90; Protein: 2.9g; Fiber: 3.2g; Fat: 6.1g; Carbs: 7.5g

Onion Dip

Preparation time: 10 minutes
Cooking time: 45 minutes
Servings: 10
Ingredients:
2/3 cup onion, chopped
1 cup cheddar jack cheese, shredded
½ cup swiss cheese, shredded
¼ cup parmesan cheese, shredded
2/3 cup whipped salad dressing
½ cup milk
Salt, as required
Directions:
In a large bowl, add all the ingredients and mix well.
Transfer the mixture into a baking pan and spread in an even layer.
Press "power button" of air fry oven and turn the dial to select the "air bake" mode.
Press the time button and again turn the dial to set the cooking time to 45 minutes.
Now push the temp button and rotate the dial to set the temperature at 375 degrees f.
Press "start/pause" button to start.
When the unit beeps to show that it is preheated, open the lid.
Arrange pan over the "wire rack" and insert in the oven.
Serve hot.
Nutrition: Calories 87 Total fat 6 g Saturated fat 3.5 g Cholesterol 18 mg Sodium 140 mg Total carbs 2.3 g Fiber 0.3g Sugar 1.1 g Protein 5.1 g

Pineapple Bites with Yogurt Dip

Preparation time: 15 minutes
Cooking time: 10 minutes
Servings: 4
Ingredients:
½ of pineapple, cut into long 1-2-inch-thick sticks
¼ cup desiccated coconut
1 tablespoon fresh mint leaves, minced
1 green chili, chopped
1 cup vanilla yogurt
1 tablespoon honey
Directions:
Preheat the air fryer to 390 o f and grease an air fryer basket.
Place the coconut in a shallow dish.
Dip pineapple sticks in the honey and then dredge in the coconut.
Transfer the pineapple sticks in the air fryer basket and cook for about 10 minutes.
For yogurt dip:
Mix together mint, chili and vanilla yogurt in a bowl.
Serve these pineapple sticks with yogurt dip.
Nutrition: Calories: 518, fat: 34.9g, carbohydrates: 20g, sugar: 0.6g, protein: 29.9g, sodium: 1475mg

Bok Choy And Butter Sauce

Preparation time: 20 minutes
Cooking Time: 15 minutes
Servings: 4
Ingredients:
2 bok choy heads; trimmed and cut into strips
1 tbsp. Butter; melted
2 tbsp. Chicken stock
1 tsp. Lemon juice
1 tbsp. Olive oil
A pinch of salt and black pepper
Directions:
In a pan that fits your air fryer, mix all the ingredients, toss, introduce the pan in the air fryer and cook at 380°f for 15 minutes.
Divide between plates and serve as a side dish
Nutrition: Calories: 141; Fat: 3g; Fiber: 2g; Carbs: 4g; Protein: 3g

Chili Dip

Preparation time: 10 minutes
Cooking time: 15 minutes
Servings: 8
Ingredients:
1 (8-oz. package cream cheese, softened
1 (16-oz.can hormel chili without beans
1 (16-oz. package mild cheddar cheese, shredded
Directions:
In a baking pan, place the cream cheese and spread in an even layer.
Top with chili evenly, followed by the cheese.

Press "power button" of air fry oven and turn the dial to select the "air bake" mode.
Press the time button and again turn the dial to set the cooking time to 15 minutes.
Now push the temp button and rotate the dial to set the temperature at 375 degrees f.
Press "start/pause" button to start.
When the unit beeps to show that it is preheated, open the lid.
Arrange pan over the "wire rack" and insert in the oven.
Serve hot.
Nutrition: Calories 388 Total fat 31.3 g Saturated fat 19.2 g Cholesterol 103 mg Sodium 674 mg Total carbs 5.6 g Fiber 0.7 g Sugar 1.1 g Protein 21.1 g

---

Goat Cheese Cauliflower

Preparation time: 25 minutes
Servings: 4
Ingredients:
8 cups cauliflower florets; roughly chopped.
4 bacon strips; chopped.
10 oz. Goat cheese, crumbled
¼ cup soft cream cheese
½ cup spring onions; chopped.
1 tbsp. Garlic; minced
Salt and black pepper to taste.
Cooking spray
Directions:
Grease a baking pan that fits the air fryer with the cooking spray and mix all the ingredients except the goat cheese into the pan.
Sprinkle the cheese on top, introduce the pan in the machine and cook at 400°f for 20 minutes
Divide between plates and serve as a side dish.
Nutrition: Calories: 203; Fat: 13g; Fiber: 2g; Carbs: 5g; Protein: 9g

---

Dill Red Cabbage

Preparation time: 25 minutes
Cooking Time: 15 minutes
Servings: 4
Ingredients:
30 oz. Red cabbage; shredded
4 oz. Butter; melted
1 tbsp. Red wine vinegar
2 tbsp. Dill; chopped.
1 tsp. Cinnamon powder
A pinch of salt and black pepper
Directions:
In a pan that fits your air fryer, mix the cabbage with the rest of the ingredients, toss, put the pan in the machine and cook at 390°f for 20 minutes
Divide between plates and serve as a side dish.
Nutrition: Calories: 201; Fat: 17g; Fiber: 2g; Carbs: 5g; Protein: 5g

Kale and Walnuts

Preparation Time: 20 Minutes
Cooking Time: 10 minutes
Servings: 4
Ingredients:
3 garlic cloves
10 cups kale; roughly chopped.
1/3 cup parmesan; grated
½ cup almond milk s
¼ cup walnuts; chopped.
1 tbsp. Butter; melted
¼ tsp. Nutmeg, ground
Salt and black pepper to taste.
Directions:
In a pan that fits the air fryer, combine all the ingredients, toss, introduce the pan in the machine and cook at 360°f for 15 minutes
Divide between plates and serve.
Nutrition: Calories: 160; Fat: 7g; Fiber: 2g; Carbs: 4g; Protein: 5g

Pesto Zucchini Pasta

Preparation time: 20 minutes
Cooking Time: 10 minutes
Servings: 4
Ingredients:
4 oz. Mozzarella; shredded
2 cups zucchinis, cut with a spiralizer
½ cup coconut cream
¼ cup basil pesto
1 tbsp. Olive oil
Salt and black pepper to taste.
Directions:
In a pan that fits your air fryer, mix the zucchini noodles with the pesto and the rest of the ingredients, toss, introduce the pan in the fryer and cook at 370°f for 15 minutes
Divide between plates and serve as a side dish.
Nutrition: Calories: 200; Fat: 8g; Fiber: 2g; Carbs: 4g; Protein: 10g

Kale and Cauliflower Mash

Preparation time: 25 minutes
Cooking Time: 10 minutes
Servings: 4
Ingredients:
1 cauliflower head, florets separated
4 garlic cloves; minced
3 cups kale; chopped.
2 scallions; chopped.
1/3 cup coconut cream
1 tbsp. Parsley; chopped.
4 tsp. Butter; melted
A pinch of salt and black pepper

Directions:
In a pan that fits the air fryer, combine the cauliflower with the butter, garlic, scallions, salt, pepper and the cream, toss, introduce the pan in the machine and cook at 380°f for 20 minutes
Mash the mix well, add the remaining ingredients, whisk, divide between plates and serve.
Nutrition: Calories: 198; Fat: 9g; Fiber: 2g; Carbs: 6g; Protein: 8g

---

Zucchini Spaghetti

Preparation time: 20 minutes
Cooking Time: 10 minutes
Servings: 4
Ingredients:
1 lb. Zucchinis, cut with a spiralizer
1 cup parmesan; grated
¼ cup parsley; chopped.
¼ cup olive oil
6 garlic cloves; minced
½ tsp. Red pepper flakes
Salt and black pepper to taste.
Directions:
In a pan that fits your air fryer, mix all the ingredients, toss, introduce in the fryer and cook at 370°f for 15 minutes
Divide between plates and serve as a side dish.
Nutrition: Calories: 200; Fat: 6g; Fiber: 3g; Carbs: 4g; Protein: 5g

---

Jalapeno Hummus

Preparation time: 10 minutes
Cooking time: 25 minutes
Servings: 4
Ingredients:
1 cup chickpeas
1 tsp dried onion, minced
1 tsp ground cumin
1/4 cup jalapeno, diced
1/2 cup fresh cilantro
1 tbsp tahini
1/2 cup avocado oil
1/2 tsp sea salt
Directions:
Add chickpeas and 2 cups water into the instant pot.
Seal pot with lid and cook on manual high pressure for 25 minutes.
Once done then allow to release pressure naturally then open the lid.
Transfer chickpeas to the food processor along with remaining ingredients and process until smooth.
Serve and enjoy.
Nutrition: Calories 246 Fat 8.8 g Carbohydrates 33.4 g Sugar 5.7 g Protein 10.9 g Cholesterol 0 mg

---

Flavorful Salsa

Preparation time: 10 minutes
Cooking time: 30 minutes
Servings: 8
Ingredients:

12 cups fresh tomatoes, peeled, seeded, and diced
3 tbsp cayenne pepper
2 tbsp garlic powder
3 tbsp sugar
1/2 cup vinegar
12 oz can tomato paste
1 cup jalapeno pepper, chopped
3 onions, chopped
2 green peppers, chopped
1 tbsp salt
Directions:
Add all ingredients into the instant pot and stir well.
Seal pot with lid and cook on manual high pressure for 30 minutes.
Once done then allow to release pressure naturally then open the lid.
Allow to cool completely then serve or store.
Nutrition: Calories 145 Fat 1.1 g Carbohydrates 32.5 g Sugar 20.3 g Protein 5.1 g Cholesterol 0 mg

Cheddar Cheese Dip

Preparation time: 10 minutes
Cooking time: 9 minutes
Servings: 16
Ingredients:
1 lb bacon slices, cooked and crumbled
1 green onion, sliced
1/4 cup heavy cream
2 cups cheddar cheese, shredded
1 cup non-alcoholic beer
1 tsp garlic powder
1 1/2 tbsp dijon mustard
1/4 cup sour cream
18 oz cream cheese, softened
Directions:
Add cream cheese, bacon, beer, garlic powder, mustard, and sour cream into the instant pot and stir well.
Seal pot with lid and cook on manual high pressure for 5 minutes.
Once done then release pressure using the quick-release method than open the lid.
Stir in heavy cream and cheese and cook on sauté mode for 3-4 minutes.
Garnish with green onion and serve.
Nutrition: Calories 195 Fat 17.4 g Carbohydrates 2 g Sugar 0.2 g Protein 6.3 g Cholesterol 54 mg

Creamy Eggplant Dip

Preparation Time: 10 minutes
Cooking Time: 8 minutes
Serving: 8
Ingredients:
2 eggplants, cut into wedges
1 tsp dried oregano
1 tbsp garlic, crushed
1/2 lemon juice
2 tbsp olive oil
1 cup of water

1/2 tsp Italian seasoning
1/4 tsp pepper
1 tsp salt
Directions:
Pour 1 cup of water into the inner pot of instant pot duo crisp. Place steamer rack in the pot.
Arrange eggplant on top of the steamer rack.
Seal the pot with a lid and cook on high for 8 minutes.
Once done, release pressure using a quick release. Remove lid.
Remove eggplant wedges from pot and peel.
Transfer eggplant and remaining ingredients into the blender and blend until smooth.
Serve and enjoy.
Nutrition:
Calories 68
Fat 3.9 g
Carbohydrates 8.7 g
Sugar 4.2 g
Protein 1.5 g
Cholesterol 0 mg

Instant Pot Salsa

Preparation Time: 10 minutes
Cooking Time: 10 minutes
Serving: 10
Ingredients:
4 cups tomatoes, peel, core, and dice
6 oz can tomato paste
15 oz can tomato sauce
1/2 cup apple cider vinegar
1 tbsp cayenne pepper sauce
1 tbsp cumin
1 tbsp garlic, minced
2 jalapeno pepper, diced
2 bell peppers, diced
1 onion, diced
2 tbsp kosher salt
Directions:
Add all ingredients into the inner pot of instant pot duo crisp and stir well.
Seal the pot with a lid and cook on high for 10 minutes.
Once done, allow to release pressure naturally. Remove lid.
Allow to cool completely then store or serve.
Nutrition:
Calories 58
Fat 0.6 g
Carbohydrates 12.3 g
Sugar 7.7 g
Protein 2.5 g
Cholesterol 0 mg

Tomatillo Salsa

Preparation Time: 10 minutes
Cooking Time: 15 minutes
Serving: 12
Ingredients:
2 lbs tomatillos, husk removed
2 cups of water
2 garlic cloves, peeled
35 dried arbol chilies, stems removed
1 tbsp olive oil
Salt
Directions:
Add oil into the inner pot of instant pot duo crisp and set pot on sauté mode.
Add garlic and chilies to the pot and sauté for 2-3 minutes.
Add remaining ingredients and stir well.
Seal the pot with pressure cooking lid and cook on high for 12 minutes.
Once done, release pressure using a quick release. Remove lid.
Blend tomatillo mixture using blender until smooth.
Season with salt and serve.
Nutrition:
Calories 40
Fat 2 g
Carbohydrates 5.6 g
Sugar 0.6 g
Protein 0.9 g
Cholesterol 0 mg

Lamb Jerky

Preparation Time: 10 minutes
Cooking Time: 6 hours
Serving: 4
Ingredients:
1 lb boneless lamb, trimmed fat and slice into thin strips
1/2 tsp onion powder
1 1/2 tbsp Worcestershire sauce
2 1/2 tbsp soy sauce
1/4 tsp black pepper
1/2 tbsp oregano
1/2 tsp garlic powder
Directions:
Add soy sauce, garlic powder, oregano, Worcestershire sauce, onion powder, and black pepper in the large bowl and mix well.
Add meat slices in the bowl and mix until coated.
Cover bowl and place in the refrigerator for overnight.
Spray the dehydrating tray with cooking spray and place in instant pot duo crisp air fryer basket.
Arrange marinated meat slices on dehydrating tray.
Place air fryer basket into the pot.
Seal the pot with air fryer lid and select dehydrate mode and cook at 145 F for 6 hours.
Serve and enjoy.
Nutrition:
Calories 226
Fat 8.4 g

Carbohydrates 2.8 g
Sugar 1.5 g
Protein 32.6 g
Cholesterol 102 mg

Buffalo Chicken Dip

Preparation Time: 10 minutes
Cooking Time: 12 minutes
Serving: 10
Ingredients:
2 lbs chicken breast, skinless, boneless and halves
1/4 cup hot sauce
8 oz cream cheese
1 cup chicken broth
Directions:
Add chicken and broth into the inner pot of instant pot duo crisp.
Seal the pot with pressure cooking lid and cook on high for 10 minutes.
Once done, allow to release pressure naturally for 10 minutes then release remaining pressure using a quick release. Remove lid.
Remove chicken from pot and shred using a fork.
Clean the instant pot.
Add shredded chicken, hot sauce, and cream cheese into the instant pot and cook on sauté mode until cheese is melted.
Serve and enjoy.
Nutrition:
Calories 187
Fat 10.3 g
Carbohydrates 0.8 g
Sugar 0.2 g
Protein 21.5 g
Cholesterol 83 mg

Jalapeno Chicken Dip

Preparation Time: 10 minutes
Cooking Time: 14 minutes
Serving: 10
Ingredients:
1 lb chicken breast, skinless and boneless
1/2 cup water
1/2 cup breadcrumbs
1/2 cup sour cream
8 oz cheddar cheese, shredded
2 jalapeno pepper, sliced
8 oz cream cheese
Directions:
Add chicken, water, cream cheese, and jalapenos into the inner pot of instant pot duo crisp.
Seal the pot with pressure cooking lid and cook on high for 12 minutes.
Once done, release pressure using a quick release. Remove lid.
Remove chicken from pot and shred using a fork. Return shredded chicken to the pot.

Add sour cream and cheddar cheese and stir well.
Sprinkle breadcrumbs on top. Seal the pot with air fryer lid and select broil mode and cook for 2 minutes.
Serve and enjoy.
Nutrition:
Calories 269
Fat 19.3 g
Carbohydrates 5.4 g
Sugar 0.6 g
Protein 18.1 g
Cholesterol 83 mg

Cauliflower Chicken Dip

Preparation Time: 10 minutes
Cooking Time: 5 minutes
Serving: 8
Ingredients:
1 medium cauliflower head, chopped
2 cups cheddar cheese, shredded
4 oz cream cheese, cubed
1 tsp paprika
1/4 cup ranch dressing
1/2 cup buffalo sauce
2 cups cooked chicken, shredded
Pepper
Salt
Directions:
Add cauliflower, ranch dressing, buffalo sauce, seasonings, and chicken into the inner pot of instant pot duo crisp. Mix well.
Seal the pot with pressure cooking lid and cook on high pressure for 5 minutes.
Once done, release pressure using a quick release. Remove lid.
Add cream cheese and cheddar cheese and stir until combined.
Serve and enjoy.
Nutrition:
Calories 238
Fat 15.5 g
Carbohydrates 5.2 g
Sugar 2.1 g
Protein 19.8 g
Cholesterol 72 mg

Ranch Mushrooms

Preparation Time: 10 minutes
Cooking Time: 11 minutes
Serving: 4
Ingredients:
16 oz mushrooms, rinsed
1 cup chicken broth
1 oz dry ranch dressing mix
1/4 cup parmesan cheese

1 tbsp garlic, minced
1/4 cup butter
Directions:
Add butter into the inner pot of instant pot duo crisp and set pot on sauté mode.
Add garlic and sauté for 1 minute.
Add mushrooms and sauté for 5 minutes.
Add remaining ingredients and stir well.
Seal the pot with pressure cooking lid and cook on high for 5 minutes.
Once done, release pressure using a quick release. Remove lid.
Stir well and serve.
Nutrition:
Calories 147
Fat 12.6 g
Carbohydrates 5.1 g
Sugar 2.3 g
Protein 5.7 g
Cholesterol 32 mg

Teriyaki Beef Jerky

Preparation Time: 10 minutes
Cooking Time: 6 hours
Serving: 4
Ingredients:
3/4 lbs beef bottom round thin meat
2 1/2 tbsp soy sauce
3 tbsp Worcestershire sauce
1/2 tsp liquid smoke
1/4 cup teriyaki sauce
1/2 tsp onion powder
1/2 tsp garlic, minced
1/2 tsp red pepper flakes
Directions:
Cut meat into the thin slices.
Add teriyaki sauce, soy sauce, Worcestershire sauce, onion powder, garlic, red pepper flakes, and liquid smoke in the large bowl.
Add meat slices in the bowl and mix until coated.
Cover bowl and place in the refrigerator for overnight.
Spray the dehydrating tray with cooking spray and place in instant pot duo crisp air fryer basket.
Arrange marinated meat slices on dehydrating tray. Place air fryer basket into the pot.
Seal the pot with air fryer lid and select dehydrate mode and cook at 160 F for 6 hours.
Store or serve.
Nutrition:
Calories 172
Fat 13.7 g
Carbohydrates 6.3 g
Sugar 5.1 g
Protein 17.7 g
Cholesterol 61 mg

Zucchinis and Walnuts

Preparation time: 25 minutes
Cooking Time: 10 minutes
Servings: 4
Ingredients:
1 lb. Zucchinis; sliced
¼ cup chives; chopped.
1 cup walnuts; chopped.
4 oz. Arugula leaves
1 tbsp. Olive oil
Salt and white pepper to the taste
Directions:
In a pan that fits the air fryer, combine all the ingredients except the arugula and walnuts, toss, put the pan in the machine and cook at 360°f for 20 minutes
Transfer this to a salad bowl, add the arugula and the walnuts, toss and serve as a side salad.
Nutrition: Calories: 170; Fat: 4g; Fiber: 1g; Carbs: 4g; Protein: 5g

Coriander Artichokes

Preparation time: 20 minutes
Cooking Time: 10 minutes
Servings: 4
Ingredients:
12 oz. Artichoke hearts
1 tbsp. Lemon juice
1 tsp. Coriander, ground
½ tsp. Cumin seeds
½ tsp. Olive oil
Salt and black pepper to taste.
Directions:
In a pan that fits your air fryer, mix all the ingredients, toss, introduce the pan in the fryer and cook at 370°f for 15 minutes
Divide the mix between plates and serve as a side dish.
Nutrition: Calories: 200; Fat: 7g; Fiber: 2g; Carbs: 5g; Protein: 8g

Tasty Eggplant Slices

Preparation Time: 10 minutes
Cooking Time: 4 hours
Serving: 4
Ingredients:
1 eggplant, cut into 1/4-inch thick slices
1/4 tsp garlic powder
1 tsp paprika
1/4 tsp onion powder
Directions:
Add all ingredients into the mixing bowl and toss until well coated.
Spray the dehydrating tray with cooking spray and place in instant pot duo crisp air fryer basket.
Arrange eggplant slices on the dehydrating tray.
Place air fryer basket into the pot.
Seal the pot with air fryer lid and select dehydrate mode and cook at 145 F for 4 hours.
Serve or store.

Nutrition:
Calories 31
Fat 0.3 g
Carbohydrates 7.3 g
Sugar 3.6 g
Protein 1.3 g
Cholesterol 0 mg

Baba Ghanoush

Preparation Time: 10 minutes
Cooking Time: 13 minutes
Serving: 6
Ingredients:
1 eggplant, pierce with a fork
2 tbsp sesame seeds
2 tbsp sesame oil
2 tsp lemon juice
1/2 tsp ground cumin
1 garlic clove, minced
1/2 onion, chopped
1 tsp sea salt
Directions:
Pour 1 cup of water into the inner pot of instant pot duo crisp. Place steamer rack in the pot.
Place eggplant on top of the steamer rack.
Seal the pot with pressure cooking lid and cook on high pressure for 8 minutes.
Once done, release pressure using a quick release. Remove lid.
Remove eggplant from pot and clean the pot. Peel and slice cooked eggplant.
Add oil into the pot and set a pot on sauté mode.
Add onion and eggplant and sauté for 3-5 minutes.
Add remaining ingredients and stir everything well to combine.
Turn off the instant pot. Blend eggplant mixture using blender until smooth.
Serve and enjoy.
Nutrition:
Calories 82
Fat 6.2 g
Carbohydrates 6.3 g
Sugar 2.7 g
Protein 1.5 g
Cholesterol 0 mg

Healthy Beet Hummus

Preparation time: 10 minutes
Cooking time: 40 minutes
Servings: 16
Ingredients:
1 cup chickpeas
1/3 cup water
1/4 cup olive oil
1/4 cup fresh lemon juice

3 beets, peeled and diced
2 garlic cloves, peeled
1/4 cup sunflower seeds
1 1/2 tsp kosher salt
Directions:
Add beets, chickpeas, 1 tsp salt, 3 cups water, garlic, and sunflower seeds into the instant pot.
Seal pot with lid and cook on manual high pressure for 40 minutes.
Strain beet, chickpeas, garlic, and sunflower seeds and place in a food processor along with lemon juice and remaining salt and process until smooth.
Add oil and 1/3 cup water and process until smooth.
Serve and enjoy.
Nutrition: Calories 86 Fat 4.3 g Carbohydrates 9.8 g Sugar 2.9 g Protein 2.9 g Cholesterol 0 mg

Chicken Jalapeno Popper Dip

Preparation time: 10 minutes
Cooking time: 14 minutes
Servings: 10
Ingredients:
1 lb chicken breast, boneless
1/2 cup water
1/2 cup breadcrumbs
3/4 cup sour cream
3 jalapeno pepper, sliced
8 oz cream cheese
8 oz cheddar cheese
Directions:
Add chicken, jalapeno, water, and cream cheese into the instant pot.
Seal pot with lid and cook on manual high pressure for 12 minutes.
Once done then release pressure using the quick-release method than open the lid.
Stir in cream and cheddar cheese.
Transfer instant pot mixture to the baking dish and top with breadcrumbs and broil for 2 minutes.
Serve and enjoy.
Nutrition: Calories 282 Fat 20.5 g Carbohydrates 5.8 g Sugar 0.7 g Protein 18.3 g Cholesterol 85 mg

Broccoli and Cauliflower

Preparation time: 25 minutes
Cooking Time: 5 minutes
Servings: 4
Ingredients:
15 oz. Broccoli florets
5 oz. Mozzarella cheese; shredded
10 oz. Cauliflower florets
2 oz. Butter; melted
1 cup sour cream
1 leek; chopped.
2 spring onions; chopped.
Salt and black pepper to taste.
2 tbsp. Mustard
Directions:
In a baking pan that fits the air fryer, add the butter and spread it well.
Add the broccoli, cauliflower and the rest of the ingredients except the mozzarella and toss

Sprinkle the cheese on top, introduce the pan in the air fryer and cook at 380°f for 20 minutes. Divide between plates and serve as a side dish.
Nutrition: Calories: 242; Fat: 13g; Fiber: 2g; Carbs: 4g; Protein: 8g

---

Buffalo Cauliflower

Preparation time: 10 minutes
Cooking Time: 15 minutes
Servings: 4
Ingredients:
½ (1-oz.dry ranch seasoning packet
¼ cup buffalo sauce
4 cups cauliflower florets
2 tbsp. Salted butter; melted.
Directions:
Take a large bowl, toss cauliflower with butter and dry ranch.
Place into the air fryer basket.
Adjust the temperature to 400 degrees f and set the timer for 5 minutes.
Shake the basket two-or three-times during cooking.
When tender, remove cauliflower from fryer basket and toss in buffalo sauce.
Serve warm.
Nutrition: Calories: 87; Protein: 2.1g; Fiber: 2.1g; Fat: 5.6g; Carbs: 7.3g

---

Roasted Eggplant

Preparation time: 30 minutes
Cooking Time: 15 minutes
Servings: 4
Ingredients:
1 large eggplant
2 tbsp. Olive oil
½ tsp. Garlic powder.
¼ tsp. Salt
Directions:
Remove top and bottom from eggplant. Slice eggplant into ¼-inch-thick round slices.
Brush slices with olive oil.
Sprinkle with salt and garlic powder
Place eggplant slices into the air fryer basket.
Adjust the temperature to 390 degrees f and set the timer for 15 minutes.
Serve immediately.
Nutrition: Calories: 91; Protein: 1.3g; Fiber: 3.7g; Fat: 6.7g; Carbs: 7.5g

---

Spinach Dip

Preparation time: 15 minutes
Cooking time: 35 minutes
Servings: 8
Ingredients:
1 (8-oz. package cream cheese, softened
1 cup mayonnaise
1 cup parmesan cheese, grated
1 cup frozen spinach, thawed and squeezed

1/3 cup water chestnuts, drained and chopped
½ cup onion, minced
¼ teaspoon garlic powder
Ground black pepper, as required
Directions:
In a bowl, add all the ingredients and mix until well combined.
Transfer the mixture into a baking pan and spread in an even layer.
Press "power button" of air fry oven and turn the dial to select the "air fry" mode.
Press the time button and again turn the dial to set the cooking time to 35 minutes.
Now push the temp button and rotate the dial to set the temperature at 300 degrees f.
Press "start/pause" button to start.
When the unit beeps to show that it is preheated, open the lid.
Arrange pan over the "wire rack" and insert in the oven.
Stir the dip once halfway through.
Serve hot.
Nutrition: Calories 258 Total fat 22.1 g Saturated fat 8.9 g Cholesterol 47 mg Sodium 384 mg Total carbs 9.4 g Fiber 0.3 g Sugar 2.3 g Protein 6.7 g

Zucchini Gratin

Preparation time: 30 minutes
Cooking Time: 10 minutes
Servings: 4
Ingredients:
4 cups zucchinis; sliced
1 ½ cups mozzarella; shredded
½ cup coconut cream
½ tbsp. Parsley; chopped.
2 tbsp. Butter; melted
½ tsp. Garlic powder
Directions:
In a baking pan that fits the air fryer, mix all the ingredients except the mozzarella and the parsley and toss.
Sprinkle the mozzarella and parsley, introduce in the air fryer and cook at 370°f for 25 minutes.
Divide between plates and serve as a side dish
Nutrition: Calories: 220; Fat: 14g; Fiber: 2g; Carbs: 5g; Protein: 9g

Spiced Cauliflower

Preparation time: 20 minutes
Cooking Time: 10 minutes
Servings: 4
Ingredients:
1 cauliflower head, florets separated
1 tbsp. Olive oil
1 tbsp. Butter; melted
¼ tsp. Cinnamon powder
¼ tsp. Cloves, ground
¼ tsp. Turmeric powder
½ tsp. Cumin, ground
A pinch of salt and black pepper
Directions:
Take a bowl and mix cauliflower florets with the rest of the ingredients and toss.
Put the cauliflower in your air fryer's basket and cook at 390°f for 15 minutes

Divide between plates and serve as a side dish.
Nutrition: Calories: 182; Fat: 8g; Fiber: 2g; Carbs: 4g; Protein: 8g

---

Roasted Tomatoes

Preparation time: 20 minutes
Cooking Time: 10 minutes
Servings: 4
Ingredients:
4 tomatoes; halved
½ cup parmesan; grated
1 tbsp. Basil; chopped.
½ tsp. Onion powder
½ tsp. Oregano; dried
½ tsp. Smoked paprika
½ tsp. Garlic powder
Cooking spray
Directions:
Take a bowl and mix all the ingredients except the cooking spray and the parmesan.
Arrange the tomatoes in your air fryer's pan, sprinkle the parmesan on top and grease with cooking spray
Cook at 370°f for 15 minutes, divide between plates and serve.
Nutrition: Calories: 200; Fat: 7g; Fiber: 2g; Carbs: 4g; Protein: 6g

---

Roasted Red Pepper Hummus

Preparation Time: 10 minutes
Cooking Time: 40 minutes
Serving: 4
Ingredients:
1 cup chickpeas, dry and rinsed
2 tbsp olive oil
1/4 tsp cumin
2 garlic cloves
2 1/2 tbsp tahini
3 tbsp fresh lemon juice
1/2 cup roasted red peppers
3 cups chicken broth
1/2 tsp salt
Directions:
Add chickpeas and broth into the inner pot of instant pot duo crisp and stir well.
Seal the pot with pressure cooking lid and cook on high for 40 minutes.
Once done, allow to release pressure naturally. Remove lid.
Drain chickpeas well and reserved half cup broth.
Transfer chickpeas, reserved broth, and remaining ingredients into the food processor and process until smooth.
Serve and enjoy.
Nutrition:
Calories 338
Fat 16.3 g
Carbohydrates 35.2 g
Sugar 7.2 g
Protein 15.3 g
Cholesterol 0 mg

Spicy Spinach Dip

Preparation Time: 10 minutes
Cooking Time: 8 minutes
Serving: 8
Ingredients:
1 lb fresh spinach
1 tbsp hot sauce
1 tsp cumin
1 tsp chili powder
1 tsp onion powder
1/2 cup olives, sliced
2 jalapeno pepper, minced
1 cup cheddar cheese, shredded
1 cup mozzarella cheese, shredded
4 oz cream cheese, cubed
1/4 cup half and half
1/4 cup sour cream
1 tbsp olive oil
2 large tomatoes, chopped
4 garlic cloves, minced
1/4 tsp pepper
1/2 tsp salt
Directions:
Add oil into the instant pot duo crisp and set pot on sauté mode.
Add tomatoes, spinach, and garlic and sauté until spinach is cooked.
Turn off the sauté mode. Add remaining ingredients and stir well.
Seal the pot with pressure cooking lid and cook on high pressure for 4 minutes.
Once done, release pressure using a quick release. Remove lid.
Serve and enjoy.
Nutrition:
Calories 194
Fat 15.8 g
Carbohydrates 7 g
Sugar 1.9 g
Protein 8.4 g
Cholesterol 38 mg

Roasted fennel

Preparation time: 20 minutes
Cooking Time: 10 minutes
Servings: 4
Ingredients:
1 lb. Fennel; cut into small wedges
3 tbsp. Olive oil
2 tbsp. Sunflower seeds
Juice of ½ lemon
Salt and black pepper to taste.
Directions:
Take a bowl and mix the fennel wedges with all the ingredients except the sunflower seeds, put them in your air fryer's basket and cook at 400°f for 15 minutes
Divide the fennel between plates, sprinkle the sunflower seeds on top and serve as a side dish.
Nutrition: Calories: 152; Fat: 4g; Fiber: 2g; Carbs: 4g; Protein: 7g

Balsamic Asparagus

Preparation time: 25 minutes
Cooking Time: 10 minutes
Servings: 4
Ingredients:
1 lb. Asparagus stalks
¼ cup olive oil+ 1 tsp.
2 tbsp. Balsamic vinegar
1 tbsp. Lime juice
1 tbsp. Smoked paprika
Salt and black pepper to taste.
Directions:
Take a bowl and mix the asparagus with salt, pepper and 1 tsp. Oil, toss, transfer to your air fryer's basket and cook at 370°f for 20 minutes.
Meanwhile, in a bowl, mix all the other ingredients and whisk them well
Divide the asparagus between plates, drizzle the balsamic vinaigrette all over and serve as a side dish.
Nutrition: Calories: 187; Fat: 6g; Fiber: 2g; Carbs: 4g; Protein: 9g

Avocado Fries

Preparation Time: 10 minutes
Cooking Time: 25 minutes
Serving: 4
Ingredients:
2 eggs, beaten
2 avocado, chopped into wedges
1/4 cup sunflower seeds, crushed
1/2 cup almond flour
1/2 tsp onion powder
1 tsp salt
Directions:
In a bowl, add beaten eggs.
In another bowl, add almond flour, sunflower seed, onion powder, and salt.
Dip avocado slices in egg mixture then coat with almond flour mixture and place into the instant pot air fryer basket.
Place basket in the pot. Seal the pot with air fryer lid and select bake mode and cook at 400 F for 25 minutes.
Serve and enjoy.
Nutrition:
Calories 338
Fat 29.9 g
Carbohydrates 12.6 g
Sugar 0.9 g
Protein 8.3 g
Cholesterol 82 mg

Radishes and Sesame Seeds

Preparation time: 20 minutes
Cooking Time: 15 minutes
Servings: 4
Ingredients:

20 radishes; halved
2 spring onions; chopped.
3 green onions; chopped.
2 tbsp. Olive oil
1 tbsp. Olive oil
3 tsp. Black sesame seeds
Salt and black pepper to taste.
Directions:
Take a bowl and mix all the ingredients and toss well.
Put the radishes in your air fryer's basket, cook at 400°f for 15 minutes, divide between plates and serve as a side dish
Nutrition: Calories: 150; Fat: 4g; Fiber: 2g; Carbs: 3g; Protein: 5g

Herbed Radish Sauté

Preparation time: 20 minutes
Cooking Time: 15 minutes
Servings: 4
Ingredients:
2 bunches red radishes; halved
2 tbsp. Parsley; chopped.
2 tbsp. Balsamic vinegar
1 tbsp. Olive oil
Salt and black pepper to taste.
Directions:
Take a bowl and mix the radishes with the remaining ingredients except the parsley, toss and put them in your air fryer's basket.
Cook at 400°f for 15 minutes, divide between plates, sprinkle the parsley on top and serve as a side dish
Nutrition: Calories: 180; Fat: 4g; Fiber: 2g; Carbs: 3g; Protein: 5g

Cream Cheese Zucchini

Preparation time: 20 minutes
Cooking Time: 15 minutes
Servings: 4
Ingredients:
1 lb. Zucchinis; cut into wedges
1 green onion; sliced
1 cup cream cheese, soft
1 tbsp. Butter; melted
2 tbsp. Basil; chopped.
1 tsp. Garlic powder
A pinch of salt and black pepper
Directions:
In a pan that fits your air fryer, mix the zucchinis with all the other ingredients, toss, introduce in the air fryer and cook at 370°f for 15 minutes
Divide between plates and serve as a side dish.
Nutrition: Calories: 129; Fat: 6g; Fiber: 2g; Carbs: 5g; Protein: 8g

Sausage Mushroom Caps

Preparation time: 18 minutes
Cooking Time: 15 minutes
Servings: 2
Ingredients:
½ lb. Italian sausage
6 large portobello mushroom caps
¼ cup grated parmesan cheese.
¼ cup chopped onion
2 tbsp. Blanched finely ground almond flour
1 tsp. Minced fresh garlic

Directions:
Use a spoon to hollow out each mushroom cap, reserving scrapings.
In a medium skillet over medium heat, brown the sausage about 10 minutes or until fully cooked and no pink remains. Drain and then add reserved mushroom scrapings, onion, almond flour, parmesan and garlic.
Gently fold ingredients together and continue cooking an additional minute, then remove from heat
Evenly spoon the mixture into mushroom caps and place the caps into a 6-inch round pan. Place pan into the air fryer basket
Adjust the temperature to 375 degrees f and set the timer for 8 minutes. When finished cooking, the tops will be browned and bubbling. Serve warm.
Nutrition: Calories: 404; Protein: 24.3g; Fiber: 4.5g; Fat: 25.8g; Carbs: 18.2g

Minty Summer Squash

Preparation time: 30 minutes
Cooking Time: 15 minutes
Servings: 4
Ingredients:
4 summer squash; cut into wedges
½ cup mint; chopped.
1 cup mozzarella; shredded
¼ cup olive oil
¼ cup lemon juice
Salt and black pepper to taste.
Directions:
In a pan that fits your air fryer, mix the squash with the rest of the ingredients, toss, introduce the pan in the air fryer and cook at 370°f for 25 minutes
Divide between plates and serve as a side dish.
Nutrition: Calories: 201; Fat: 7g; Fiber: 2g; Carbs: 4g; Protein: 9g

Chapter 5: Poultry Recipes

Chicken Casserole

Preparation time:10 Minutes
Cooking Time: 9 minutes
Serving: 6
Ingredients:
3 cup chicken, shredded
12 oz. bag egg noodles
1/2 large onion
1/2 cup chopped carrots
1/4 cup frozen peas
1/4 cup frozen broccoli pieces
2 stalks celery chopped
5 cup chicken broth
1 teaspoon garlic powder
salt and pepper to taste
1 cup cheddar cheese, shredded
1 package French's onions
1/4 c sour cream
1 can cream of chicken and mushroom soup
Directions:
Add chicken, broth, black pepper, salt, garlic powder, vegetables, and egg noodles to the Instant Pot Duo.
Put on the pressure-cooking lid and seal it.
Hit the "Pressure Button" and select 4 minutes of cooking time, then press "Start."
Once the Instant Pot Duo beeps, do a quick release and remove its lid.
Stir in cheese, 1/3 of French's onions, can of soup and sour cream.
Mix well and spread the remaining onion top.
Put on the Air Fryer lid and seal it.
Hit the "Air fryer Button" and select 5 minutes of cooking time, then press "Start."
Once the Instant Pot Duo beeps, remove its lid.
Serve.
Nutrition:
Calories 494
Total Fat 19.1g
Saturated Fat 9.6g
Cholesterol 142mg
Sodium 1233mg
Total Carbohydrate 29g
Dietary Fiber 2.6g
Total Sugars 3.7g
Protein 48.9g

Ranch Chicken Wings

Preparation time: 10 minutes
Cooking Time: 35 minutes
Serving: 6
Ingredients:
12 chicken wings
1 tablespoon olive oil
1 cup chicken broth
1/4 cup butter
1/2 cup Red Hot Sauce
1/4 teaspoon Worcestershire sauce
1 tablespoon white vinegar
1/4 teaspoon cayenne pepper
1/8 teaspoon garlic powder
Seasoned salt to taste
Ranch dressing for dipping
Celery for garnish
Directions:
Set the Air Fryer Basket in the Instant Pot Duo and pour the broth in it.
Spread the chicken wings in the basket and put on the pressure-cooking lid.
Hit the "Pressure Button" and select 10 minutes of cooking time, then press "Start."
Meanwhile, prepare the sauce and add butter, vinegar, cayenne pepper, garlic powder, Worcestershire sauce, and hot sauce in a small saucepan.
Stir cook this sauce for 5 minutes on medium heat until it thickens.
Once the Instant Pot Duo beeps, do a quick release and remove its lid.
Remove the wings and empty the Instant Pot Duo.
Toss the wings with oil, salt, and black pepper.
Set the Air Fryer Basket in the Instant Pot Duo and arrange the wings in it.
Put on the Air Fryer lid and seal it.
Hit the "Air Fryer Button" and select 20 minutes of cooking time, then press "Start."
Once the Instant Pot Duo beeps, remove its lid.
Transfer the wings to the sauce and mix well.
Serve.
Nutrition:
Calories 414
Total Fat 31.6g
Saturated Fat 11g
Cholesterol 98mg
Sodium 568mg
Total Carbohydrate 11.2g
Dietary Fiber 0.3g
Total Sugars 0.2g
Protein 20.4g

Roasted Chicken

Preparation Time: 10 minutes
Cooking Time: 15 minutes
Serving: 4
Ingredients:
4 chicken thighs
5 oz jar roasted red peppers, drained and sliced
1 cups grape tomatoes

1/2 lb potatoes, cut into small chunks
2 tbsp olive oil
2 tbsp fresh parsley, chopped
1/2 tsp dried oregano
3 garlic cloves, crushed
2 tbsp capers, drained
Pepper
Salt
Directions:
Line instant pot multi-level air fryer basket with aluminum foil.
Season chicken with pepper and salt and place into the air fryer basket and place basket into the instant pot.
Mix together remaining ingredients and pour over chicken and mix well.
Seal pot with air fryer lid and select roast mode then set the temperature to 380 F and timer for 40-45 minutes. Stir halfway through.
Serve and enjoy.
Nutrition:
Calories 435
Fat 18.1 g
Carbohydrates 18.2 g
Sugar 1.9 g
Protein 45.2 g
Cholesterol 130 mg

Chicken Rice

Preparation time: 10 minutes
Cooking time: 12 minutes
Servings: 6
Ingredients:
2 lbs. chicken thighs, skinless, boneless, and cut into pieces
18 oz enchilada sauce
15 oz frozen mixed vegetables
1 oz taco seasoning
2 cups rice, uncooked
1 cup chicken stock
Directions:
Spray instant pot duo crisp inner pot with cooking spray and set the pot on sauté mode.
Season chicken with taco seasoning and place in the pot.
Sear chicken until brown from all the sides, about 10 minutes.
Add rice, stock, enchilada sauce, and vegetables and stir well.
Seal the pot with pressure cooking lid and cook on high for 2 minutes.
Once done, allow to release pressure naturally for 10 minutes then release remaining pressure using a quick release. Remove lid.
Stir well and serve.
Nutrition: Calories 787 Fat 15.2 g Carbohydrates 114.6 g Sugar 2.9 g Protein 60.2 g Cholesterol 136 mg

Yummy Hawaiian Chicken

Preparation Time: 10 minutes
Cooking Time: 12 minutes
Serving: 6
Ingredients:

2 lbs chicken breasts, skinless, boneless, and cut into chunks
2 tbsp cornstarch
1 cup chicken broth
20 oz can pineapple tidbits
1 tbsp garlic, crushed
2 tbsp brown sugar
6 tbsp soy sauce
1/2 tsp ground ginger
1/2 tsp salt
Directions:
Add all ingredients except cornstarch into the inner pot of instant pot duo crisp and stir well.
Seal the pot with pressure cooking lid and cook on high pressure for 10 minutes.
Once done, release pressure using a quick release. Remove lid.
In a small bowl, whisk together 1/4 cup water and cornstarch and pour into the pot.
Set pot on sauté mode. Cook chicken on sauce mode until sauce thickens.
Serve over rice and enjoy.
Nutrition:
Calories 377
Fat 11.5 g
Carbohydrates 18.7 g
Sugar 12.1 g
Protein 46 g
Cholesterol 135 mg

Spicy Chicken Wings

Preparation Time: 10 minutes
Cooking Time: 20 minutes
Serving: 4
Ingredients:
2 lbs frozen chicken wings
2 tbsp apple cider vinegar
2 tbsp butter, melted
1/2 cup hot pepper sauce
1/2 cup water
1/2 tsp paprika
1 oz ranch seasoning
Directions:
Add water, vinegar, butter, and hot pepper sauce into the instant pot duo crisp.
Add chicken wings and stir well.
Seal the pot with pressure cooking lid and cook on high for 5 minutes.
Once done, release pressure using a quick release. Remove lid.
Sprinkle paprika and ranch seasoning over the chicken.
Seal the pot with air fryer lid and select air fry mode and cook at 375 F for 15 minutes.
Toss wings in sauce and serve.
Nutrition:
Calories 521
Fat 38.2 g
Carbohydrates 0.2 g
Sugar 0.1 g
Protein 36.6 g
Cholesterol 167 mg

Paprika Chicken

Preparation Time: 10 minutes
Cooking Time: 30 minutes
Serving: 4
Ingredients:
4 chicken breasts, skinless and boneless, cut into chunks
2 tsp garlic, minced
2 tbsp smoked paprika
3 tbsp olive oil
2 tbsp lemon juice
Pepper
Salt
Directions:
In a small bowl, mix together garlic, lemon juice, paprika, oil, pepper, and salt.
Rub chicken with garlic mixture.
Add chicken into the instant pot air fryer basket and place basket in the pot.
Seal the pot with air fryer lid and select bake mode and cook at 350 F for 30 minutes.
Serve and enjoy.
Nutrition:
Calories 381
Fat 21.8 g
Carbohydrates 2.6 g
Sugar 0.5 g
Protein 42.9 g
Cholesterol 130 mg

Easy Cheesy Chicken

Preparation time: 10 minutes
Cooking time: 17 minutes
Servings: 6
Ingredients:
1 1/2 lbs chicken tenders
25 oz tomato sauce
2 tbsp butter
1/2 cup olive oil
1/2 tsp garlic powder
1/2 cup parmesan cheese, grated
2 cups mozzarella cheese, shredded
Directions:
Add olive oil into the inner pot of instant pot duo crisp and set pot on sauté mode.
Add chicken and sauté until lightly brown from both the sides.
Add garlic powder, tomato sauce, butter, and parmesan cheese on top of chicken.
Seal the pot with pressure cooking lid and cook on high for 15 minutes.
Once done, release pressure using a quick release. Remove lid.
Sprinkle mozzarella cheese on top of chicken. Cover pot with air fryer lid and select broil mode and cook for 1-2 minutes.
Serve and enjoy.
Nutrition: Calories 457 Fat 31.4 g Carbohydrates 6.9 g Sugar 5.1 g Protein 37.9 g Cholesterol 118 mg

Creamy Italian Chicken

Preparation time: 10 minutes
Cooking time: 10 minutes
Servings: 8
Ingredients:
2 lbs. chicken breasts, skinless and boneless
1 cup chicken stock
1/4 cup butter
14 oz can cream of chicken soup
8 oz cream cheese
1 tbsp Italian seasoning
Directions:
Add the chicken stock into the inner pot of instant pot duo crisp.
Add cream of chicken soup, Italian seasoning, and butter into the pot and stir well.
Seal the pot with pressure cooking lid and cook on high for 10 minutes.
Once done, release pressure using a quick release. Remove lid.
Add cream cheese and stir until cheese is melted
Serve and enjoy.
Nutrition: Calories 416 Fat 27.5 g Carbohydrates 4.6 g Sugar 0.6 g Protein 36.3 g Cholesterol 153 mg

Paprika Chicken

Preparation time: 10 minutes
Cooking time: 30 minutes
Servings: 4
Ingredients:
4 chicken breasts, skinless and boneless, cut into chunks
2 tsp garlic, minced
2 tbsp smoked paprika
3 tbsp olive oil
2 tbsp lemon juice
Pepper
Salt
Directions:
In a small bowl, mix together garlic, lemon juice, paprika, oil, pepper, and salt.
Rub chicken with garlic mixture.
Add chicken into the instant pot air fryer basket and place basket in the pot.
Seal the pot with air fryer lid and select bake mode and cook at 350 f for 30 minutes.
Serve and enjoy.
Nutrition: Calories 381 Fat 21.8 g Carbohydrates 2.6 g Sugar 0.5 g Protein 42.9 g Cholesterol 130 mg

Chicken Fajitas

Preparation time: 10 minutes
Cooking time: 10 minutes
Servings: 6
Ingredients:
4 chicken breasts, skinless and boneless
1/2 cup bell pepper, sliced
1/2 cup water
1 packet fajita seasoning
1 onion, sliced

1/4 tsp garlic powder
Directions:
Add all ingredients into the inner pot of instant pot duo crisp and stir well.
Seal the pot with pressure cooking lid and cook on high for 10 minutes.
Once done, release pressure using a quick release. Remove lid.
Shred chicken using a fork and stir well.
Serve and enjoy.
Nutrition: Calories 198 Fat 7.3 g Carbohydrates 3.1 g Sugar 1.3 g Protein 28.5 g Cholesterol 87 mg

Jamaican Chicken

Preparation time: 10 minutes
Cooking time: 15 minutes
Servings: 6
Ingredients:
6 chicken drumsticks
1 tbsp jerk seasoning
3 tbsp soy sauce
1/4 cup red wine vinegar
1/4 cup brown sugar
1/2 cup ketchup
1 tsp salt
Directions:
Add all ingredients except chicken into the inner pot of instant pot duo crisp and stir well.
Add chicken and stir to coat.
Seal the pot with pressure cooking lid and cook on high for 10 minutes.
Once done, release pressure using a quick release. Remove lid.
Remove chicken from pot. Set pot on sauté mode and cook sauce for 5 minutes.
Pour sauce over chicken and serve.
Nutrition: Calories 126 Fat 2.7 g Carbohydrates 11.7 g Sugar 10.6 g Protein 13.5 g Cholesterol 40 mg

Flavorful Lemon Chicken

Preparation time: 10 minutes
Cooking time: 4 hours 5 minutes
Servings: 4
Ingredients:
20 oz chicken breasts, skinless, boneless, and cut into pieces
1 tsp dried parsley
2 tbsp olive oil
2 tbsp butter
3 tbsp flour
1/4 cup chicken broth
1/2 cup fresh lemon juice
1/8 tsp dried thymefla
1/4 tsp dried basil
1/2 tsp dried oregano
1 tsp salt
Directions:
In a bowl, toss chicken with flour.
Heat butter and oil in a pan over medium-high heat.
Add chicken to the pan and sear until brown.
Transfer chicken into the inner pot of instant pot duo crisp.

Add remaining ingredients on top of chicken.
Seal the pot with pressure cooking lid and select slow cook mode and cook on low for 4 hours.
Serve and enjoy.
Nutrition: Calories 412 Fat 23.7 g Carbohydrates 5.3 g Sugar 0.7 g Protein 42.3 g Cholesterol 141 mg

Dijon Chicken

Preparation time: 10 minutes
Cooking time: 50 minutes
Servings: 4
Ingredients:
1 1/2 lbs. chicken thighs, skinless and boneless
2 tbsp dijon mustard
1/4 cup French mustard
4 tbsp maple syrup
2 tsp olive oil
Directions:
In a large bowl, mix together maple syrup, olive oil, dijon mustard, and french mustard.
Add chicken to the bowl and mix until chicken is well coated.
Transfer chicken into the instant pot air fryer basket and place basket in the pot.
Seal the pot with air fryer lid and select bake mode and cook at 375 f for 45-50 minutes.
Serve and enjoy.
Nutrition: Calories 401 Fat 15.3 g Carbohydrates 13.8 g Sugar 12 g Protein 49.6 g Cholesterol 151 mg

Mango Chicken

Preparation time: 10 minutes
Cooking time: 15 minutes
Servings: 2
Ingredients:
2 chicken breasts, skinless and boneless
1 ripe mango, peeled and diced
1/2 tbsp turmeric
1/2 cup chicken broth
2 garlic cloves, minced
1/2 tsp ginger, grated
1 fresh lime juice
1/2 tsp pepper
1/2 tsp salt
Directions:
Add chicken into the inner pot of instant pot duo crisp and top with mango.
Add lime juice, broth, turmeric, pepper, and salt.
Seal the pot with pressure cooking lid and cook on high for 15 minutes.
Once done, allow to release pressure naturally. Remove lid.
Shred chicken using a fork and stir well.
Serve and enjoy.
Nutrition: Calories 407 Fat 12.1 g Carbohydrates 30 g Sugar 23.6 g Protein 45.3 g Cholesterol 130 mg

Honey Cashew Butter Chicken

Preparation time: 10 minutes
Cooking time: 7 minutes

Servings: 3
Ingredients:
1 lb chicken breast, cut into chunks
2 tbsp rice vinegar
2 tbsp honey
2 tbsp coconut aminos
1/4 cup cashew butter
2 garlic cloves, minced
1/4 cup chicken broth
1/2 tbsp sriracha
Directions:
Add chicken into the inner pot of instant pot duo crisp.
In a small bowl, mix together cashew butter, garlic, broth, sriracha, vinegar, honey, and coconut aminos and pour over chicken.
Seal the pot with pressure cooking lid and cook on high for 7 minutes.
Once done, release pressure using a quick release. Remove lid.
Stir well and serve.
Nutrition: Calories 366 Fat 2.1 g Carbohydrates 20.7 g Sugar 11.6 g Protein 36.4 g Cholesterol 97 mg

Sweet & Tangy Tamarind Chicken

Preparation time: 10 minutes
Cooking time: 15 minutes
Servings: 4
Ingredients:
2 lbs chicken breasts, skinless, boneless, and cut into pieces
1 tbsp ketchup
1 tbsp vinegar
2 tbsp ginger, grated
1 garlic clove, minced
3 tbsp olive oil
1 tbsp arrowroot powder
1/2 cup tamarind paste
2 tbsp brown sugar
1 tsp salt
Directions:
Add oil into the inner pot of instant pot duo crisp and set the pot on sauté mode.
Add ginger and garlic and sauté for 30 seconds.
Add chicken and sauté for 3-4 minutes.
In a small bowl, mix together the tamarind paste, brown sugar, ketchup, vinegar, and salt and pour over chicken and stir well.
Seal the pot with pressure cooking lid and cook on high for 8 minutes.
Once done, release pressure using a quick release. Remove lid.
In a small bowl, whisk arrowroot powder with 2 tbsp water and pour it into the pot.
Set pot on sauté mode and cook chicken for 1-2 minutes.
Serve and enjoy.
Nutrition: Calories 598 Fat 27.6 g Carbohydrates 18.9 g Sugar 14 g Protein 66.4 g Cholesterol 202 mg

Garlic Lemon Chicken

Preparation Time: 10 minutes
Cooking Time: 40 minutes
Serving: 4

Ingredients:
2 lbs chicken drumsticks
4 tbsp butter
2 tbsp parsley, chopped
1 fresh lemon juice
10 garlic cloves, minced
2 tbsp olive oil
Pepper
Salt
Directions:
Add butter, parsley, lemon juice, garlic, oil, pepper, and salt into the mixing bowl and mix well.
Add chicken to the bowl and toss until well coated.
Transfer chicken into the instant pot air fryer basket and place basket in the pot.
Seal the pot with air fryer lid and select bake mode and cook at 400 F for 40 minutes.
Serve and enjoy.
Nutrition:
Calories 560
Fat 31.6 g
Carbohydrates 2.9 g
Sugar 0.4 g
Protein 63.1 g
Cholesterol 230 mg

Flavorful Herb Chicken

Preparation Time: 10 minutes
Cooking Time: 4 hours
Serving: 6
Ingredients:
6 chicken breasts, skinless and boneless
1 onion, sliced
14 oz can tomatoes, diced
1 tsp dried basil
1 tsp dried rosemary
1 tbsp olive oil
1/2 cup balsamic vinegar
1/2 tsp thyme
1 tsp dried oregano
4 garlic cloves
Pepper
Salt
Directions:
Add all ingredients into the inner pot of instant pot duo crisp and stir well.
Seal the pot with pressure cooking lid and select slow cook mode and cook on high for 4 hours.
Stir well and serve.
Nutrition:
Calories 328
Fat 13.3 g
Carbohydrates 6.3 g
Sugar 3.1 g
Protein 43.2 g
Cholesterol 130 mg

Asian Style Chicken Meal

Preparation time: 5-10 Minutes
Cooking Time: 30 Minutes
Serving: 2-3
Ingredients: ¼ cup honey
½ cup rice vinegar
1 pound chicken wings
1 teaspoon sea salt
2 cloves garlic, minced
1 teaspoon ginger, grated
1 small orange, zest, and juice
2 teaspoons red chili pepper paste
Directions:
Place Instant Pot Air Fryer Crisp over kitchen platform. In the inner pot, add 2 cups water and arrange trivet and place the chicken wings over.
Close the Pressure Lid and press the "Pressure" setting. Set the "Hi" pressure level and set the timer to 2 minutes. Press "Start."
Instant Pot will start building pressure. Quick-release pressure after cooking time is over (just press the button on the lid), and open the lid. Take out the wings and empty water.
In a mixing bowl, combine the orange zest, orange juice, rice vinegar, honey, red pepper paste, ginger, garlic, and salt.
Add the sauce in the pot and place trivet; place the chicken over the trivet.
Close the Crisp Lid and press the "Air Fry" setting. Set temperature to 390°F and set the timer to 30 minutes. Press "Start."
Halfway down, open the Crisp Lid, shake the basket and close the lid to continue cooking for the remaining time.
Open the Crisp Lid after cooking time is over. Serve the chicken with the honey sauce.
Nutrition: Calories: 448
Fat: 17g
Saturated Fat: 6g
Trans Fat: 0.5g
Carbohydrates: 41g
Fiber: 2g
Sodium: 1087mg
Protein: 24g

Korean chicken wings

Preparation time: 5 minutes
Cooking time: 10 minutes
Servings: 8
Ingredients:
Wings:
1 tsp. Pepper
1 tsp. Salt
2 pounds chicken wings
Sauce:
2 packets splenda
1 tbsp. Minced garlic
1 tbsp. Minced ginger
1 tbsp. Sesame oil
1 tsp. Agave nectar
1 tbsp. Mayo
2 tbsp. Gochujang

Finishing:
¼ c. Chopped green onions
2 tsp. Sesame seeds
Directions:
Preparing the ingredients. Ensure instant crisp air fryer is preheated to 400 degrees.
Line a small pan with foil and place a rack onto the pan, then place into instant crisp air fryer.
Season wings with pepper and salt and place onto the rack.
Air frying. Lock the air fryer lid. Set temperature to 160°f, and set time to 20 minutes and air fry 20 minutes, turning at 10 minutes.
As chicken air fries, mix together all the sauce components.
Once a thermometer says that the chicken has reached 160 degrees, take out wings and place into a bowl.
Pour half of the sauce mixture over wings, tossing well to coat.
Put coated wings back into instant crisp air fryer for 5 minutes or till they reach 165 degrees.
Remove and sprinkle with green onions and sesame seeds. Dip into extra sauce.
Nutrition: Calories: 356; Fat: 26g; Protein:23g; Sugar:2g

Mustard Chicken

Preparation Time: 10 minutes
Cooking Time: 20 minutes
Serving: 4
Ingredients:
1 lbs chicken tenders
1 garlic clove, minced
1/2 oz fresh lemon juice
2 tbsp fresh tarragon, chopped
1/2 cup whole grain mustard
1/2 tsp paprika
1/2 tsp pepper
1/4 tsp kosher salt
Directions:
Add all ingredients except chicken to the large bowl and mix well.
Add chicken to the bowl and stir until well coated.
Place the dehydrating tray in a multi-level air fryer basket and place basket in the instant pot.
Place chicken tenders on dehydrating tray.
Seal pot with air fryer lid and select bake mode then set the temperature to 380 F and timer for 20 minutes. Turn chicken halfway through.
Serve and enjoy.
Nutrition:
Calories 242
Fat 9.5 g
Carbohydrates 3.1 g
Sugar 0.1 g
Protein 33.2 g
Cholesterol 101 mg

BBQ Chicken Wings

Preparation Time: 10 minutes
Cooking Time: 35 minutes
Serving: 4
Ingredients:

1 lb chicken wings
1/2 cup BBQ sauce
1 tbsp olive oil
1/2 cup hot sauce
Pepper
Salt
Directions:
Toss chicken wings with olive oil and season with pepper and salt.
Spray instant pot multi-level air fryer basket with cooking spray.
Add chicken wings into the air fryer basket and place basket into the instant pot.
Seal pot with air fryer lid and select air fry mode then set the temperature to 400 F and timer for 30 minutes. Stir halfway through.
In a large bowl, mix together hot sauce and BBQ sauce.
Add chicken wings in sauce mixture and toss until well coated.
Serve and enjoy.
Nutrition:
Calories 296
Fat 12.1 g
Carbohydrates 11.9 g
Sugar 8.5 g
Protein 33 g
Cholesterol 101 mg

Lemon Chicken Potatoes

Preparation time: 5-10 Minutes
Cooking Time: 20 Minutes
Serving: 5-6
Ingredients: ½ cup chicken broth
12 chicken thighs, bone-in
1 ½ pound yellow potatoes, quartered
⅓ cup olive oil
⅓ cup lemon juice
1 teaspoon lemon zest
1 teaspoon dried parsley
1 teaspoon black pepper
1 tablespoon garlic, minced
2 teaspoons dried oregano
2 teaspoons kosher salt
Lemon wedges to serve
Directions:
In a mixing bowl, whisk the lemon juice, olive oil, garlic, parsley, oregano, pepper, lemon zest, and salt.
Place Instant Pot Air Fryer Crisp over kitchen platform. In the inner pot, add the broth and chicken. Arrange the potatoes on top and pour the lemon mixture.
Close the Pressure Lid and press the "Pressure" setting. Set the "Hi" pressure level and set the timer to 15 minutes. Press "Start."
Instant Pot will start building pressure. Quick-release pressure after cooking time is over (just press the button on the lid), and open the lid. Add the chicken mixture to a serving plate along with the lemon sauce.
Add back the chicken to the pot. Close the Crisp Lid and press the "Air Fry" setting. Set temperature to 400°F and set the timer to 4 minutes. Press "Start."
Halfway down, open the Crisp Lid, shake the basket and close the lid to continue cooking for the remaining time.
Open the Crisp Lid after cooking time is over. Add the chicken to the potato mixture and serve warm.

Nutrition: **Calories: 612**

Fat: 38.5g
Saturated Fat: 12g
Trans Fat: 0g
Carbohydrates: 23g
Fiber: 6g
Sodium: 983mg
Protein: 43g

Boneless Air Fryer Turkey Breasts

Preparation time: 10 minutes
Cooking time: 50 minutes
Serving 4
6 Ingredients
3 lb boneless breast
¼ cup mayonnaise
2 tsp poultry seasoning
1 tsp salt
½ tsp garlic powder
¼ tsp black pepper

Directions
Choose the Air Fry option on the Instant Pot Duo Crisp Air fryer. Set the temperature to 360°F and push start. The preheating will start.
Season your boneless turkey breast with mayonnaise, poultry seasoning, salt, garlic powder, and black pepper.
Once preheated, Air Fry the turkey breasts on 360°F for 1 hour, turning every 15 minutes or until internal temperature has reached a temperature of 165°F.
Nutrition: Calories 558, Total Fat 18g, Total Carbs 1g, Protein 98g

Spicy Chicken Breast

Preparation Time: 10 minutes
Cooking Time: 35 minutes
Serving: 2
Ingredients:
2 chicken breasts, bone-in, and skin-on
1 tbsp ground fennel
1 tbsp chili powder
1 tbsp olive oil
1 tsp ground cumin
1 tsp garlic powder
1 tsp onion powder
1 tbsp paprika
1/2 tsp black pepper
1 tsp sea salt
Directions:
In a small bowl, mix together all dried spices.
Brush chicken with olive oil and rub with spice mixture.
Place chicken in the instant pot air fryer basket and place basket in the pot.
Seal the pot with air fryer lid and select air fry mode and cook at 375 F for 35 minutes.
Serve and enjoy.
Nutrition:
Calories 108

Fat 8.9 g
Carbohydrates 8.3 g
Sugar 1.4 g
Protein 2.3 g
Cholesterol 1 mg

Tasty Butter Chicken

Preparation Time: 10 minutes
Cooking Time: 8 minutes
Serving: 6
Ingredients:
3 lbs chicken breasts, boneless, skinless, and cut into cubes
1/2 cup butter, cut into cubes
2 tbsp tomato paste
1 tsp turmeric powder
2 tbsp garam masala
1 tbsp ginger paste
1 tbsp garlic paste
1 onion, diced
1/4 cup fresh cilantro, chopped
1/2 cup heavy cream
1 1/4 cup tomato sauce
2/3 cup chicken stock
1 1/2 tsp olive oil
1 tsp kosher salt
Directions:
Add 3 tbsp butter and oil in the inner pot of instant pot duo crisp and set pot on sauté mode.
Add garlic paste and onion and sauté for a minute.
Add chicken, tomato sauce, stock, tomato paste, turmeric, garam masala, ginger paste, and salt and stir to combine.
Seal the pot with pressure cooking lid and cook on high for 5 minutes.
Once done, release pressure using a quick release. Remove lid.
Set pot on sauté mode. Add remaining butter and heavy cream and cook for 2 minutes.
Stir well and serve.
Nutrition:
Calories 643
Fat 37.3 g
Carbohydrates 7.2 g
Sugar 3.8 g
Protein 67.4 g
Cholesterol 256 mg

Easy Cheesy Chicken

Preparation Time: 10 minutes
Cooking Time: 17 minutes
Serving: 6
Ingredients:
1 1/2 lbs chicken tenders
25 oz tomato sauce
2 tbsp butter
1/2 cup olive oil

1/2 tsp garlic powder
1/2 cup parmesan cheese, grated
2 cups mozzarella cheese, shredded

Directions:

Add olive oil into the inner pot of instant pot duo crisp and set pot on sauté mode.
Add chicken and sauté until lightly brown from both the sides.
Add garlic powder, tomato sauce, butter, and parmesan cheese on top of chicken.
Seal the pot with pressure cooking lid and cook on high for 15 minutes.
Once done, release pressure using a quick release. Remove lid.
Sprinkle mozzarella cheese on top of chicken. Cover pot with air fryer lid and select broil mode and cook for 1-2 minutes.
Serve and enjoy.

Nutrition:
Calories 457
Fat 31.4 g
Carbohydrates 6.9 g
Sugar 5.1 g
Protein 37.9 g
Cholesterol 118 mg

Turkey Legs

Preparation Time: 10 minutes
Cooking Time: 25 minutes
Serving: 4

Ingredients:

4 turkey legs
1/4 tsp rosemary
1 tbsp butter
1/4 tsp thyme
1/4 tsp oregano
Pepper
Salt

Directions:

Season turkey legs with pepper and salt.
In a small bowl, mix together butter, thyme, oregano, rosemary, pepper, and salt.
Rub the butter mixture all over turkey legs.
Place the dehydrating tray in a multi-level air fryer basket and place basket in the instant pot.
Place turkey legs on dehydrating tray.
Seal pot with air fryer lid and select air fry mode then set the temperature to 350 F and timer for 25 minutes. Turn turkey legs halfway through.
Serve and enjoy.

Nutrition:
Calories 174
Fat 9.9 g
Carbohydrates 0.2 g
Sugar 0 g
Protein 19.8 g
Cholesterol 68 mg

Asian Wings

Preparation Time: 10 minutes
Cooking Time: 25 minutes
Serving: 4
Ingredients:
1 lb chicken wings
1/4 tsp pepper
1/2 tsp salt
For sauce:
1 tbsp sugar
1/2 tbsp garlic, minced
1/2 tbsp mayonnaise
1 tbsp gochujang
1/2 tbsp ginger, minced
1/2 tbsp sesame oil
1/2 tsp honey
Directions:
Season chicken wings with pepper and salt.
Spray instant pot multi-level air fryer basket with cooking spray.
Add chicken wings into the air fryer basket and place basket into the instant pot.
Seal pot with air fryer lid and select air fry mode then set the temperature to 400 F and timer for 25 minutes. Turn chicken wings halfway through.
Meanwhile, in a bowl, mix together all sauce ingredients.
Add chicken wings to the sauce bowl and toss well.
Serve and enjoy.
Nutrition:
Calories 262
Fat 10.8 g
Carbohydrates 6.4 g
Sugar 4.7 g
Protein 33.1 g
Cholesterol 101 mg

Crispy Crust Whole Chicken

Preparation Time: 10 minutes
Cooking Time: 45 minutes
Serving: 4
Ingredients:
1 whole chicken
1 1/2 cups chicken broth
2 tbsp Montreal steak seasoning
1 tsp Italian seasoning
1 tsp paprika
1 tsp onion powder
1 tsp garlic powder
2 tbsp olive oil
Directions:
Pour broth into the instant pot.
Mix together Montreal steak seasoning, Italian seasoning, paprika, onion powder, and garlic powder.
Brush chicken with olive oil and rub with seasoning. Place chicken in the air fryer basket and place basket in the instant pot.
Seal the pot with pressure cooking lid and cook on high pressure for 25 minutes.

Once done, allow to release pressure naturally for 15 minutes then release remaining pressure using quick release. Remove lid.
Remove liquid from the instant pot.
Seal pot with air fryer lid and select air fry mode and set the temperature to 400 F and timer for 10 minutes.
Turn chicken to the other side and air fry for 10 minutes more.
Serve and enjoy.
Nutrition:
Calories 925
Fat 40.4 g
Carbohydrates 1.8 g
Sugar 0.8 g
Protein 128.7 g
Cholesterol 390 mg

Tasty Butter Chicken

Preparation time: 10 minutes
Cooking time: 8 minutes
Servings: 6
Ingredients:
3 lbs. chicken breasts, boneless, skinless, and cut into cubes
1/2 cup butter, cut into cubes
2 tbsp tomato paste
1 tsp turmeric powder
2 tbsp garam masala
1 tbsp ginger paste
1 tbsp garlic paste
1 onion, diced
1/4 cup fresh cilantro, chopped
1/2 cup heavy cream
1 1/4 cup tomato sauce
2/3 cup chicken stock
1 1/2 tsp olive oil
1 tsp kosher salt
Directions:
Add 3 tbsp butter and oil in the inner pot of instant pot duo crisp and set pot on sauté mode.
Add garlic paste and onion and sauté for a minute.
Add chicken, tomato sauce, stock, tomato paste, turmeric, garam masala, ginger paste, and salt and stir to combine.
Seal the pot with pressure cooking lid and cook on high for 5 minutes.
Once done, release pressure using a quick release. Remove lid.
Set pot on sauté mode. Add remaining butter and heavy cream and cook for 2 minutes.
Stir well and serve.
Nutrition: Calories 643 Fat 37.3 g Carbohydrates 7.2 g Sugar 3.8 g Protein 67.4 g Cholesterol 256 mg

Chicken Pasta

Preparation time: 10 minutes
Cooking time: 15 minutes
Servings: 4
Ingredients:
1 lb. chicken breasts, boneless and skinless, cut into bite-size pieces
1 tbsp garlic, minced

2 bell peppers, seeded and diced
2 tbsp olive oil
1 onion, diced
1 cup chicken stock
3 tbsp fajita seasoning
8 oz penne pasta, dry
7 oz can tomato

Directions:

Add olive oil in the inner pot of instant pot duo crisp and set pot on sauté mode.
Add chicken and half fajita seasoning in the pot and sauté chicken for 3-5 minutes.
Add garlic, bell pepper, onions, and remaining fajitas seasoning and sauté for 2 minutes.
Add tomatoes, stock, and pasta and stir well.
Seal the pot with pressure cooking lid and cook on high for 6 minutes.
Once done, release pressure using a quick release. Remove lid.
Set pot on sauté mode and cook for 1-2 minutes.
Serve and enjoy.

Nutrition: Calories 509 Fat 17 g Carbohydrates 46.2 g Sugar 6.1 g Protein 40.9 g Cholesterol 142 mg

Cheesy Chicken Wings

Preparation Time: 10 minutes
Cooking Time: 18 minutes
Serving: 4

Ingredients:

2 lbs chicken wings
1/2 cup chicken stock
1 tsp season salt

For sauce:

1/2 cup parmesan cheese, grated
1 tbsp garlic, crushed
1 stick butter, melted
1/2 tsp black pepper
1/2 tsp dried parsley flakes
1 tsp garlic powder

Directions:

Season chicken wings with seasoned salt.
Add chicken wings to the inner pot of instant pot duo crisp along with the chicken stock.
Seal the pot with pressure cooking lid and cook on high for 8 minutes.
Meanwhile, mix together butter, pepper, parmesan cheese, parsley flakes, garlic powder, and garlic. Set aside.
Once chicken wings done then release pressures using a quick release. Remove lid.
Remove chicken wings from the pot and clean the pot.
Spray instant pot air fryer basket with cooking spray and place in the pot.
Toss chicken wings with melted butter and add into the air fryer basket.
Seal the pot with air fryer lid and select broil mode and cook for 10 minutes.
Serve and enjoy.

Nutrition:
Calories 652
Fat 40.6 g
Carbohydrates 1.6 g
Sugar 0.3 g
Protein 67.3 g
Cholesterol 265 mg

Creamy Italian Chicken

Preparation Time: 10 minutes
Cooking Time: 10 minutes
Serving: 8
Ingredients:
2 lbs chicken breasts, skinless and boneless
1 cup chicken stock
1/4 cup butter
14 oz can cream of chicken soup
8 oz cream cheese
1 tbsp Italian seasoning
Directions:
Add the chicken stock into the inner pot of instant pot duo crisp.
Add cream of chicken soup, Italian seasoning, and butter into the pot and stir well.
Seal the pot with pressure cooking lid and cook on high for 10 minutes.
Once done, release pressure using a quick release. Remove lid.
Add cream cheese and stir until cheese is melted
Serve and enjoy.
Nutrition:
Calories 416
Fat 27.5 g
Carbohydrates 4.6 g
Sugar 0.6 g
Protein 36.3 g
Cholesterol 153 mg

Air Fryer Spicy Chicken Thighs

Preparation: 10 minutes, 25 minutes
Cooking Time: 15 minutes
Servings: 4
Ingredients:
2 pounds (4 Nos.) chicken thighs with bone and skin.
⅓ cup soy sauce, low sodium
2 tablespoons chili garlic sauce
1 tablespoon lime zest
2 garlic cloves, finely grated
2 teaspoon minced ginger
2 tablespoons honey
½ cup green onions, finely chopped
4 tablespoon sesame seeds, toasted
¼ cup virgin olive oil
¼ teaspoon kosher salt

Directions:
Clean, wash, and pat dry the chicken thighs.
Combine olive oil, chili garlic sauce, honey soy sauce, lime juice, minced ginger, grated garlic, and salt thoroughly.
Keep half a cup of the marinade for later use.
Put the chicken thighs into the bowl and coat the marinade well.
Transfer it into a container, cover, and refrigerate for 30 minutes.
For making the dish juicier, it would be better to broil the chicken.
For broiling, use the separator available with the Instant Pot Air Fryer.
Place the air fryer basket in the inner pot and place the separator in the air fryer basket.

Now place the marinated chicken thighs on the separator.
Close the crisp cover.
In the AIR FRYER section, select the BROIL option.
You don't need to select the temperature, because by default the heat will set to 400°F.
Set the timer for 20 minutes.
Press START to begin cooking.
While the frying is on, you can make the sauce.
Put the reserved marinade in a saucepan and bring to boiling.
Simmer for about 5 minutes and allow the sauce to becomes thick.
When the sauce becomes thick, remove it from the heat.
Now take out the broiled chicken thighs and brush the marinade sauce over the thighs.
Serve by garnishing with toasted sesame seeds and chopped green onions.
Enjoy your juicy, chicken thighs.
Nutrition: Calories: 712, Total fat: 52.3g, Saturated fat: 12.5g, Trans fat: 0.2g, Cholesterol: 227mg, Sodium: 883mg, Total carbs: 19g, Dietary fiber: 2g, Sugars: 14g, Protein: 41g

Garlic Ranch Chicken Wings

Preparation Time: 10 minutes
Cooking Time: 25 minutes
Serving: 4
Ingredients:
1 lb chicken wings
3 garlic cloves, minced
2 tbsp butter, melted
1 1/2 tbsp ranch seasoning
Directions:
Add chicken wings into the large bowl. Mix together butter, ranch seasoning, and garlic and pour over chicken wings and toss well.
Cover bowl and place in the refrigerator overnight.
Place marinated chicken wings into the air fryer basket and place basket in the pot.
Seal pot with air fryer lid and select air fry mode then set the temperature to 360 F and timer for 20 minutes. Mix halfway through.
Turn temperature to 390 F and air fry for 5 minutes more.
Serve and enjoy.
Nutrition:
Calories 281
Fat 14.2 g
Carbohydrates 0.7 g
Sugar 0 g
Protein 33 g
Cholesterol 116 mg

Classic Honey Mustard Chicken

Preparation time:5-10 Minutes
Cooking Time: 20 Minutes
Serving: 5-6
Ingredients: 3 tablespoons honey
2 tablespoons Dijon mustard
6 (6-ounces each) boneless, skinless chicken breasts 2 tablespoons rosemary, minced
¼ teaspoon ground black pepper

¾ teaspoon salt

Directions:

In a mixing bowl, combine the honey, Dijon mustard, black pepper, rosemary, and salt. Rub the chicken breasts with the mixture.

Grease Air Fryer Basket with some cooking spray. Arrange the chicken breasts.

Place Instant Pot Air Fryer Crisp over kitchen platform. Press Air Fry, set the temperature to 400°F and set the timer to 5 minutes to preheat. Press "Start" and allow it to preheat for 5 minutes.

In the inner pot, place the Air Fryer basket.

Close the Crisp Lid and press the "Air Fry" setting. Set temperature to 350°F and set the timer to 20-22 minutes. Press "Start."

Halfway down, open the Crisp Lid, shake the basket and close the lid to continue cooking for the remaining time.

Open the Crisp Lid after cooking time is over. Serve warm with veggies or cooked rice.

Nutrition: **Calories:**
Fat: g
Saturated Fat: g
Trans Fat: 0g
Carbohydrates: g
Fiber: g
Sodium: mg
Protein: g

Parmesan Chicken Wings

Preparation Time: 10 minutes
Cooking Time: 25 minutes
Serving: 4
Ingredients:
1 lb chicken wings
2 tbsp cornstarch
1/4 cup parmesan cheese, grated
1/2 tbsp garlic powder
1/2 tsp onion powder
1/2 tsp paprika
Pepper
Salt

Directions:

In a bowl, mix together cornstarch, garlic powder, onion powder, paprika, parmesan cheese, pepper, and salt.

Add chicken wings in cornstarch mixture and toss until well coated.

Place the dehydrating tray in a multi-level air fryer basket and place basket in the instant pot.

Place chicken wings on dehydrating tray.

Seal pot with air fryer lid and select air fry mode then set the temperature to 380 F and timer for 25 minutes. Turn chicken halfway through.

Serve and enjoy.

Nutrition:
Calories 254
Fat 9.7 g
Carbohydrates 5 g
Sugar 0.4 g
Protein 34.9 g
Cholesterol 105 mg

Barbecue Air Fried Chicken

Preparation time: 5 minutes
Cooking time: 26 minutes
Serving 10
10 Ingredients
1 teaspoon Liquid Smoke
2 cloves Fresh Garlic smashed
1/2 cup Apple Cider Vinegar
3 pounds Chuck Roast well-marbled with intramuscular fat
1 Tablespoon Kosher Salt
1 Tablespoon Freshly Ground Black Pepper
2 teaspoons Garlic Powder
1.5 cups Barbecue Sauce
1/4 cup Light Brown Sugar + more for sprinkling
2 Tablespoons Honey optional and in place of 2 TBL sugar
Directions
Add meat to the Instant Pot Duo Crisp Air Fryer Basket, spreading out the meat.
Select the option Air Fry.
Close the Air Fryer lid and cook at 300 degrees F for 8 minutes. Pause the Air Fryer and flip meat over after 4 minutes.
Remove the lid and baste with more barbecue sauce and sprinkle with a little brown sugar.
Again, Close the Air Fryer lid and set the temperature at 400°F for 9 minutes. Watch meat though the lid and flip it over after 5 minutes.
Nutrition: Calories 360, Total Fat 16g, Total Carbs 27g, Protein 27g

Balsamic Chicken

Preparation Time: 10 minutes
Cooking Time: 17 minutes
Serving: 6
Ingredients:
2 lbs chicken breasts
1/3 cup balsamic vinegar
1 onion, chopped
1/2 cup chicken broth
1 tbsp Dijon mustard
1/2 tsp dried thyme
1 tsp garlic, chopped
Directions:
Mix together Dijon, chicken broth, and vinegar and pour into the inner pot of instant pot duo crisp.
Add chicken, thyme, garlic, and onion and stir well.
Seal the pot with pressure cooking lid and cook on high pressure for 12 minutes.
Once done, release pressure using a quick release. Remove lid.
Remove chicken from pot and shred using a fork. Pour the leftover liquid of pot over shredded chicken.
Line air fryer basket with foil.
Add shredded chicken to the air fryer basket and place basket in the pot.
Seal the pot with air fryer lid and select broil mode and cook for 5 minutes.
Serve and enjoy.
Nutrition:
Calories 303
Fat 11.4 g
Carbohydrates 2.3 g
Sugar 0.9 g
Protein 44.5 g

Cholesterol 135 mg

Italian Chicken Wings

Preparation Time: 10 minutes
Cooking Time: 15 minutes
Serving: 4
Ingredients:
12 chicken wings
1 tbsp chicken seasoning
3 tbsp olive oil
1 tbsp garlic powder
1 tbsp basil
1/2 tbsp oregano
3 tbsp tarragon
Pepper
Salt
Directions:
Add all ingredients into the mixing bowl and toss well.
Pour 1 cup water into the inner pot of instant pot duo crisp then place steamer rack in the pot.
Arrange chicken wings on top of the steamer rack.
Seal the pot with pressure cooking lid and cook on high pressure for 10 minutes.
Once done, release pressure using a quick release. Remove lid.
Remove chicken wings from the pot. Dump leftover liquid from the pot.
Add chicken wings into the air fryer basket then place a basket in the pot.
Seal the pot with air fryer lid and select broil mode and cook for 5 minutes.
Serve and enjoy.
Nutrition:
Calories 588
Fat 29.6 g
Carbohydrates 2.6 g
Sugar 0.5 g
Protein 74.6 g
Cholesterol 227 mg

Herbed Turkey Dinner

Preparation time: 5-10 Minutes
Cooking Time: 40 Minutes
Serving: 5-6
Ingredients: 2 pounds turkey breast with skin
1 teaspoon rosemary, chopped
1 teaspoon thyme, finely chopped
4 tablespoons melted butter
3 garlic cloves, grated
½ teaspoon kosher salt
1 teaspoon ground black pepper
Directions:
Rub the salt and black pepper over the turkey breasts. In a bowl, combine the rosemary, melted butter, thyme, and garlic in a medium bowl. Add the turkey and coat well.

Place Instant Pot Air Fryer Crisp over kitchen platform. Press Air Fry, set the temperature to 400°F and set the timer to 5 minutes to preheat. Press "Start" and allow it to preheat for 5 minutes.
In the inner pot, place the Air Fryer basket. In the basket, add the turkey.
Close the Crisp Lid and press the "Air Fry" setting. Set temperature to 375°F and set the timer to 40 minutes. Press "Start."
Halfway down, open the Crisp Lid, shake the basket and close the lid to continue cooking for the remaining time.
Open the Crisp Lid after cooking time is over. Slice and serve warm.

Nutrition: Calories: 327
Fat: 21.5g
Saturated Fat: 9g
Trans Fat: 0g
Carbohydrates: 6.5g
Fiber: 1g
Sodium: 983mg
Protein: 39g

Garlic Lemon Chicken

Preparation time: 10 minutes
Cooking time: 40 minutes
Servings: 4
Ingredients:
2 lbs. chicken drumsticks
4 tbsp butter
2 tbsp parsley, chopped
1 fresh lemon juice
10 garlic cloves, minced
2 tbsp olive oil
Pepper
Salt
Directions:
Add butter, parsley, lemon juice, garlic, oil, pepper, and salt into the mixing bowl and mix well.
Add chicken to the bowl and toss until well coated.
Transfer chicken into the instant pot air fryer basket and place basket in the pot.
Seal the pot with air fryer lid and select bake mode and cook at 400 f for 40 minutes.
Serve and enjoy.
Nutrition: Calories 560 Fat 31.6 g Carbohydrates 2.9 g Sugar 0.4 g Protein 63.1 g Cholesterol 230 mg

Flavorful Herb Chicken

Preparation time: 10 minutes
Cooking time: 4 hours
Servings: 6
Ingredients:
6 chicken breasts, skinless and boneless
1 onion, sliced
14 oz can tomato, diced
1 tsp dried basil
1 tsp dried rosemary
1 tbsp olive oil
1/2 cup balsamic vinegar
1/2 tsp thyme

1 tsp dried oregano
4 garlic cloves
Pepper
Salt

Directions:
Add all ingredients into the inner pot of instant pot duo crisp and stir well.
Seal the pot with pressure cooking lid and select slow cook mode and cook on high for 4 hours.
Stir well and serve.

Nutrition: Calories 328 Fat 13.3 g Carbohydrates 6.3 g Sugar 3.1 g Protein 43.2 g

---

Broccoli Chicken Casserole

Preparation time:10 minutes
Cooking Time: 22 minutes
Serving: 6
Ingredients:
1 1/2 lbs. chicken, cubed
2 teaspoon chopped garlic
2 tablespoon butter
1 1/2 cups chicken broth
1 1/2 cups long-grain rice
1 (10.75 oz) can cream of chicken soup
2 cups broccoli florets
1 cup crushed Ritz cracker
2 tablespoon melted butter
2 cups shredded cheddar cheese

Directions:
Add 1 cup water to the Instant Pot Dup and place a basket in it.
Place the broccoli in the basket evenly.
Put on the pressure-cooking lid and seal it.
Hit the "Pressure Button" and select 1 minute of cooking time, then press "Start."
Once the Instant Pot Duo beeps, do a quick release and remove its lid.
Remove the broccoli and empty the Instant Pot Duo.
Hit the sauté button then add 2 tablespoon butter.
Toss in chicken and stir cook for 5 minutes, then add garlic and sauté for 30 seconds.
Stir in rice, chicken broth, and cream of chicken soup.
Put on the pressure-cooking lid and seal it.
Hit the "Pressure Button" and select 12 minutes of cooking time, then press "Start."
Once the Instant Pot Duo beeps, do a quick release and remove its lid.
Add cheese and broccoli, then mix well gently.
Toss the cracker with 2 tablespoon butter in a bowl and spread over the chicken in the Pot.
Put on the Air Fryer lid and seal it.
Hit the "Air Fryer Button" and select 4 minutes of cooking time, then press "Start."
Once the Instant Pot Duo beeps, remove its lid.
Serve.

Nutrition:
Calories 609
Total Fat 24.4g
Saturated Fat 12.6g
Cholesterol 142mg
Sodium 924mg
Total Carbohydrate 45.5g
Dietary Fiber 1.4g
Total Sugars 1.6g

Protein 49.2g

Chicken Tikka Kebab

Preparation time:10 minutes
Cooking Time: 17 minutes
Serving: 4
Ingredients:
1 lb. chicken thighs boneless skinless, cubed
1 tablespoon oil
1/2 cup red onion, cubed
1/2 cup green bell pepper, cubed
1/2 cup red bell pepper, cubed
lime wedges to garnish
onion rounds to garnish
For marinade:
1/2 cup yogurt Greek
3/4 tablespoon ginger, grated
3/4 tablespoon garlic, minced
1 tablespoon lime juice
2 teaspoon red chili powder mild
1/2 teaspoon ground turmeric
1 teaspoon garam masala
1 teaspoon coriander powder
1/2 tablespoon dried fenugreek leaves
1 teaspoon salt
Directions:
Prepare the marinade by mixing yogurt with all its Ingredients: in a bowl.
Fold in chicken, then mix well to coat and refrigerate for 8 hours.
Add bell pepper, onions, and oil to the marinade and mix well.
Thread the chicken, peppers, and onions on the skewers.
Set the Air Fryer Basket in the Instant Pot Duo.
Put on the Air Fryer lid and seal it.
Hit the "Air Fry Button" and select 10 minutes of cooking time, then press "Start."
Once the Instant Pot Duo beeps, and remove its lid.
Flip the skewers and continue Air frying for 7 minutes.
Serve.
Nutrition:
Calories 241
Total Fat 14.2g
Saturated Fat 3.8g
Cholesterol 92mg
Sodium 695mg
Total Carbohydrate 8.5g
Dietary Fiber 1.6g
Total Sugars 3.9g
Protein 21.8g

Chicken Fritters

Preparation Time: 10 minutes
Cooking Time: 25 minutes
Serving: 4
Ingredients:
1 lb ground chicken
1 1/2 cups mozzarella cheese, shredded
1/2 cup shallots, chopped
2 cups broccoli, chopped
3/4 cup breadcrumbs
1 garlic clove, minced
1 egg, lightly beaten
Pepper
Salt
Directions:
Add all ingredients into the large bowl and mix until well combined.
Place the dehydrating tray in a multi-level air fryer basket and place basket in the instant pot.
Make small patties from meat mixture and place on dehydrating tray.
Seal pot with air fryer lid and select bake mode then set the temperature to 380 F and timer for 25 minutes. Turn patties halfway through.
Serve and enjoy.
Nutrition:
Calories 281
Fat 14.2 g
Carbohydrates 0.7 g
Sugar 0 g
Protein 33 g
Cholesterol 116 mg

Chicken Kabab

Preparation Time: 10 minutes
Cooking Time: 15 minutes
Serving: 4
Ingredients:
1 lb chicken thighs, skinless, boneless & cut into 1/2-inch cubes
1 cup bell pepper, cut into 2-inch cubes
1/2 cup onion, cut into 2-inch cubes
1 tbsp olive oil
For marinade:
1/2 tbsp dried fenugreek leaves
1 tsp coriander powder
1 tsp garam masala
1/2 tsp turmeric
2 tsp chili powder
1 tbsp fresh lime juice
1 tbsp ginger garlic paste
1/2 cup yogurt
1 tsp salt
Directions:
In a bowl, mix together all marinade ingredients. Add chicken mix well and marinate for 30 minutes.
Add bell pepper, onion, and oil into the chicken marinade and mix well.
Thread marinated chicken, onion, and peppers in the wooden skewers.

Spray instant pot air fryer basket with cooking spray and place skewers in the basket. Do not overcrowd.
Place basket in the instant pot.
Seal pot with air fryer lid and select air fry mode and set the temperature of 400 F and timer for 8 minutes.
Turn skewers to the other side and air fry for 7 minutes more.
Serve and enjoy.
Nutrition:
Calories 301
Fat 13 g
Carbohydrates 9.1 g
Sugar 4.6 g
Protein 35.8 g
Cholesterol 103 mg

Air Fryer Garlic Herb Turkey Breast

Preparation: 10 minutes
Cooking: 40 minutes
Servings: 6
Ingredients:
2 pounds turkey breast with skin.
4 tablespoons melted butter
3 garlic cloves, grated
1 teaspoon fresh rosemary, chopped
1 teaspoon thyme, finely chopped
1 teaspoon ground black pepper
½ teaspoon kosher salt
Vegetable cooking spray

Directions:
Clean, wash and pat dry the turkey breasts.
Rub salt and pepper on all sides of turkey breasts.
Combine rosemary, melted butter, thyme, and garlic in a medium bowl.
Brush the mix all over the turkey breast.
Spray some cooking oil in the air fryer basket.
Place the seasoned turkey in the air fryer basket and put it in the inner pot of the Instant Pot Air fryer.
Close the crisp lid and select the temperature to 375°F in AIR FRY mode.
Set the timer to 40 minutes and press START to begin the frying.
After 20 minutes of frying, open the crisp lid and flip the turkey breast spray some cooking oil.
Close the crisp lid to resume cooking.
Once the frying is over, allow it to settle down the heat before you want to slice and serve.
Nutrition: Calories: 406, Total fat: 26.5g, Saturated fat: 10g, Trans fat: 0.3g, Cholesterol: 143mg, Sodium: 1761mg, Total carbs: 1g, Dietary fiber: 0g, Sugars: 0g, Protein: 42g

Spicy Chicken Breast

Preparation time: 10 minutes
Cooking time: 35 minutes
Servings: 2
Ingredients:
2 chicken breasts, bone-in, and skin-on
1 tbsp ground fennel
1 tbsp chili powder

1 tbsp olive oil
1 tsp ground cumin
1 tsp garlic powder
1 tsp onion powder
1 tbsp paprika
1/2 tsp black pepper
1 tsp sea salt

Directions:

In a small bowl, mix together all dried spices.
Brush chicken with olive oil and rub with spice mixture.
Place chicken in the instant pot air fryer basket and place basket in the pot.
Seal the pot with air fryer lid and select air fry mode and cook at 375 f for 35 minutes.
Serve and enjoy.

Nutrition: Calories 108 Fat 8.9 g Carbohydrates 8.3 g Sugar 1.4 g Protein 2.3 g Cholesterol 1 mg

---

Zucchini Tomato Chicken

Preparation Time: 10 minutes
Cooking Time: 30 minutes
Serving: 4

Ingredients:

1 lb chicken tenders
1 tbsp olive oil
1 dill sprigs
1/2 zucchini, sliced
1/2 cup cherry tomatoes

For topping:
1/2 tbsp fresh lemon juice
1/2 tbsp fresh dill, chopped
1 tbsp feta cheese, crumbled
1/2 tbsp olive oil

Directions:

In a bowl, toss chicken with oil, dill, zucchini, and cherry tomatoes.
Line instant pot multi-level air fryer basket with aluminum foil.
Add chicken mixture into the air fryer basket and place basket into the instant pot.
Seal pot with air fryer lid and select bake mode then set the temperature to 380 F and timer for 30 minutes. Stir halfway through.
Mix together topping ingredients and sprinkle over chicken and vegetables.
Serve and enjoy.

Nutrition:
Calories 261
Fat 12.5 g
Carbohydrates 2 g
Sugar 1.2 g
Protein 33.7 g
Cholesterol 103 mg

Garlicky Chicken

Preparation Time: 10 minutes
Cooking Time: 30 minutes
Serving: 4

Ingredients:
1 lb chicken drumsticks
1 tbsp parsley, minced
1/2 fresh lemon juice
4 garlic cloves, minced
1 tbsp olive oil
Pepper
Salt
Directions:
Season chicken with pepper and salt.
Mix together parsley, lemon juice, garlic, and oil and rub over chicken.
Place the dehydrating tray in a multi-level air fryer basket and place basket in the instant pot.
Place chicken drumsticks on dehydrating tray.
Seal pot with air fryer lid and select bake mode then set the temperature to 380 F and timer for 30 minutes. Turn chicken halfway through.
Serve and enjoy.
Nutrition:
Calories 228
Fat 10.1 g
Carbohydrates 1.2 g
Sugar 0.2 g
Protein 31.5 g
Cholesterol 100 mg

Spicy Chicken Wings

Preparation time: 10 minutes
Cooking time: 20 minutes
Servings: 4
Ingredients:
2 lbs. frozen chicken wings
2 tbsp apple cider vinegar
2 tbsp butter, melted
1/2 cup hot pepper sauce
1/2 cup water
1/2 tsp paprika
1 oz ranch seasoning
Directions:
Add water, vinegar, butter, and hot pepper sauce into instant pot air fryer crisp.
Add chicken wings and stir well.
Seal the pot with pressure cooking lid and cook on high for 5 minutes.
Once done, release pressure using a quick release. Remove lid.
Sprinkle paprika and ranch seasoning over the chicken.
Seal the pot with air fryer lid and select air fry mode and cook at 375 f for 15 minutes.
Toss wings in sauce and serve.
Nutrition: Calories 521 Fat 38.2 g Carbohydrates 0.2 g Sugar 0.1 g Protein 36.6 g Cholesterol 167 mg

Cheesy Chicken Wings

Preparation time: 10 minutes
Cooking time: 18 minutes
Servings: 4

Ingredients:
2 lbs chicken wings
1/2 cup chicken stock
1 tsp season salt
For sauce:
1/2 cup parmesan cheese, grated
1 tbsp garlic, crushed
1 stick butter, melted
1/2 tsp black pepper
1/2 tsp dried parsley flakes
1 tsp garlic powder
Directions:
Season chicken wings with seasoned salt.
Add chicken wings to the inner pot of instant pot duo crisp along with the chicken stock.
Seal the pot with pressure cooking lid and cook on high for 8 minutes.
Meanwhile, mix together butter, pepper, parmesan cheese, parsley flakes, garlic powder, and garlic. Set aside.
Once chicken wings done then release pressures using a quick release. Remove lid.
Remove chicken wings from the pot and clean the pot.
Spray instant pot air fryer basket with cooking spray and place in the pot.
Toss chicken wings with melted butter and add into the air fryer basket.
Seal the pot with air fryer lid and select broil mode and cook for 10 minutes.
Serve and enjoy.
Nutrition: Calories 652 Fat 40.6 g Carbohydrates 1.6 g Sugar 0.3 g Protein 67.3 g Cholesterol 265 mg

Chicken Vegetable Fajitas

Preparation Time: 10 minutes
Cooking Time: 20 minutes
Serving: 4
Ingredients:
8 oz chicken thighs, boneless, skinless, and cut into strips
1 tbsp olive oil
1 jalapeno pepper, sliced
1/2 cup onion, sliced
1 1/2 cups bell peppers, sliced
1 tbsp taco seasoning
Directions:
Add chicken and remaining ingredients into the mixing bowl and toss well.
Spray instant pot multi-level air fryer basket with cooking spray.
Add chicken vegetable mixture into the air fryer basket and place basket into the instant pot.
Seal pot with air fryer lid and select bake mode then set the temperature to 380 F and timer for 20 minutes. Mix halfway through.
Serve and enjoy.
Nutrition:
Calories 281
Fat 14.2 g
Carbohydrates 0.7 g
Sugar 0 g
Protein 33 g
Cholesterol 116 mg

Fennel Chicken

Preparation Time: 10 minutes
Cooking Time: 15 minutes
Serving: 4
Ingredients:
1 lb chicken thighs, boneless and cut into three pieces
1 tsp cayenne
1 tsp turmeric
1 tsp garam masala
1 tsp ground fennel seeds
1 tsp paprika
2 tsp garlic, minced
2 tsp ginger, minced
1 tbsp olive oil
1 onion, sliced
Pepper
Salt
Directions:
Add chicken and remaining ingredients into the mixing bowl and toss well and place it in the refrigerator overnight.
Spray instant pot multi-level air fryer basket with cooking spray.
Add marinated chicken mixture into the air fryer basket and place basket into the instant pot.
Seal pot with air fryer lid and select air fry mode then set the temperature to 360 F and timer for 15 minutes. Mix halfway through.
Serve and enjoy.
Nutrition:
Calories 281
Fat 14.2 g
Carbohydrates 0.7 g
Sugar 0 g
Protein 33 g
Cholesterol 116 mg

Chicken Mac and Cheese

Preparation time:10 minutes
Cooking Time: 9 minutes
Serving: 6
Ingredients:
2 1/2 cup macaroni
2 cup chicken stock
1 cup cooked chicken, shredded
1 1/4 cup heavy cream
8 tablespoon butter
2 2/3 cups cheddar cheese, shredded
1/3 cup parmesan cheese, shredded
1 bag Ritz crackers
1/4 teaspoon garlic powder
Salt and pepper to taste
Directions:
Add chicken stock, heavy cream, chicken, 4 tablespoon butter, and macaroni to the Instant Pot Duo.
Put on the pressure-cooking lid and seal it.
Hit the "Pressure Button" and select 4 minutes of cooking time, then press "Start."

Crush the crackers and mix them well with 4 tablespoons melted butter.
Once the Instant Pot Duo beeps, do a quick release and remove its lid.
Put on the Air Fryer lid and seal it.
Hit the "Air Fryer Button" and select 5 minutes of cooking time, then press "Start."
Once the Instant Pot Duo beeps, remove its lid.
Serve.
Nutrition:
Calories 611
Total Fat 43.6g
Saturated Fat 26.8g
Cholesterol 147mg
Sodium 739mg
Total Carbohydrate 29.5g
Dietary Fiber 1.2g
Total Sugars 1.7g
Protein 25.4g

Broccoli Chicken Casserole

Preparation time:10 minutes
Cooking Time: 22 minutes
Serving: 6
Ingredients:
1 1/2 lbs. chicken, cubed
2 teaspoon chopped garlic
2 tablespoon butter
1 1/2 cups chicken broth
1 1/2 cups long-grain rice
1 (10.75 oz) can cream of chicken soup
2 cups broccoli florets
1 cup crushed Ritz cracker
2 tablespoon melted butter
2 cups shredded cheddar cheese
Directions:
Add 1 cup water to the Instant Pot Dup and place a basket in it.
Place the broccoli in the basket evenly.
Put on the pressure-cooking lid and seal it.
Hit the "Pressure Button" and select 1 minute of cooking time, then press "Start."
Once the Instant Pot Duo beeps, do a quick release and remove its lid.
Remove the broccoli and empty the Instant Pot Duo.
Hit the sauté button then add 2 tablespoon butter.
Toss in chicken and stir cook for 5 minutes, then add garlic and sauté for 30 seconds.
Stir in rice, chicken broth, and cream of chicken soup.
Put on the pressure-cooking lid and seal it.
Hit the "Pressure Button" and select 12 minutes of cooking time, then press "Start."
Once the Instant Pot Duo beeps, do a quick release and remove its lid.
Add cheese and broccoli, then mix well gently.
Toss the cracker with 2 tablespoon butter in a bowl and spread over the chicken in the Pot.
Put on the Air Fryer lid and seal it.
Hit the "Air Fryer Button" and select 4 minutes of cooking time, then press "Start."
Once the Instant Pot Duo beeps, remove its lid.
Serve.
Nutrition:
Calories 609

Total Fat 24.4g
Saturated Fat 12.6g
Cholesterol 142mg
Sodium 924mg
Total Carbohydrate 45.5g
Dietary Fiber 1.4g
Total Sugars 1.6g
Protein 49.2g

Chapter 6: Soups and stews

No Bean Beef Chili

Preparation Time: 10 minutes
Cooking Time: 45 minutes
Serving: 10
Ingredients:
2 1/2 ground beef
1 cup beef broth
4 oz can green chilies, diced
6 oz can tomato paste
14 oz can tomato, diced
14 oz can fire-roasted tomatoes, diced
1 tsp cumin
2 tbsp chili powder
1 1/2 tbsp garlic, minced
1/2 cup onion, diced
2 tbsp olive oil
Pepper
Salt
Directions:
Add oil into the instant pot duo crisp and set pot on sauté mode.
Add onion and sauté for 3-5 minutes. Add garlic and sauté for a minute.
Add ground meat and cook until browned, about 6-10 minutes.
Add remaining ingredients and stir well.
Seal the pot with pressure cooking lid and cook on high pressure for 30 minutes.
Once done, allow to release pressure naturally. Remove lid.
Serve and enjoy.
Nutrition:
Calories 113
Fat 4.6 g
Carbohydrates 10 g
Sugar 4.8 g
Protein 8.6 g
Cholesterol 19 mg

Vegan Cauliflower Soup

Preparation Time: 10 minutes
Cooking Time: 6 minutes
Serving: 4
Ingredients:
5 cups cauliflower florets
1 tbsp fresh lemon juice
3 cups vegetable broth
1/2 tsp cinnamon
1/2 tsp turmeric

1/2 cup cashews
1 tbsp garlic, minced
1 onion, diced
1 tbsp olive oil
1 tsp salt
Directions:
Add oil into the instant pot duo crisp and set pot on sauté mode.
Add garlic and onion and sauté for 3 minutes.
Add broth, cinnamon, turmeric, cashews, cauliflower, and salt and stir well.
Seal the pot with pressure cooking lid and cook on high pressure for 3 minutes.
Once done, allow to release pressure naturally for 10 minutes then release remaining pressure using a quick release. Remove lid.
Add lemon juice and stir well.
Blend soup using immersion blender until smooth.
Serve and enjoy.
Nutrition:
Calories 205
Fat 12.7 g
Carbohydrates 16.7 g
Sugar 5.7 g
Protein 9.2 g
Cholesterol 0 mg

Flavors Squash Soup

Preparation Time: 10 minutes
Cooking Time: 8 minutes
Serving: 6
Ingredients:
6 cups butternut squash, peeled and cubed
1/4 cup heavy cream
1/8 tsp nutmeg
1/2 tsp cayenne pepper
2 tsp thyme
3 cups vegetable stock
1 onion, chopped
2 tbsp butter
Pepper
Salt
For Herb Garlic Croutons:
2 cups of bread cubes
1 tbsp olive oil
1/4 tsp dried thyme
1/4 tsp dried basil
1/4 tsp dried oregano
1 garlic clove, minced
Pepper
Salt
Directions:
Add butter into the instant pot and set the pot on sauté mode.
Add onion and sauté for 3 minutes.
Add squash, nutmeg, cayenne, thyme, stock, and salt. Stir well.
Seal pot with pressure cooking lid and cook on high for 5 minutes.
Once done, release pressure using quick release. Remove lid.

Stir in heavy cream. Puree the soup using a blender until smooth.
For Croutons:
In a bowl, toss bread cubes with remaining ingredients.
Spray instant pot multi-level air fryer basket with cooking spray.
Add bread cubes into the air fryer basket and place basket into the instant pot.
Seal pot with air fryer lid and select bake mode then set the temperature to 350 F and timer for 10 minutes. Stir halfway through.
Top soup with croutons and serve.
Nutrition:
Calories 126
Fat 6 g
Carbohydrates 19 g
Sugar 4.3 g
Protein 2 g
Cholesterol 17 mg

Garlic Carrot Soup

Preparation Time: 10 minutes
Cooking Time: 10 minutes
Serving: 6
Ingredients:
8 carrots, peel and cut into pieces
1/2 onion, chopped
1/4 tsp ginger
1 1/2 tsp curry powder
4 cups vegetable stock
1/2 fresh lemon juice
2 tbsp butter
2 garlic cloves
1 tsp salt
For Rosemary Croutons:
2 cups of bread cubes
1 tbsp olive oil
1/2 tsp dried rosemary
1/2 tsp garlic powder
Pepper
Salt
Directions:
Add butter into the instant pot and set the pot on sauté mode.
Add onion and garlic to the pot and sauté for 2 minutes.
Add 1 cup stock, curry powder, and carrots. Stir.
Seal pot with pressure cooking lid and cook on high for 8 minutes.
Once done, release pressure using quick release. Remove lid.
Add remaining stock and puree the soup using a blender until smooth.
Add lemon juice, ginger, and salt and stir well.
For Croutons:
In a bowl, toss bread cubes with remaining ingredients.
Spray instant pot multi-level air fryer basket with cooking spray.
Add bread cubes into the air fryer basket and place basket into the instant pot.
Seal pot with air fryer lid and select bake mode then set the temperature to 350 F and timer for 15-20 minutes. Stir halfway through.
Top soup with croutons and serve.
Nutrition:

Calories 79
Fat 4 g
Carbohydrates 10.2 g
Sugar 5 g
Protein 1.2 g
Cholesterol 10 mg

Thyme Carrot Cauliflower Soup

Preparation Time: 10 minutes
Cooking Time: 15 minutes
Serving: 4
Ingredients:
2 cups cauliflower florets
2 2/3 cups vegetable stock
1/8 tsp dried thyme
1 1/2 tbsp curry powder
1 carrot, diced
1 cup onion, diced
1 1/3 tbsp olive oil
1/8 tsp pepper
1/8 tsp salt
For Italian Seasoned Bread Croutons:
1 1/2 cups bread cubes
1 tsp Italian seasoning
1 tbsp olive oil
Salt
Directions:
Add oil into the instant pot and set the pot on saute mode.
Add carrots, cauliflower, and onion into the pot and sauté for 4-5 minutes.
Add spices and stock and stir well.
Seal pot with pressure cooking lid and cook on high for 10 minutes.
Once done, release pressure using quick release. Remove lid.
Stir in milk. Puree the soup using a blender until smooth.
For Croutons:
In a bowl, toss bread cubes, Italian seasoning, oil, and salt.
Spray instant pot multi-level air fryer basket with cooking spray.
Add bread cubes into the air fryer basket and place basket into the instant pot.
Seal pot with air fryer lid and select bake mode then set the temperature to 350 F and timer for 20 minutes. Stir halfway through.
Top soup with croutons and serve.
Nutrition:
Calories 82
Fat 5.2 g
Carbohydrates 8.9 g
Sugar 3.7 g
Protein 2 g
Cholesterol 0 mg

Summer Vegetable Soup

Preparation Time: 10 minutes
Cooking Time: 10 minutes
Serving: 6
Ingredients:
1 summer squash, sliced
1 onion, diced
1/4 cup basil, chopped
2 bell peppers, sliced
1/2 cup green beans, cut into pieces
8 cups vegetable broth
1 zucchini, sliced
2 tomatoes, sliced
1 eggplant, sliced
2 garlic cloves, smashed
3/4 cup corn
Pepper
Salt
For Garlic Buttery Croutons
2 cups of bread cubes
1/2 tsp garlic powder
1 tbsp olive oil
1 tbsp butter, melted
Directions:
Add all ingredients into the instant pot and stir well.
Seal pot with pressure cooking lid and cook on high for 10 minutes.
Once done, release pressure using quick release. Remove lid.
Puree the soup using a blender until smooth.
For Croutons:
In a bowl, toss bread cubes, garlic powder, butter, and oil.
Spray instant pot multi-level air fryer basket with cooking spray.
Add bread cubes into the air fryer basket and place basket into the instant pot.
Seal pot with air fryer lid and select bake mode then set the temperature to 350 F and timer for 15-20 minutes. Stir halfway through.
Top soup with croutons and serves.
Nutrition:
Calories 128
Fat 2.5 g
Carbohydrates 18.6 g
Sugar 9.2 g
Protein 9.7 g
Cholesterol 0 mg

Flavorful Fish Stew

Preparation Time: 10 minutes
Cooking Time: 30 minutes
Serving: 5
Ingredients:
1 1/2 lbs white fish, remove bones and cut into 1-inch pieces
1 tbsp fresh parsley, chopped
1 tbsp fresh lime juice
2 tbsp coconut oil

1/2 tsp cayenne pepper
1 tbsp paprika
1 tbsp ground cumin
6 oz can coconut milk
8 oz fish broth
14 oz can tomato, crushed
1 tbsp garlic, minced
1 red bell pepper, sliced
1 onion, diced
1/4 tsp pepper
1 tsp salt

Directions:
Add oil into the instant pot duo crisp and set pot on sauté mode.
Add garlic, bell pepper, and onion and sauté for 3-5 minutes.
Add tomatoes, broth, coconut milk, cumin, paprika, cayenne, pepper, and salt and stir well.
Seal the pot with pressure cooking lid and cook on high pressure for 10 minutes.
Once done, release pressure using a quick release. Remove lid.
Set pot on sauté mode and cook the stew for 10 minutes.
Add fish and stir until fish is cooked, about 5 minutes.
Turn off the instant pot. Add lime juice and stir well.
Garnish with parsley and serve.

Nutrition:
Calories 620
Fat 53.5 g
Carbohydrates 14.5 g
Sugar 7 g
Protein 24.1 g
Cholesterol 10 mg

Buffalo Chicken Soup

Preparation Time: 10 minutes
Cooking Time: 10 minutes
Serving: 6

Ingredients:
1 lb chicken, cooked and shredded
1/2 cup heavy cream
5 oz cream cheese, cubed
2 1/2 tbsp buffalo sauce
4 cups chicken broth
1 tbsp garlic, minced
1/2 cup celery, diced
1/2 onion, diced
1 tbsp olive oil
Pepper
Salt

Directions:
Add oil into the instant pot duo crisp and set pot on sauté mode.
Add celery and onion and sauté until onion is softened about 5 minutes.
Add garlic and sauté for a minute. Add shredded chicken, buffalo sauce, and broth and stir well.
Seal the pot with pressure cooking lid and cook on high pressure for 5 minutes.
Once done, allow to release pressure naturally for 5 minutes then release remaining pressure using a quick release. Remove lid.
Transfer 1 cup of soup and cream cheese into the blender and blend until smooth. Return blended soup to the pot.

Add heavy cream and stir well.
Serve and enjoy.
Nutrition:
Calories 289
Fat 17.5 g
Carbohydrates 3.9 g
Sugar 1 g
Protein 27.4 g
Cholesterol 98 mg

Creamy & Tasty Chicken Soup

Preparation Time: 10 minutes
Cooking Time: 25 minutes
Serving: 6
Ingredients:
1 lb chicken breast, skinless and boneless
1 cup cheddar cheese, shredded
1/2 cup cream cheese
1 cup heavy cream
1 1/2 cups chicken broth
1 tsp paprika
1 tsp chili powder
1 tsp dried oregano
1 tsp cumin powder
1 bell pepper, sliced
1 tbsp garlic, minced
1 onion, chopped
1 tbsp olive oil
1 small jar sun-dried tomatoes, drained
Pepper
Salt
Directions:
Add oil into the instant pot duo crisp and set pot on sauté mode.
Add garlic and onion and sauté for 3-5 minutes.
Add remaining ingredients except for cheddar cheese, cream cheese, and heavy cream and stir well.
Seal the pot with pressure cooking lid and cook on high pressure for 20 minutes.
Once done, release pressure using a quick release. Remove lid.
Remove chicken from pot and shred using a fork. Return shredded chicken to the pot.
Set pot on sauté mode. Add cheddar cheese, cream cheese, and heavy cream and stir until cheese is melted.
Season soup with pepper and salt.
Serve and enjoy.
Nutrition:
Calories 372
Fat 25.5 g
Carbohydrates 11 g
Sugar 5.6 g
Protein 25.8 g
Cholesterol 117 mg

Lamb Stew

Preparation time: 10 minutes
Cooking time: 30 minutes
Servings: 3
Ingredients:
1 lb. lamb loin, cut into pieces
2 cups chicken stock
1 chili pepper, chopped
1 cup cabbage, shredded
1 zucchini, sliced
1/2 tsp dried thyme
1 tsp oregano
½ tsp chili powder
3 tbsp olive oil
2 garlic cloves, crushed
1 tsp salt
Directions:
Add oil into the instant pot and set the pot on sauté mode.
Add garlic and meat and sauté for a minute.
Season with thyme, oregano, chili powder, and salt.
Stir everything well and cook for 5 minutes.
Add zucchini and cook for 3-4 minutes.
Add cabbage, chili pepper, and stock. Stir well.
Seal pot with lid and cook on manual high pressure for 12 minutes.
Once done then allow to release pressure naturally for 10 minutes then release using the quick-release method.
Open the lid.
Stir and serve.
Nutrition: Calories 455 Fat 29.4 g Carbohydrates 5.5 g Sugar 2.5 g Protein 42 g Cholesterol 132 mg

Creamy Cauliflower Soup

Preparation Time: 10 minutes
Cooking Time: 10 minutes
Serving: 6
Ingredients:
1 medium cauliflower head, cut into florets
2 tbsp green onion, chopped
1 1/2 cups cheddar cheese, shredded
1/2 cup sour cream
3 cups vegetable broth
1 tsp garlic, minced
1 celery stalk, chopped
1 onion, chopped
1 tbsp olive oil
6 bacon slices, cooked and chopped
Pepper
Salt
Directions:
Add oil into the instant pot and set the pot on sauté mode.
Add garlic, celery, onion, pepper, and salt and sauté for 3-5 minutes.
Add cauliflower and broth and stir well.
Seal the pot with pressure cooking lid and cook on high pressure for 5 minutes.
Once done, allow to release pressure naturally for 10 minutes then release remaining pressure using a quick release.
Remove lid.

Add 1 cup shredded cheese and sour cream and stir well.
Blend soup using immersion blender until smooth.
Top with bacon, green onion, and remaining cheese.
Serve and enjoy.
Nutrition:
Calories 330
Fat 24.5 g
Carbohydrates 9.1 g
Sugar 3.7 g
Protein 19.3 g
Cholesterol 59 mg

Chicken Broccoli Soup

Preparation Time: 10 minutes
Cooking Time: 10 minutes
Serving: 8
Ingredients:
6 cups broccoli florets
2 cups cooked chicken, chopped
1 cup cheddar cheese, shredded
1/2 cup coconut milk
4 cups chicken stock
1 tbsp garlic, minced
1/2 onion, chopped
2 tbsp coconut oil
1/2 tsp sea salt
Directions:
Add oil into the instant pot duo crisp and set pot on sauté mode.
Add onion, garlic, and cumin and sauté until onion is softened.
Add broccoli, stock, pepper, and salt and stir well.
Seal the pot with pressure cooking lid and cook on high pressure for 4 minutes.
Once done, release pressure using a quick release. Remove lid.
Blend soup using immersion blender until smooth.
Set pot on sauté mode. Add cheese and chicken and stir until cheese is melted.
Serve and enjoy.
Nutrition:
Calories 206
Fat 13.3 g
Carbohydrates 6.9 g
Sugar 2.4 g
Protein 16.4 g
Cholesterol 42 mg

Broccoli Asparagus Soup

Preparation Time: 10 minutes
Cooking Time: 8 minutes
Serving: 6
Ingredients:
15 asparagus spears, cut the ends and chopped

1 tsp dried mixed herbs
1/4 cup nutritional yeast
1/2 cup coconut milk
3 1/2 cups vegetable broth
2 cups cauliflower florets
2 cups broccoli florets
2 tsp garlic, chopped
1 cup onion, chopped
2 tbsp olive oil
Pepper
Salt
Directions:
Add oil into the instant pot duo crisp and set pot on sauté mode.
Add onion and garlic and sauté for 3-5 minutes.
Add broth and all vegetables and stir well.
Seal the pot with pressure cooking lid and cook on high pressure for 3 minutes.
Once done, allow to release pressure naturally. Remove lid.
Blend soup using blender until smooth.
Add coconut milk, nutritional yeast, herbs, pepper, and salt and stir well.
Serve warm and enjoy.
Nutrition:
Calories 172
Fat 10.8 g
Carbohydrates 13 g
Sugar 4.4 g
Protein 9.5 g
Cholesterol 0 mg

Easy Chicken Soup

Preparation Time: 10 minutes
Cooking Time: 40 minutes
Serving: 8
Ingredients:
1 1/2 lbs chicken breasts, boneless and cut into chunks
4 cups of water
4 cups chicken broth
2 tsp thyme
2 tsp basil
1 onion, chopped
1 tbsp garlic, minced
2 celery stalks, chopped
5 carrots, peeled and chopped
1/2 tsp pepper
2 tsp salt
Directions:
Add all ingredients into the inner pot of instant pot duo crisp. Stir well.
Seal the pot with pressure cooking lid and cook on high pressure for 40 minutes.
Once done, release pressure using a quick release. Remove lid.
Stir well and serve immediately.
Nutrition:
Calories 205
Fat 7 g
Carbohydrates 6.2 g

Sugar 2.9 g
Protein 27.6 g
Cholesterol 76 mg

Tasty Mexican Chicken Soup

Preparation Time: 10 minutes
Cooking Time: 15 minutes
Serving: 5
Ingredients:
1 lb chicken breast, skinless and boneless
1 cup cheddar cheese, shredded
1/2 cup cream cheese
1 cup half and half
1 1/2 cups chicken stock
1 tsp paprika
1 1/2 tsp chili powder
1 tsp dried oregano
1 1/2 tsp cumin powder
1 bell pepper, chopped
1 tbsp garlic, minced
1 onion, chopped
2 tsp olive oil
14 oz can fire-roasted tomatoes
Salt
Directions:
Add oil into the instant pot duo crisp and set pot on sauté mode.
Add onion and garlic and sauté until onion is softened.
Add paprika, oregano, chilli powder, and cumin powder and sauté for 1 minute.
Add stock, roasted tomatoes, and salt and stir well. Add chicken breast.
Seal the pot with pressure cooking lid and cook on high pressure for 8 minutes.
Once done, allow to release pressure naturally for 10 minutes then release remaining pressure using a quick release. Remove lid.
Remove chicken from pot and shred using a fork.
Return shredded chicken to the pot along with bell pepper, half and half, cheddar cheese, and cream cheese and stir until cheese is melted.
Serve and enjoy.
Nutrition:
Calories 403
Fat 25.9 g
Carbohydrates 12.6 g
Sugar 4.7 g
Protein 29.8 g
Cholesterol 125 mg

Curried Chicken Soup

Preparation Time: 10 minutes
Cooking Time: 10 minutes
Serving: 6
Ingredients:

2 lbs chicken breast, boneless and cut into 1-inch cubes
1/4 cup fresh cilantro, chopped
1 cup of coconut milk
2 1/2 cups spinach, chopped
1 cup can tomato, diced
4 cups chicken broth
2 tbsp curry powder
1 tbsp ginger, minced
1 tbsp garlic, minced
1 cup onion, chopped
2 tbsp butter
Pepper
Salt
Directions:
Add butter into the instant pot duo crisp and set pot on sauté mode.
Add onion and sauté for 2 minutes.
Add ginger and garlic and sauté for 30 seconds.
Add remaining ingredients except for spinach, coconut milk, and cilantro and stir well.
Seal the pot with pressure cooking lid and cook on high pressure for 5 minutes.
Once done, allow to release pressure naturally for 10 minutes then release remaining pressure using a quick release. Remove lid.
Set pot on sauté mode. Add coconut milk and spinach and stir until spinach is wilted.
Turn off the instant pot.
Garnish with cilantro and serve.
Nutrition:
Calories 355
Fat 18.5 g
Carbohydrates 9.4 g
Sugar 4.1 g
Protein 37.6 g
Cholesterol 107 mg

Lemon Asparagus Soup

Preparation Time: 10 minutes
Cooking Time: 7 minutes
Serving: 4
Ingredients:
12 oz asparagus, trimmed and chopped
1 tsp nutritional yeast
2 tsp fresh lemon juice
1/4 tsp lemon zest
1/4 tsp dried mint
2 1/2 cups vegetable stock
1 tsp garlic, chopped
1 small onion, chopped
1 tsp olive oil
Pepper
Salt
Directions:
Add oil into the instant pot duo crisp and set pot on sauté mode.
Add garlic and onion and sauté for 2-3 minutes.
Add asparagus, lemon zest, mint, pepper, and salt and sauté for minute.
Add stock and stir well.

Seal the pot with pressure cooking lid and cook on high pressure for 3 minutes.
Once done, release pressure using a quick release. Remove lid.
Blend soup using blender until smooth. Add nutritional yeast and lemon juice and stir well.
Serve and enjoy.
Nutrition:
Calories 41
Fat 1.9 g
Carbohydrates 6.2 g
Sugar 2.9 g
Protein 2.5 g
Cholesterol 0 mg

Creamy Sweet Potato Soup

Preparation Time: 10 minutes
Cooking Time: 15 minutes
Serving: 6
Ingredients:
2 lbs sweet potatoes, peeled and diced
2 cups of water
4 cups vegetable broth
1/2 onion, chopped
1 tbsp olive oil
1/2 tsp cinnamon
1 tsp paprika
3 garlic cloves, minced
Pepper
Salt
For Croissant Croutons:
1 croissant, cut into 1/2-inch cubes
2 tbsp parmesan cheese, grated
1/2 tsp dried oregano
1 tbsp olive oil
Pepper
Salt
Directions:
Add oil into the instant pot and set the pot on saute mode.
Add onion and sweet potato and saute for 5 minutes.
Add remaining ingredients and stir well.
Seal pot with pressure cooking lid and cook on high for 10 minutes.
Once done, release pressure using quick release. Remove lid.
Puree the soup using a blender until smooth.
For Croutons:
In a bowl, toss croissant cubes with remaining ingredients.
Spray instant pot multi-level air fryer basket with cooking spray.
Add croissant cubes into the air fryer basket and place basket into the instant pot.
Seal pot with air fryer lid and select bake mode then set the temperature to 350 F and timer for 10 minutes. Stir halfway through.
Top soup with croutons and serve.
Nutrition:
Calories 231
Fat 3.6 g
Carbohydrates 44.5 g

Sugar 1.7 g
Protein 5.8 g

Spinach Soup

Preparation Time: 10 minutes
Cooking Time: 10 minutes
Serving: 2
Ingredients:
3 cups spinach, chopped
3 cups vegetable broth
1 cup cauliflower, chopped
1 tsp garlic powder
2 tbsp olive oil
1/4 cup coconut cream
1/2 tsp pepper
1/4 tsp sea salt
For Hot Dog Bun Croutons:
2 hot dog buns, cut into cubes
2 tbsp olive oil
1/4 tsp black pepper
1/2 tsp dried parsley
1/2 tsp garlic powder
Salt
Directions:
Add olive oil into the instant pot and set the pot on sauté mode.
Add cauliflower, broth, spinach, garlic powder, pepper, and salt and stir well.
Seal pot with pressure cooking lid and cook on high for 10 minutes.
Once done, release pressure using quick release. Remove lid.
Puree the soup using a blender until smooth.
Stir in coconut cream.
For Croutons:
In a bowl, toss bun cubes with remaining ingredients.
Spray instant pot multi-level air fryer basket with cooking spray.
Add bread cubes into the air fryer basket and place basket into the instant pot.
Seal pot with air fryer lid and select bake mode then set the temperature to 375 F and timer for 15 minutes. Stir halfway through.
Top soup with croutons and serve.
Nutrition:
Calories 275
Fat 23.5 g
Carbohydrates 8.7 g
Sugar 3.8 g
Protein 10.5 g
Cholesterol 0 mg

Creamy Corn Soup

Preparation Time: 10 minutes
Cooking Time: 10 minutes
Serving: 4
Ingredients:

2 1/2 cups corn kernels
2 tsp olive oil
1/2 tbsp soy sauce
3/4 cup cabbage, minced
2 garlic cloves, minced
1 carrot, minced
5 cups vegetable broth
1 tsp ground cumin
1 1/2 tsp ginger, grated
Pepper
Salt
For Pumpernickel Croutons:
2 cups pumpernickel bread cubes
2 tbsp butter, melted
1/4 tsp garlic powder
1/4 tsp salt
Directions:
Add all ingredients into the instant pot and stir well.
Seal pot with pressure cooking lid and cook on high for 10 minutes.
Once done, release pressure using quick release. Remove lid.
Remove 3 cups of soup from the pot and Puree the soup using a blender until smooth.
Return blended soup into the pot and stir well. Season with pepper and salt.
For Croutons:
In a bowl, toss pumpernickel bread cubes with remaining ingredients.
Spray instant pot multi-level air fryer basket with cooking spray.
Add pumpernickel bread cubes into the air fryer basket and place basket into the instant pot.
Seal pot with air fryer lid and select bake mode then set the temperature to 375 F and timer for 10 minutes. Stir halfway through.
Top soup with croutons and serve.
Nutrition:
Calories 168
Fat 5.4 g
Carbohydrates 22.9 g
Sugar 5.3 g
Protein 9.9 g
Cholesterol 0 mg

Flavorful Mushroom Soup

Preparation Time: 10 minutes
Cooking Time: 11 minutes
Serving: 2
Ingredients:
1 cup mushrooms, chopped
1 onion, chopped
1 1/2 tsp garam masala
2 tbsp olive oil
1 tsp fresh lemon juice
1/4 tsp chili powder
5 cups chicken stock
2 fresh celery stalks, chopped
2 garlic cloves, crushed
For Croissant Croutons:
1 croissant, cut into 1/2-inch cubes

2 tbsp parmesan cheese, grated
1/2 tsp dried oregano
1 tbsp olive oil
Pepper
Salt

Directions:
Add oil into the instant pot and set the pot on sauté mode.
Add garlic and onion and sauté for 5 minutes.
Add chili powder and garam masala and cook for a minute.
Add remaining ingredients and stir well.
Seal the pot with pressure cooking lid and cook on high pressure for 5 minutes.
Once done, release pressure using quick release. Remove lid.
Puree the soup using a blender until smooth.

For Croutons:
In a bowl, toss croissant cubes with remaining ingredients.
Spray instant pot multi-level air fryer basket with cooking spray.
Add croissant cubes into the air fryer basket and place basket into the instant pot.
Seal pot with air fryer lid and select bake mode then set the temperature to 350 F and timer for 10 minutes. Stir halfway through.
Top soup with croutons and serve.

Nutrition:
Calories 183
Fat 15.7 g
Carbohydrates 9.8 g
Sugar 5 g
Protein 3.8 g
Cholesterol 0 mg

Curried Squash Soup

Preparation Time: 10 minutes
Cooking Time: 40 minutes
Serving: 4

Ingredients:
3 lbs butternut squash, peeled and cubed
3 cups of water
2 garlic cloves, minced
1 onion, minced
1 tsp olive oil
1 tbsp curry powder
1/2 cup coconut milk

For Caesar Croutons:
2 cup bread cubes
1/8 tsp dried thyme
1/4 tsp dried oregano
1/4 tsp garlic powder
1/2 tsp dried parsley
1 tbsp parmesan cheese, grated
1 tbsp olive oil
Pepper
Salt

Directions:
Add olive oil into the instant pot and set the pot on sauté mode.
Add onion to the pot and sauté for 8 minutes.

Add curry powder and garlic and sauté for a minute.
Add squash, water, and salt and stir well.
Seal pot with pressure cooking lid and cook on high for 30 minutes.
Once done, release pressure using quick release. Remove lid.
Puree the soup using a blender until smooth.
Stir in coconut milk.
For Croutons:
In a bowl, toss bread cubes with remaining ingredients.
Spray instant pot multi-level air fryer basket with cooking spray.
Add bread cubes into the air fryer basket and place basket into the instant pot.
Seal pot with air fryer lid and select bake mode then set the temperature to 375 F and timer for 10 minutes. Stir halfway through.
Top soup with croutons and serve.
Nutrition:
Calories 250
Fat 8.9 g
Carbohydrates 45.4 g
Sugar 9.7 g
Protein 4.7 g

Creamy Peanut Butter Carrot Soup

Preparation Time: 10 minutes
Cooking Time: 15 minutes
Serving: 4
Ingredients:
8 carrots, peeled and chopped
1 1/2 cup chicken stock
1/4 cup peanut butter
1 tbsp curry paste
1 onion, chopped
3 garlic cloves, peeled
14 oz coconut milk
Pepper
Salt
For Parmesan Croutons:
2 cups of bread cubes
2 tbsp parmesan cheese, grated
2 tbs butter, melted
1 garlic clove, minced
1 tbsp olive oil
Pepper
Salt
Directions:
Add all ingredients into the instant pot and stir well.
Seal pot with pressure cooking lid and cook on high for 15 minutes.
Once done, release pressure using quick release. Remove lid.
Puree the soup using a blender until smooth.
Season soup with pepper and salt.
For Croutons:
In a bowl, toss bread cubes with butter, garlic, oil, pepper, and salt.
Spray instant pot multi-level air fryer basket with cooking spray.
Add bread cubes into the air fryer basket and place basket into the instant pot.

Seal pot with air fryer lid and select bake mode then set the temperature to 375 F and timer for 15 minutes. Stir halfway through.
Toss bread cubes with parmesan cheese until well coated.
Top soup with croutons and serve.
Nutrition:
Calories 416
Fat 34.2 g
Carbohydrates 25.3 g
Sugar 12.3 g
Protein 8.2 g
Cholesterol 0 mg

Tasty Tomato Soup

Preparation Time: 10 minutes
Cooking Time: 5 minutes
Serving: 4
Ingredients:
6 tomatoes, chopped
14 oz coconut milk
1 tsp turmeric
1/2 tsp cayenne pepper
1 tsp garlic, minced
1/4 cup fresh parsley, chopped
1 onion, diced
1 tsp ginger, minced
1 tsp salt
For Cornbread Croutons:
1 1/4 cups cornbread cubes
2 tbsp olive oil
Pepper
Salt
Directions:
Add all ingredients to the instant pot and stir well.
Seal the pot with pressure cooking lid and cook high for 5 minutes.
Once done, release pressure using quick release. Remove lid.
Puree the soup using a blender until smooth.
For Croutons:
In a bowl, toss cornbread cubes with remaining ingredients.
Spray instant pot multi-level air fryer basket with cooking spray.
Add cornbread cubes into the air fryer basket and place basket into the instant pot.
Seal pot with air fryer lid and select bake mode then set the temperature to 350 F and timer for 15 minutes. Stir halfway through.
Top soup with croutons and serve.
Nutrition:
Calories 279
Fat 24.2 g
Carbohydrates 16.5 g
Sugar 9.4 g
Protein 4.5 g
Cholesterol 0 mg

Lentil Carrot Soup

Preparation Time: 10 minutes
Cooking Time: 16 minutes
Serving: 4
Ingredients:
3/4 cup red lentils, rinsed
1/2 onion, diced
1/4 tsp black pepper
4 cups vegetable stock
4 carrots, peeled and chopped
1 1/2 tbsp curry powder
1 tbsp ginger, grated
2 tsp vegetable oil
1 tsp kosher salt
For Garlic Buttery Croutons
2 cups of bread cubes
1/2 tsp garlic powder
1 tbsp olive oil
1 tbsp butter, melted
Directions:
Add oil into the instant pot and set the pot on sauté mode.
Add onion to the pot and sauté for 5 minutes.
Add curry powder and ginger and sauté for 30 seconds.
Add lentils, stock, carrots, pepper, and salt and stir well to combine.
Seal pot with pressure cooking lid and cook on high for 10 minutes.
Once done, release pressure using quick release. Remove lid.
Puree the soup using a blender until smooth.
For Croutons:
In a bowl, toss bread cubes, garlic powder, butter, and oil.
Spray instant pot multi-level air fryer basket with cooking spray.
Add bread cubes into the air fryer basket and place basket into the instant pot.
Seal pot with air fryer lid and select bake mode then set the temperature to 350 F and timer for 15-20 minutes. Stir halfway through.
Top soup with croutons and serve.
Nutrition:
Calories 196
Fat 3.2 g
Carbohydrates 32.2 g
Sugar 5.1 g
Protein 10.8 g
Cholesterol 0 mg

Chapter 7: Meat Recipes

Roast Beef

Preparation time: 10 minutes
Cooking Time: 15 minutes
Serving: 4
Ingredients:
2 lb. beef roast top
oil for spraying
Rub
1 tbsp kosher salt
1 teaspoon black pepper
2 teaspoon garlic powder
1 teaspoon summer savory
Directions:
Whisk all the rub Ingredients: in a small bowl.
Liberally rub this mixture over the roast.
Place an Air Fryer Basket in the Instant Pot Duo and layer it with cooking oil.
Set the seasoned roast in the Air Fryer Basket.
Put on the Air Fryer lid and seal it.
Hit the "Air fry Button" and select 20 minutes of cooking time, then press "Start."
Once the Instant Pot Duo beeps, remove its lid.
Turn the roast and continue Air fryer for another 15 minutes.
Serve warm.
Nutrition:
Calories 427
Total Fat 14.2g
Saturated Fat 5.3g
Cholesterol 203mg
Sodium 1894mg
Total Carbohydrate 1.4g
Dietary Fiber 0.3g
Total Sugars 0.3g
Protein 69.1g

Steak Tips with Potatoes

Preparation Time: 10 minutes
Cooking Time: 20 minutes
Serving: 2
Ingredients:
1/2 lb steak, cut into 1/2-inch cubes
1/4 lb potatoes, cut into 1/2-inch cubes
1/4 tsp garlic powder
1/2 tsp Worcestershire sauce
1 tbsp butter, melted
Pepper

Salt

Directions:

Cook potatoes into the boiling water for 5 minutes. Drain well and set aside.

In a mixing bowl, toss together steak cubes, potatoes, garlic powder, Worcestershire sauce, butter, pepper, and salt.

Spray instant pot multi-level air fryer basket with cooking spray.

Add steak potato mixture into the air fryer basket and place basket into the instant pot.

Seal pot with air fryer lid and select air fry mode then set the temperature to 400 F and timer for 20 minutes. mix halfway through.

Serve and enjoy.

Nutrition:

Calories 318
Fat 11.5 g
Carbohydrates 9.4 g
Sugar 1 g
Protein 42 g
Cholesterol 117 mg

Asian Beef Broccoli

Preparation Time: 10 minutes
Cooking Time: 15 minutes
Serving: 3

Ingredients:

1/2 lb steak, cut into strips
1 tsp garlic, minced
1 tsp ginger, minced
2 tbsp sesame oil
2 tbsp soy sauce
1/3 cup oyster sauce
1 lb broccoli florets

Directions:

Add steak into the mixing bowl. Add remaining ingredients and mix well and set aside for 1 hour.

Spray instant pot multi-level air fryer basket with cooking spray.

Add marinated steak pieces and broccoli into the air fryer basket and place basket into the instant pot.

Seal pot with air fryer lid and select air fry mode then set the temperature to 350 F and timer for 15 minutes. mix halfway through.

Serve and enjoy.

Nutrition:

Calories 295
Fat 13.4 g
Carbohydrates 12.4 g
Sugar 2.8 g
Protein 32.4 g
Cholesterol 68 mg

Simple Steak

Preparation time: 6minutes
Cooking time: 14 minutes
Servings: 2
Ingredients:

½ pound quality cuts steak
Salt and freshly ground black pepper, to taste
Directions:
Preparing the ingredients. Preheat the instant crisp air fryer to 390 degrees f.
Rub the steak with salt and pepper evenly.
Air frying. Place the steak in the instant crisp air fryer basket, close air fryer lid and cook for about 14 minutes crispy.

Garlic-Cumin and Orange Juice Marinated Steak

Preparation time: 6 minutes
Cooking time: 60 minutes
Servings: 4
Ingredients:
¼ cup orange juice
1 teaspoon ground cumin
2 pounds skirt steak, trimmed from excess fat
2 tablespoons lime juice
2 tablespoons olive oil
4 cloves of garlic, minced
Salt and pepper to taste
Directions:
Preparing the ingredients. Place all ingredients in a mixing bowl and allow to marinate in the fridge for at least 2 hours
Preheat the instant crisp air fryer to 390°f.
Place the grill pan accessory in the instant crisp air fryer.
Air frying. Close air fryer lid. Grill for 15 minutes per batch and flip the beef every 8 minutes for even grilling. Meanwhile, pour the marinade on a saucepan and allow to simmer for 10 minutes or until the sauce thickens. Slice the beef and pour over the sauce.
Nutrition: Calories: 568; Fat: 34.7g; Protein:59.1g; Sugar:1g

Bacon Wrapped Hot Dog.

Preparation time: 15 minutes
Cooking time: 10 minutes
Servings: 4
Ingredients:
4 slices sugar-free bacon.
4 beef hot dogs
Directions:
Wrap each hot dog with slice of bacon and secure with toothpick. Place into the air fryer basket.
Adjust the temperature to 370 degrees f and set the timer for 10 minutes. Flip each hot dog halfway through the cooking time.
When fully cooked, bacon will be crispy.
Serve warm.
Nutrition: Calories: 197; Protein: 9.2g; Fiber: 0.0g; Fat: 15.0g; Carbs: 1.3g

Beef and Broccoli Stir-Fry

Preparation time: 1 hour 20 minutes
Cooking time: 10 minutes
Servings: 2

Ingredients:
- ½ lb. Sirloin steak, thinly sliced
- 2 tbsp. Soy sauce (or liquid aminos
- ¼ tsp. Grated ginger
- ¼ tsp. Finely minced garlic
- 1 tbsp. Coconut oil
- 2 cups broccoli florets
- ¼ tsp. Crushed red pepper
- ⅛ tsp. Xanthan gum
- ½ tsp. Sesame seeds

Directions:

To marinate beef, place it into a large bowl or storage bag and add soy sauce, ginger, garlic and coconut oil. Allow to marinate for 1 hour in refrigerator.

Remove beef from marinade, reserving marinade and place beef into the air fryer basket. Adjust the temperature to 320 degrees f and set the timer for 20 minutes

After 10 minutes, add broccoli and sprinkle red pepper into the fryer basket and shake.

Pour the marinade into a skillet over medium heat and bring to a boil, then reduce to simmer.

Stir in xanthan gum and allow to thicken

When air fryer timer beeps, quickly empty fryer basket into skillet and toss.

Sprinkle with sesame seeds. Serve immediately.

Nutrition: Calories: 342; Protein: 27.0g; Fiber: 2.7g; Fat: 18.9g; Carbs: 9.6g

---

Lamb Loin and Tomato Vinaigrette

Preparation time: 40 minutes
Cooking time: 10 minutes
Servings: 4
Ingredients:
- 4 lamb loin slices
- 3 garlic cloves; minced
- 1/3 cup parsley; chopped
- 1/3 cup sun-dried tomatoes; chopped
- 2 tbsp. Balsamic vinegar
- 2 tbsp. Water
- 2 tbsp. Olive oil
- 2 tsp. Thyme; chopped
- A pinch of salt and black pepper

Directions:

In a blender, combine all the ingredients except the lamb slices and pulse well.

Take a bowl and mix the lamb with the tomato vinaigrette and toss well

Put the lamb in your air fryer's basket and cook at 380°f for 15 minutes on each side

Divide everything between plates and serve.

Nutrition: Calories: 273; Fat: 13g; Fiber: 4g; Carbs: 6g; Protein: 17g

---

Beef Taco Fried Egg Rolls

Preparation time: 10 minutes
Cooking time: 12 minutes
Servings: 8
Ingredients
- 1 tsp. Cilantro
- 2 chopped garlic cloves

1 tbsp. Olive oil
1 c. Shredded Mexican cheese
½ packet taco seasoning
½ can cilantro lime rotel
½ chopped onion
16 egg roll wrappers
1-pound lean ground beef

Directions:

Preparing the ingredients. Ensure that your instant crisp air fryer is preheated to 400 degrees.

Add onions and garlic to a skillet, cooking till fragrant. Then add taco seasoning, pepper, salt, and beef, cooking till beef is broke up into tiny pieces and cooked thoroughly.

Add rotel and stir well.

Lay out egg wrappers and brush with water to soften a bit.

Load wrappers with beef filling and add cheese to each.

Fold diagonally to close and use water to secure edges.

Brush filled egg wrappers with olive oil and add to the instant crisp air fryer.

Air frying. Close air fryer lid. Set temperature to 400°f, and set time to 8 minutes. Cook 8 minutes, flip, and cook another 4 minutes.

Served sprinkled with cilantro.

Nutrition: Calories: 348; Fat: 11g; Protein:24g; Sugar:1g

Air Fryer Meatloaf

Preparation: 10 minutes
Cooking time: 25 minutes
Servings: 4

Ingredients:

1-pound lean beef
1 egg, medium, lightly beaten
3 tablespoons breadcrumbs
1 onion, small, finely chopped
1 tablespoon fresh thyme, chopped
1 teaspoon kosher salt
½ teaspoon ground black pepper
2 mushrooms, medium, sliced
1 tablespoon olive oil

Directions:

Wash beef and pat dry.

In a medium-large bowl, combine beef, egg, breadcrumbs, salt, thyme, onion, and pepper. Knead and mix the ingredients well.

Transfer this mix into a baking pan and place the mushroom on top of the mix.

Coat this mix with olive oil and place the pan in the air fryer basket.

Now put the air fryer basket in the inner pot of instant pot air fryer.

Close the crisp cover.

Under the roast mode, set the timer for 25 minutes and let the meatloaf roast. The smart roast option will automatically select the temperature to 380°f.

Press the start button to resume the cooking.

After cooking, allow the meatloaf to settle down the heat before you can slice and serve it.

Slice it into small portions and serve.

Nutrition: Calories 297, carbohydrates: 5.9g, fat 18.8g, protein: 24.8g, cholesterol 126mg, sodium:706mg, sugars: 1g. Saturate fat: 6g, potassium: 361mg, calcium: 33mg

Baked Carrot Beef

Preparation time: 5-10 Minutes
Cooking Time: 60 Minutes
Serving: 5-6
Ingredients: 2 carrots, chopped
2 sticks celery, chopped
3 pounds beef
Olive oil to taste
2 medium onions, sliced
Garlic cloves from 1 bunch
1 bunch mixed fresh herbs (thyme, rosemary, bay, sage etc.) **Directions**:
Grease a baking pan with some cooking spray. Add the vegetables, beef roast, olive oil, and herbs; combine well.
Place Instant Pot Air Fryer Crisp over kitchen platform. Press Air Fry, set the temperature to 400°F and set the timer to 5 minutes to preheat. Press "Start" and allow it to preheat for 5 minutes.
In the inner pot, place the Air Fryer basket. In the basket, add the pan.
Close the Crisp Lid and press the "Bake" setting. Set temperature to 380°F and set the timer to 60 minutes. Press "Start."
Open the Crisp Lid after cooking time is over. Serve warm.
Nutrition: **Calories: 306**
Fat: 21g
Saturated Fat: 7g
Trans Fat: 0g
Carbohydrates: 10g
Fiber: 3g
Sodium: 324mg
Protein: 32g

Smoky Steak

Preparation Time: 10 minutes
Cooking Time: 5 minutes
Serving: 2
Ingredients:
12 oz steaks
1 tsp liquid smoke
1 tbsp soy sauce
1/2 tbsp cocoa powder
1 tbsp Montreal steak seasoning
Pepper
Salt
Directions:
Add steak, liquid smoke, and soy sauce in a zip-lock bag and shake well.
Season steak with seasonings and place in the refrigerator overnight.
Place the dehydrating tray in a multi-level air fryer basket and place basket in the instant pot.
Place marinated steak on dehydrating tray.
Seal pot with air fryer lid and select air fry mode then set the temperature to 375 F and timer for 5 minutes.
Serve and enjoy.
Nutrition:
Calories 356
Fat 8.7 g
Carbohydrates 1.4 g
Sugar 0.2 g
Protein 62.2 g

Cholesterol 153 mg

Herb Garlic Lamb Chops

Preparation Time: 10 minutes
Cooking Time: 6 minutes
Serving: 3
Ingredients:
3 lamb loin chops
1 tbsp lemon juice
1 tbsp lemon zest, grated
2 tsp dried rosemary
1 tsp dried thyme
1 tbsp olive oil
2 tsp garlic, minced
Directions:
Mix together lemon juice, lemon zest, rosemary, thyme, oil, and garlic and rub over lamb chops.
Place the dehydrating tray in a multi-level air fryer basket and place basket in the instant pot.
Place lamb chops on dehydrating tray.
Seal pot with air fryer lid and select air fry mode then set the temperature to 400 F and timer for 6 minutes. Turn lamb chops halfway through.
Serve and enjoy.
Nutrition:
Calories 300
Fat 14.8 g
Carbohydrates 1.9 g
Sugar 0.3 g
Protein 38.2 g
Cholesterol 122 mg

Delicious Lamb Chops

Preparation Time: 10 minutes
Cooking Time: 8 minutes
Serving: 4
Ingredients:
1 lb lamb chops
2 tbsp lemon juice
2 tbsp olive oil
1 tsp ground coriander
1 tsp oregano
1 tsp thyme
1 tsp rosemary
1 tsp salt
Directions:
Add lamb chops and remaining ingredients into the zip-lock bag. Shake well and place it in the refrigerator for 1 hour.
Place the dehydrating tray in a multi-level air fryer basket and place basket in the instant pot.
Place lamb chops on dehydrating tray.
Seal pot with air fryer lid and select air fry mode then set the temperature to 400 F and timer for 8 minutes. Turn lamb chops halfway through.

Serve and enjoy.
Nutrition:
Calories 276
Fat 15.5 g
Carbohydrates 0.8 g
Sugar 0.2 g
Protein 32 g

Garlic Roasted Pork Tenderloin

Preparation time: 5-10 Minutes
Cooking Time: 18 Minutes
Serving: 5-6
Ingredients:
¼ teaspoon ground black pepper
¼ teaspoon garlic powder
¼ teaspoon salt
1 ½ pound pork tenderloin
1 tablespoon olive oil
Directions:
In a mixing bowl, add the olive oil, black pepper, salt, and garlic powder. Combine the ingredients to mix well with each other. Rub the mixture evenly over the pork tenderloin.
Place Instant Pot Air Fryer Crisp over kitchen platform. Press Air Fry, set the temperature to 400°F and set the timer to 5 minutes to preheat. Press "Start" and allow it to preheat for 5 minutes.
In the inner pot, place the Air Fryer basket. In the basket, add the tenderloins.
Close the Crisp Lid and press the "Roast" setting. Set temperature to 400°F and set the timer to 25 minutes. Press "Start."
Halfway down, open the Crisp Lid, flip the tenderloin and close the lid to continue cooking for the remaining time.
Open the Crisp Lid after cooking time is over. Slice and serve warm.
Nutrition: **Calories: 203**
Fat: 6g
Saturated Fat: 1.5g
Trans Fat: 0g
Carbohydrates: 2g
Fiber: 0g
Sodium: 173mg

Crispy Breaded Pork Chops in the Air Fryer

Preparation: 10 minutes
Cooking: 12 minutes
Servings: 6
Ingredients:
6 pork chops, center cut, boneless
1 egg, large, beaten
½ cup panko breadcrumbs
⅓ cup corn flakes crumbs, crushed
2 tablespoons parmesan cheese, grated
1¼ teaspoon sweet paprika
1½ teaspoon garlic powder
¼ teaspoon chili powder
½ teaspoon onion powder
½ teaspoon ground black pepper

1 teaspoon kosher salt
Olive oil cooking spray
Directions:
Cut and remove excess fat of the pork.
Wash and pat dry.
Spray the air fryer basket with cooking oil and place it in the inner pot of the Instant Pot Air Fryer.
Close the crisp cover.
Set the air fryer temperature to 400°F and preheat for 5 minutes in the AIR FRY mode.
Press START to begin the preheating.
In the meantime, season the pork chops by rubbing half teaspoon salt on both sides and keep aside.
In a large shallow bowl, combine panko breadcrumbs, cornflakes, cheese, salt, garlic powder, paprika, chili powder, onion powder, and pepper.
In a medium shallow bowl, beat the egg.
Now batch by batch, do the breading and seasoning.
First, dip the pork chops in the beaten egg and then dredge in the breadcrumbs mix and press it gently so that it will have good breadcrumb coating on all sides.
Once the preheat timer goes off, put the pork chops in the air fryer basket in batches and spritz some more cooking oil.
Close the crisp cover.
In the AIR FRY mode, at 400°F, select the timer for 40 minutes.
Press START to begin the cooking.
Halfway through the cooking, open the air fryer, and flip the pork chop.
To complete the remaining portion of the cooking, close the crisp cover. The Instant Pot will automatically resume cooking, from the point you have interrupted.
Once done, keep it aside and repeat the process with the rest of the batch.
Nutrition: Calories 376, Total fat: 18.8g, Saturated fat: 6.1g, Trans fat: 0.2g, Cholesterol: 164mg, Sodium: 555mg, Total carbs: 7g, Dietary fiber: 1g, Sugars: 1g, Protein: 42g

Easy Air Fryer Pork Chops

Preparation: 10 minutes
Cooking: 20 minutes
Servings: 4
Ingredients:
5 ounces (4 pieces) pork chops, center-cut
½ cup parmesan cheese, grated
1 teaspoon parsley, dried
1 teaspoon ground paprika
½ teaspoon ground black pepper
1 teaspoon garlic powder
1 teaspoon salt
2 tablespoon olive oil, extra-virgin
Olive cooking oil spray
Directions:
Wash pork chops and pat dry.
In a large bowl, combine the parmesan cheese, pepper, parsley, salt, garlic powder, and paprika.
Coat the pork chops with the olive oil and then dredge them in the parmesan mixture one by one and place it on a plate.
Spritz cooking oil in the air fryer basket and place in the inner pot of the Instant Pot Air Fryer.
Place these chops in the air fryer basket in batches.
Close the crisp lid.
Under the ROAST mode, select the timer for 25 minutes. The temperature by default will remain at 400°F.
Press START to begin the cooking.
Flip it halfway through for even cooking.

Once the cooking over, transfer the pork chop on a cutting board and let it rest for about 5 minutes before you slice and serve.
Nutrition: Calories 305, Carbohydrates: 1.5g, fat 16.6g, Protein: 35.3g, Cholesterol 90mg, Sodium: 685mg, Potassium: 457mg, Sugars: 0g, Saturated fat: 5g, Calcium: 121mg

---

Rogan Josh

Preparation time: 10 minutes
Cooking time: 35 minutes
Servings: 4
Ingredients:
1 lb leg of lamb, cut into cubes
2 garlic cloves, minced
1/4 tsp ground cinnamon
1 small onion, diced
1 tbsp tomato paste
1/2 cup yogurt
1/4 cup water
1/2 tsp turmeric
1 tsp paprika
2 tsp garam masala
1/4 cup cilantro, chopped
1/2 tsp cayenne pepper
2 tsp ginger, minced
1 tsp salt
Directions:
Add all ingredients into the bowl and stir well.
Place bowl in the refrigerator for 2 hours.
Add marinated meat with marinade into the instant pot.
Seal pot with lid and cook on manual high pressure for 20 minutes.
Once done then allow to release pressure naturally for 10 minutes then release using the quick-release method.
Open the lid.
Serve and enjoy.
Nutrition: Calories 620 Fat 42.9 g Carbohydrates 10.5 g Sugar 2.7 g Protein 44.8 g Cholesterol 161 mg

---

Cheesy Lamb Chops

Preparation time: 10 minutes
Cooking time: 18 minutes
Servings: 3
Ingredients:
3 lamb chops
1/2 tsp garlic powder
1 tbsp olive oil
3/4 cup parmesan cheese
1/4 tsp dried basil, crushed
1 cup of water
1/4 tsp dried oregano, crushed
Pepper
Salt
Directions:
Season lamb chops with pepper, garlic powder, and salt.
Place lamb chops into the instant pot and cook for 4 minutes on each side.

Remove lamb chops from pot and place on a plate.
Pour water to the pot then place a trivet in the pot.
Place lamb chops on the trivet.
Seal pot with lid and cook on manual high pressure for 10 minutes.
Once done then release pressure using the quick-release method than open the lid.
Serve and enjoy.
Nutrition: Calories 530 Fat 19.3 g Carbohydrates 10.5 g Sugar 2.7 g Protein 44.8 g Cholesterol 161 mg

---

Garlicky Lamb

Preparation time: 10 minutes
Cooking time: 17 minutes
Servings: 6
Ingredients:
2 lbs. lamb steak, cut into strips
1 tbsp olive oil
2 1/2 scallions, chopped
3 tbsp water
2 tbsp arrowroot
1/2 cup soy sauce, low-sodium
1/2 cup water
4 garlic cloves, minced
Directions:
Add oil into the instant pot and set the pot on sauté mode.
Add meat to the pot and cook for 5 minutes.
Add the ginger and garlic and cook for 1-2 minutes.
Add remaining ingredients and stir well.
Seal pot with lid and cook on manual high for 12 minutes.
Once done then release pressure using the quick-release method than open the lid.
Serve and enjoy.
Nutrition: Calories 319 Fat 13.5 g Carbohydrates 3.1 g Sugar 0.5 g Protein 44.1 g Cholesterol 136 mg

---

Pork Tenderloin in the Air Fryer

Preparation: 20 minutes
Cooking: 18 minutes
Servings: 6
Ingredients:
1½ pound pork tenderloin
1 tablespoon olive oil
¼ teaspoon ground black pepper
¼ teaspoon garlic powder
¼ teaspoon salt
Directions:
Wash and pat dry the pork tenderloin.
In a small bowl, mix the olive oil, black pepper, and garlic powder well and add salt as needed.
Rub the seasoning mixture over the tenderloin.
Transfer the meat in the air fryer basket.
Place the air fryer basket in the inner pot of the Instant Pot Air Fryer.
Close the crisp cover.
In the ROAST mode, set the timer to 25 minutes. The default heat will show 400°F, which you cannot change in the smart cooking option.
Press START to begin the cooking.

Flip the tenderloin midway for even cooking.
After cooking, allow the meat to cool down before you can slice and serve.
Nutrition: Calories: 183, Total fat: 6.2g, Saturated fat: 1.7g, Trans fat: 0g, Cholesterol: 83mg, Sodium: 162mg, Total carbs: 0g, Dietary fiber: 0g, Sugars: 0g, Protein: 30g

---

Air-fried Garlic-rosemary Lamb Chops

Preparation Time: 3 minutes
Cooking Time: 12 minutes
Servings: 2
Ingredients
2 lamb chops
1 clove of garlic
2 tsps. olive oil
2 tsps. garlic puree
A sprig of fresh rosemary
Salt and pepper to taste
Directions
Place lamb chops in a bowl and season with salt and pepper and brush or spray with olive oil.
Top each lamb chop with garlic puree.
Between each chops place fresh rosemary and unpeeled garlic.
Leave the bowl with the lamb chops in the refrigerator for about an hour to marinate.
Transfer the marinated lamb chops to the instant pot duo crisp air fryer basket and air-fry at 360 degrees F for 6 minutes.
Flip lamb chops for even cooking and cook for another 6 minutes without changing the cooking temperature.
Leave to rest for a minute or 2.
Discard the fresh garlic and rosemary and serve.
Nutrition: Calories – 426; Carbohydrates – 1g; Fat – 10g; Protein – 83g; Sodium – 200mg;

Rosemary Lamb Chops

Preparation Time: 10 minutes
Cooking Time: 12 minutes
Serving: 4
Ingredients:
4 lamb chops
2 tsp garlic paste
1 tbsp rosemary, chopped
1 tbsp olive oil
Pepper
Salt
Directions:
Coat lamb chops with olive oil and rubs with garlic paste, rosemary, pepper, and salt.
Place the dehydrating tray in a multi-level air fryer basket and place basket in the instant pot.
Place lamb chops on dehydrating tray.
Seal pot with air fryer lid and select air fry mode then set the temperature to 360 F and timer for 12 minutes. Turn lamb chops halfway through.
Serve and enjoy.
Nutrition:
Calories 286
Fat 13.5 g
Carbohydrates 1 g
Sugar 0 g

Protein 38 g
Cholesterol 122 mg

Greek Lamb Chops

Preparation Time: 10 minutes
Cooking Time: 10 minutes
Serving: 4
Ingredients:
1 lb lamb chops
1 tsp garlic, minced
1 tsp dried oregano
2 tbsp lemon juice
2 tbsp olive oil
Pepper
Salt
Directions:
Add lamb chops into the mixing bowl. Add remaining ingredients and coat well.
Place the dehydrating tray in a multi-level air fryer basket and place basket in the instant pot.
Place lamb chops on dehydrating tray.
Seal pot with air fryer lid and select air fry mode then set the temperature to 400 F and timer for 10 minutes. Turn lamb chops halfway through.
Serve and enjoy.
Nutrition:
Calories 275
Fat 15.4 g
Carbohydrates 0.7 g
Sugar 0.2 g
Protein 32 g
Cholesterol 102 mg

Herb Butter Lamb Chops

Preparation Time: 10 minutes
Cooking Time: 5 minutes
Serving: 4
Ingredients:
4 lamb chops
1 tsp rosemary, diced
1 tbsp butter
Pepper
Salt
Directions:
Season lamb chops with pepper and salt.
Place the dehydrating tray in a multi-level air fryer basket and place basket in the instant pot.
Place lamb chops on dehydrating tray.
Seal pot with air fryer lid and select air fry mode then set the temperature to 400 F and timer for 5 minutes.
Mix together butter and rosemary and spread overcooked lamb chops.
Serve and enjoy.
Nutrition:
Calories 278

Fat 12.8 g
Carbohydrates 0.2 g
Sugar 0 g
Protein 38 g
Cholesterol 129 mg

Asian Lamb Curry

Preparation time: 10 minutes
Cooking time: 30 minutes
Servings: 4
Ingredients:
1 1/2 lbs lamb chunks
2 tsp ginger garlic paste
1 1/2 cups can tomato, chopped
1/2 tsp fennel powder
1/2 tsp coriander powder
1/2 tsp garam masala
1 tsp chili powder
2 bay leaves
2 onion, chopped
1 tbsp oil
3/4 tsp cumin powder
Salt
Directions:
Add oil into the instant pot and set the pot on sauté mode.
Add bay leaves and onion to the pot and cook for 5 minutes.
Add ginger-garlic paste, meat, and all spices and stir well.
Add remaining ingredients and stir well to combine.
Seal pot with lid and cook on manual high pressure for 5 minutes.
Once done then allow to release pressure naturally for 10 minutes then release using the quick-release method.
Open the lid.
Stir and serve.
Nutrition: Calories 433 Fat 20.8 g Carbohydrates 12.3 g Sugar 5.4 g Protein 47.4 g Cholesterol 148 mg

---

Indian Lamb Curry

Preparation time: 10 minutes
Cooking time: 20 minutes
Servings: 6
Ingredients:
2 lbs lamb meat, bone-in
2 1/2 tbsp green curry paste
1/2 cup coconut cream
1/4 cup cilantro, chopped
1/2 tbsp lime juice
6 oz green beans, chopped
1/2 tbsp soy sauce
1/2 tbsp fish sauce
2 garlic cloves, crushed
1/2 cup chicken broth
4.5 oz coconut milk

1 small onion, minced
1 tbsp olive oil
Pepper
Salt
Directions:
Season meat with pepper and salt.
Add oil into the instant pot and set the pot on sauté mode.
Add garlic and onion to the pot and sauté for 3-4 minutes.
Add curry paste and coconut cream and cook for 4-5 minutes.
Add meat, fish sauce, soy sauce, broth, and coconut milk. Stir well.
Seal pot with lid and cook on manual high pressure for 8 minutes.
Once done then release pressure using the quick-release method than open the lid.
Add lime juice and green beans and cook on sauté mode for 4 minutes.
Garnish with cilantro and serve.
Nutrition: Calories 413 Fat 28.6 g Carbohydrates 7 g Sugar 1.8 g Protein 29.9 g Cholesterol 107 mg

Pulled Pork

Preparation Time: 10 minutes
Cooking Time: 8 hours
Serving: 12
Ingredients:
4 lbs pork shoulder
1 tsp garlic powder
1 tsp cayenne pepper
1 tsp pepper
2 tbsp paprika
3/4 cup water
1/4 cup apple cider vinegar
1 tsp onion powder
1 tsp kosher salt
Directions:
Add water and vinegar into the inner pot of instant pot duo crisp. Place pork into the pot.
Add remaining ingredients into the pot.
Seal the pot with pressure cooking lid and select slow cook mode and cook on low for 8 hours.
Remove meat from pot and shred using a fork.
Serve and enjoy.
Nutrition:
Calories 448
Fat 32.5 g
Carbohydrates 1.2 g
Sugar 0.3 g
Protein 35.5 g
Cholesterol 136 mg

Swedish Meatballs

Preparation time: 10 minutes
cooking time: 14 minutes
Servings: 4
Ingredients:
For the meatballs:

1 pound 93% lean ground beef
1 (1-ounce packet lipton onion recipe soup & dip mix
⅓ cup breadcrumbs
1 egg, beaten
Salt
Pepper
For the gravy:
1 cup beef broth
⅓ cup heavy cream
Tablespoons all-purpose flour
Directions:
Preparing the ingredients. In a large bowl, combine the ground beef, onion soup mix, breadcrumbs, egg, and salt and pepper to taste. Mix thoroughly.
Using 2 tablespoons of the meat mixture, create each meatball by rolling the beef mixture around in your hands. This should yield about 10 meatballs.
Air frying. Place the meatballs in the instant crisp air fryer. It is okay to stack them. Close air fryer lid and cook for 14 minutes.
While the meatballs cook, prepare the gravy. Heat a saucepan over medium-high heat.
Add the beef broth and heavy cream. Stir for 1 to 2 minutes.
Add the flour and stir. Cover and allow the sauce to simmer for 3 to 4 minutes, or until thick.
Drizzle the gravy over the meatballs and serve.
Nutrition: Calories: 178; Fat: 14g; Protein:9g; Fiber:0g

Air Fryer Pork Chops

Preparation: 5 minutes
Cooking time: 20 minutes
Servings: 4
Ingredients:
4 pork chops, boneless
7 tablespoons shredded parmesan cheese
1 teaspoon kosher salt
1 teaspoon paprika
1 teaspoon garlic powder
1 teaspoon onion powder
½ teaspoon ground black pepper
2 tablespoons extra-virgin olive oil
Directions:
Remove excess fat if anything on the pork chop, wash, and dry with paper towels.
Coat both sides of the meat with olive oil.
Take a medium bowl and combine the parmesan with all the spices thoroughly.
Marinate this mixture evenly on both sides of the meat.
Place the air fryer basket in the inner pot of the instant pot air fryer.
Put the marinated pork chops in the air fryer basket.
Close the crisp cover.
Under air fryer, select the smart option roast and set the timer to 20 minutes. The default temperature with smart option roast is 380°f.
Press start to begin the cooking.
After 10 minutes of cooking, open the crisp lid and flip the chop for even cooking.
Close the crisp cover to resume for the remaining period.
Once the cooking over, you can serve the pork chops hot.
Nutrition: Calories: 400, total fat: 22.9g, saturated fat: 7.3g, trans fat: 0.2g, cholesterol: 142mg, sodium: 887mg, total carbs: 3g, dietary fiber: 0g, sugars: 0g, protein: 43g

Rice and Meatball Stuffed Bell Peppers

Preparation time: 13 minutes
Cooking time: 15 minutes
Servings: 4
Ingredients
4 bell peppers
1 tablespoon olive oil
1 small onion, chopped
2 cloves garlic, minced
1 cup frozen cooked rice, thawed
16 to 20 small frozen precooked meatballs, thawed
½ cup tomato sauce
Tablespoons dijon mustard
Directions:
Preparing the ingredients. To prepare the peppers, cut off about ½ inch of the tops. Carefully remove the membranes and seeds from inside the peppers. Set aside.
In a 6-by-6-by-2-inch pan, combine the olive oil, onion, and garlic.
Air frying. Close air fryer lid. Bake in the instant crisp air fryer for 2 to 4 minutes or until crisp and tender. Remove the vegetable mixture from the pan and set aside in a medium bowl.
Add the rice, meatballs, tomato sauce, and mustard to the vegetable mixture and stir to combine. Stuff the peppers with the meat-vegetable mixture.
Place the peppers in the instant crisp air fryer basket and bake for 9 to 13 minutes or until the filling is hot and the peppers are tender.
Nutrition: Calories: 487; Fat: 21g; Protein:26g; Fiber:6g

Pub Style Corned Beef Egg Rolls

Preparation time: 15 minutes
Cooking time: 10 minutes
Servings: 10
Ingredients
Olive oil
½ c. Orange marmalade
5 slices of swiss cheese
4 c. Corned beef and cabbage
1 egg
10 egg roll wrappers
Brandy mustard sauce:
1/16th tsp. Pepper
2 tbsp. Whole grain mustard
1 tsp. Dry mustard powder
1 c. Heavy cream
½ c. Chicken stock
¼ c. Brandy
¾ c. Dry white wine
¼ tsp. Curry powder
½ tbsp. Cilantro
1 minced shallot
2 tbsp. Ghee
Directions:
Preparing the ingredients. To make mustard sauce, add shallots and ghee to skillet, cooking until softened. Then add brandy and wine, heating to a low boil. Cook 5 minutes for liquids to reduce. Add stock and seasonings. Simmer 5 minutes.
Turn down heat and add heavy cream. Cook on low till sauce reduces and it covers the back of a spoon.

Place sauce in the fridge to chill.
Crack the egg in a bowl and set to the side.
Lay out an egg wrapper with the corner towards you. Brush the edges with egg wash.
Place 1/3 cup of corned beef mixture into the center along with 2 tablespoons of marmalade and ½ a slice of swiss cheese.
Fold the bottom corner over filling. As you are folding the sides, make sure they are stick well to the first flap you made.
Place filled rolls into prepared instant crisp air fryer basket. Spritz rolls with olive oil.
Air frying. Close air fryer lid set temperature to 390°f, and set time to 10 minutes. Cook 10 minutes at 390 degrees, shaking halfway through cooking.
Serve rolls with brandy mustard sauce.
Nutrition: Calories: 415; Fat: 13g; Protein:38g; Sugar:4g

Lamb and Pine Nuts Meatballs

Preparation time: 35 minutes
Cooking time: 10 minutes
Servings: 4
Ingredients:
1 ½ lb. Lamb, ground
2 garlic cloves; minced
1 egg, whisked
1 scallion; chopped
½ cup pine nuts, toasted and chopped.
1 tbsp. Olive oil
1 tbsp. Thyme; chopped
A pinch of salt and black pepper
Directions:
Take a bowl and mix the lamb with the rest of the ingredients except the oil, stir well and shape medium meatballs out of this mix
Grease the meatballs with the oil, put them in your air fryer's basket and cook at 380°f for 15 minutes on each side.
Divide between plates and serve with a side salad
Nutrition: Calories: 287; Fat: 12g; Fiber: 3g; Carbs: 6g; Protein: 17g

Air Fryer Roast Beef

Preparation: 5 minutes
Cooking time: 15 minutes
Servings: 6
Ingredients:
2½ pound beef
1 tablespoon Montreal steak seasoning
1 tablespoon olive oil
Directions:
Tie up the beef to make it compact enough to cook.
Rub some olive oil all over the beef roast
Sprinkle the seasoning over the meat.
Put the air fryer basket in the inner pot of the instant pot air fryer.
Place the separator in the air fryer basket and keep the beef on the separator.
Close the crisp cover.
Select the smart option roast under air fryer and set the timer to 15 minutes.
Press the start button and let the meat cook well.
Open the crisp cover and flip it halfway through for even cooking.

After flipping close the crisp cover again to resume cooking for the remaining period.
Once done, allow it to rest for 5 minutes before you serve.
Nutrition: Calories 276, total fat: 13g, saturated fat: 3.4g, trans fat: 0.6g, cholesterol: 140mg, sodium: 266mg, total carbs: 1g, dietary fiber: 0g, sugars: 0g, protein: 39g.

Smoked Lamb Chops

Preparation time: 25 minutes
Cooking time: 10 minutes
Servings: 4
Ingredients:
4 lamb chops
4 garlic cloves; minced
2 tbsp. Olive oil
¼ tsp. Smoked paprika
½ tsp. Chili powder
A pinch of salt and black pepper
Directions:
Take a bowl and mix the lamb with the rest of the ingredients and toss well
Transfer the chops to your air fryer's basket and cook at 390°f for 10 minutes on each side. Serve with a side salad
Nutrition: Calories: 274; Fat: 12g; Fiber: 4g; Carbs: 6g; Protein: 17g

---

Spicy Beef

Preparation time: 25 minutes
Cooking time: 10 minutes
Servings: 4
Ingredients:
4 beef steaks
1 tbsp. Hot paprika
1 tbsp. Butter; melted
Salt and black pepper to taste.
Directions:
Take a bowl and mix the beef with the rest of the ingredients, rub well, transfer the steaks to your air fryer's basket and cook at 390°f for 10 minutes on each side
Divide the steaks between plates and serve with a side salad.
Nutrition: Calories: 280; Fat: 12g; Fiber: 4g; Carbs: 6g; Protein: 17g

---

Adobo Beef

Preparation time: 35 minutes
Cooking time: 10 minutes
Servings: 4
Ingredients:
1 lb. Beef roast, trimmed
1 tbsp. Olive oil
¼ tsp. Garlic powder
½ tsp. Turmeric powder
½ tsp. Oregano; dried
A pinch of salt and black pepper
Directions:
Take a bowl and mix the roast with the rest of the ingredients and rub well.

Put the roast in the air fryer's basket and cook at 390°f for 30 minutes.
Slice the roast, divide it between plates and serve with a side salad.
Nutrition: Calories: 294; Fat: 12g; Fiber: 3g; Carbs: 6g; Protein: 19g

Pork Chop Salad

Preparation time: 23 minutes
Cooking time: 10 minutes
Servings: 2
Ingredients:
2 (4-oz. pork chops; chopped into 1-inch cubes
½ cup shredded monterey jack cheese
1 medium avocado; peeled, pitted and diced
¼ cup full-fat ranch dressing
4 cups chopped romaine
1 medium roma tomato; diced
1 tbsp. Chopped cilantro
1 tbsp. Coconut oil
½ tsp. Garlic powder.
¼ tsp. Onion powder.
2 tsp. Chili powder
1 tsp. Paprika
Directions:
Take a large bowl, drizzle coconut oil over pork.
Sprinkle with chili powder, paprika, garlic powder and onion powder.
Place pork into the air fryer basket.
Adjust the temperature to 400 degrees f and set the timer for 8 minutes.
Pork will be golden and crispy when fully cooked
Take a large bowl, place romaine, tomato and crispy pork.
Top with shredded cheese and avocado.
Pour ranch dressing around bowl and toss the salad to evenly coat.
Top with cilantro.
Serve immediately.
Nutrition: Calories: 526; Protein: 34.4g; Fiber: 8.6g; Fat: 37.0g; Carbs: 13.8g

Fajita Flank Steak Rolls

Preparation time: 35 minutes
Cooking time: 10 minutes
Servings: 6
Ingredients:
2 lb. Flank steak
4 (1-oz. slices pepper jack cheese
1 medium red bell pepper; seeded and sliced into strips
¼ cup diced yellow onion
1 medium green bell pepper; seeded and sliced into strips
2 tbsp. Unsalted butter.
1 tsp. Cumin
½ tsp. Garlic powder.
2 tsp. Chili powder
Directions:
In a medium skillet over medium heat, melt butter and begin sautéing onion, red bell pepper and green bell pepper. Sprinkle with chili powder, cumin and garlic powder. Sauté until peppers are tender, about 5–7 minutes.

Lay flank steak flat on a work surface. Spread onion and pepper mixture over entire steak rectangle. Lay slices of cheese on top of onions and peppers, barely overlapping

With the shortest end toward you, begin rolling the steak, tucking the cheese down into the roll as necessary. Secure the roll with twelve toothpicks, six on each side of the steak roll. Place steak roll into the air fryer basket

Adjust the temperature to 400 degrees f and set the timer for 15 minutes. Rotate the roll halfway through the cooking time. Add an additional 1–4 minutes depending on your preferred internal temperature (135 degrees f for medium

When timer beeps, allow roll to rest 15 minutes, then slice into six even pieces.
Serve warm.
Nutrition: Calories: 439; Protein: 38.0g; Fiber: 1.2g; Fat: 26.6g; Carbs: 3.7g

Moroccan Lamb

Preparation time: 35 minutes
Cooking time: 10 minutes
Servings: 4
Ingredients:
8 lamb cutlets
½ cup mint leaves
6 garlic cloves
3 tbsp. Lemon juice
1 tbsp. Coriander seeds
4 tbsp. Olive oil
1 tbsp. Cumin, ground
Zest of 2 lemons, grated
A pinch of salt and black pepper
Directions:
In a blender, combine all the ingredients except the lamb and pulse well.
Rub the lamb cutlets with this mix, place them in your air fryer's basket and cook at 380°f for 15 minutes on each side.
Serve with a side salad
Nutrition: Calories: 284; Fat: 13g; Fiber: 3g; Carbs: 5g; Protein: 15g

Cuban Pork

Preparation Time: 10 minutes
Cooking Time: 8 hours 10 minutes
Serving: 6
Ingredients:
3 lbs pork shoulder roast
1 tsp oregano, dried
1 tsp cumin
1/2 cup fresh lime juice
1/2 cup orange juice
1 bay leaf
1 onion, sliced
1 1/2 garlic cloves, crushed
1/4 tsp red chili flakes
2 tbsp olive oil
1/8 tsp pepper
1 1/2 tsp salt
Directions:
In a bowl, mix together garlic, pepper, chili flakes, lime juice, orange juice, oil, oregano, cumin, and salt,

Place pork into the inner pot of instant pot duo crisp. Pour bowl mixture over pork.
Add bay leaf. Seal the pot with pressure cooking lid and select slow cook mode and cook on low for 8 hours.
Remove meat from pot and shred using a fork.
Clean the pot. Add shredded meat into the air fryer basket and place basket into the pot.
Seal the pot with air fryer lid and select broil mode and cook for 10 minutes.
Serve and enjoy.
Nutrition:
Calories 644
Fat 51 g
Carbohydrates 5 g
Sugar 2.6 g
Protein 38.7 g
Cholesterol 161 mg

Pork Tenderloin

Preparation Time: 10 minutes
Cooking Time: 6 hours
Serving: 8
Ingredients:
2 lbs pork tenderloin
1/2 cup balsamic vinegar
1 tbsp garlic cloves, minced
1/2 tsp red chili flakes
2 tbsp coconut amino
1 tbsp Worcestershire sauce
1 tbsp olive oil
1/2 tsp sea salt
Directions:
Add olive oil, garlic, and pork tenderloin into the inner pot of instant pot duo crisp and set pot on sauté mode.
In a bowl, mix together remaining ingredients and pour over pork.
Seal the pot with pressure cooking lid and select slow cook mode and cook on low for 6 hours.
Serve and enjoy.
Nutrition:
Calories 188
Fat 5.7 g
Carbohydrates 1.6 g
Sugar 0.5 g
Protein 29.8 g
Cholesterol 83 mg

Beef with Beans

Preparation time: 10 minutes
Cooking time: 13 minutes
Servings: 8
Ingredients:
12 ozs lean steak
1 onion, sliced
1 can chopped tomatoes
3/4 cup beef stock

4 tsp fresh thyme, chopped
1 can red kidney beans
Salt and pepper to taste
Oven safe bowl
Directions:
Preparing the ingredients. Preheat the instant crisp air fryer to 390 degrees.
Trim the fat from the meat and cut into thin 1cm strips
Add onion slices to the oven safe bowl and place in the instant crisp air fryer.
Air frying. Close air fryer lid. Cook for 3 minutes. Add the meat and continue cooking for 5 minutes. Add the tomatoes and their juice, beef stock, thyme and the beans and cook for an additional 5 minutes
Season with black pepper to taste.
Nutrition:
Calories 98
Fat 7 g
Carbohydrates 6 g
Sugar 0.4 g
Protein 11.8 g
Cholesterol 33 mg

Easy Pork Roast

Preparation Time: 10 minutes
Cooking Time: 8 hours
Serving: 6
Ingredients:
3 lbs pork shoulder roast, boneless and cut into 4 pieces
1/2 tbsp cumin
1 tbsp fresh oregano
1 cup of grapefruit juice
Pepper
Salt
Directions:
Season meat with pepper and salt and place into the inner pot of instant pot duo crisp.
Add oregano, cumin, and grapefruit juice into the blender and blend until smooth.
Pour blended mixture over meat.
Seal the pot with pressure cooking lid and select slow cook mode and cook on low for 8 hours.
Remove meat from pot and shred using a fork.
Return shredded meat into the pot and stir well.
Serve and enjoy.
Nutrition:
Calories 599
Fat 46.4 g
Carbohydrates 3.8 g
Sugar 2.7 g
Protein 38.5 g
Cholesterol 161 mg

Ranch Pork Chops

Preparation Time: 10 minutes
Cooking Time: 30 minutes
Serving: 6
Ingredients:
6 pork chops, boneless
1/4 cup olive oil
1 tsp dried parsley
2 tbsp ranch seasoning
Pepper
Salt
Directions:
Line instant pot air fryer basket with parchment paper.
Season pork chops with pepper and salt and place on parchment paper into the air fryer basket.
Mix together olive oil, parsley, and ranch seasoning.
Spoon oil mixture over pork chops.
Place air fryer basket in the pot.
Seal the pot with air fryer basket and select bake mode and cook at 400 F for 30 minutes.
Serve and enjoy.
Nutrition:
Calories 338
Fat 28.3 g
Carbohydrates 0 g
Sugar 0 g
Protein 18 g
Cholesterol 69 mg

Pork Carnitas

Preparation Time: 10 minutes
Cooking Time: 9 hours
Serving: 6
Ingredients:
3 lbs pork shoulder
3 tsp cumin
2 orange juice
1/2 cup water
2 tsp olive oil
2 tsp ground coriander
2 tsp salt
Directions:
Place the pork shoulder into the inner pot of instant pot duo crisp.
Pour remaining ingredients over the pork shoulder.
Seal the pot with pressure cooking lid and select slow cooker mode and cook on low for 9 hours.
Remove meat from pot and shred using a fork.
Serve and enjoy.
Nutrition:
Calories 693
Fat 50.4 g
Carbohydrates 3.4 g
Sugar 2.4 g
Protein 53.2 g

Cholesterol 204 mg

Pulled Pork

Preparation Time: 10 minutes
Cooking Time: 50 minutes
Serving: 6
Ingredients:
3 lbs pork butt, cut into large chunks
1/2 tsp cumin
2 tbsp paprika
1 tbsp olive oil
1/2 cup water
1/2 tsp cayenne pepper
1 tbsp oregano
1 tsp pepper
2 tsp salt
Directions:
Add the meat into the inner pot of instant pot duo crisp and top with olive oil.
In a small bowl, mix together paprika, cayenne, oregano, cumin, pepper, and salt and sprinkle over meat.
Add water and stir well.
Seal the pot with pressure cooking lid and cook on high for 40 minutes.
Once done, allow to release pressure naturally for 10 minutes then release remaining pressure using a quick release. Remove lid.
Remove meat from pot and shred using a fork.
Return shredded meat to the pot and cook on sauté mode for 10 minutes.
Stir and serve.
Nutrition:
Calories 469
Fat 17.9 g
Carbohydrates 2.2 g
Sugar 0.3 g
Protein 71.1 g
Cholesterol 209 mg

Pork Patties

Preparation Time: 10 minutes
Cooking Time: 15 minutes
Serving: 6
Ingredients:
2 lbs ground pork
1 tsp red pepper flakes
1 tbsp dried parsley
1 1/2 tbsp Italian seasoning
1 tsp fennel seed
1 tsp paprika
2 tbsp olive oil
2 tsp salt
Directions:
Line instant pot air fryer basket with parchment paper.

In a large bowl, mix together ground pork, fennel seed, paprika, red pepper flakes, parsley, Italian seasoning, olive oil, pepper, and salt.
Make small patties from meat mixture and place on place on parchment paper into the air fryer basket.
Place basket into the pot.
Seal the pot with air fryer basket and select bake mode and cook at 375 F for 15 minutes.
Serve and enjoy.
Nutrition:
Calories 270
Fat 11.2 g
Carbohydrates 1 g
Sugar 0.4 g
Protein 39.7 g
Cholesterol 113 mg

Herb Pork Tenderloin

Preparation Time: 10 minutes
Cooking Time: 30 minutes
Serving: 4
Ingredients:
1 lb pork tenderloin
1 tsp oregano, dried
1 tsp thyme, dried
1 tsp olive oil
1/2 tsp onion powder
1/2 tsp garlic powder
1/2 tsp pepper
1/2 tsp salt
Directions:
In a small bowl, mix together onion powder, garlic powder, oregano, thyme, pepper and salt.
Coat pork with oil then rub with herb mixture and place into the instant pot air fryer basket.
Place basket in the pot.
Seal the pot with air fryer lid and select roast mode and cook at 400 F for 30 minutes.
Slice and serve.
Nutrition:
Calories 177
Fat 5.2 g
Carbohydrates 1.1 g
Sugar 0.2 g
Protein 29.9 g
Cholesterol 83 mg

Teriyaki Pork

Preparation time: 10 minutes
Cooking time: 40 minutes
Servings: 4
Ingredients:
2 lb. pork loin
1/2 tsp onion powder
1 tsp ground ginger

2 tbsp brown sugar
1/2 cup water
1/4 cup soy sauce
1 cup chicken stock
1 1/2 tbsp honey
2 garlic cloves, crushed
Directions:
In a small bowl, mix together all ingredients except meat and stock.
Pour the stock into the instant pot.
Place meat into the pot then pour bowl mixture over the pork.
Seal pot with lid and cook on manual high pressure for 45 minutes.
Once done then allow to release pressure naturally then open the lid.
Serve and enjoy.
Nutrition: Calories 606 Fat 31.8 g Carbohydrates 13.4 g Sugar 11.4 g Protein 63.3 g Cholesterol 181 mg

Easy & Tasty Ribs

Preparation time: 10 minutes
Cooking time: 40 minutes
Servings: 4
Ingredients:
2 3/4 lbs. country-style pork ribs
Dry rub:
1 tsp garlic powder
1 tbsp brown sugar
1 tsp cumin
1 tsp pepper
1 cup chicken stock
1 tsp cayenne pepper
1 tsp paprika
1 tsp onion powder
1 tsp salt
Directions:
In a small bowl, mix together all rub ingredients and rub over meat.
Pour the stock into the instant pot then place ribs into the pot.
Seal pot with lid and cook on high pressure for 45 minutes.
Once done then allow to release pressure naturally then open the lid.
Stir and serve.
Nutrition: Calories 601 Fat 36.3 g Carbohydrates 4.5 g Sugar 2.9 g Protein 61.3 g Cholesterol 235 mg

Air Fryer Steak

Preparation:10 minutes
Cooking time: 35minutes
Servings: 4
Ingredients:
2 pounds bone-in-ribeye
4 tablespoon butter, softened
2 garlic cloves, minced
2 teaspoon parsley, freshly chopped
1 teaspoon chives, freshly chopped
1 teaspoon thyme, freshly chopped
1 teaspoon rosemary, freshly chopped

½ teaspoon black pepper, freshly ground
1 teaspoon kosher salt
Directions:
Wash and pat dry the ribeye.
In a small bowl, mix the butter and herbs thoroughly.
In a plastic wrap, place the butter-herb mix in the center and roll it like a log. Close both ends of the wrap to keep it airtight and refrigerate it until it hardens. It will take about 20 minutes to freeze.
Rub the salt and pepper over the steak on both sides.
Transfer the steak in the air fryer basket and place it in the inner pot of the instant pot air fryer.
Close the crisp cover.
Under the air fry mode, select the temperature to 400°f and select timer to 14 minutes.
Press start to begin the cooking.
Halfway through the cooking, open the crisp cover and flip the steak.
After flipping, close the crisp cover to resume the cooking.
Now take out the refrigerated herb mix and slice it.
After cooking, serve on a plate and top it with the herb slice mix.
Nutrition: Calories: 407, total fat: 22.1g, saturated fat: 11.1g, trans fat: 1g, cholesterol: 178mg, sodium: 823mg, total carbs: 1g, dietary fiber: 0g, sugars: 0g, protein: 52g

---

Parmesan Pork Chops

Preparation Time: 10 minutes
Cooking Time: 12 minutes
Serving: 4
Ingredients:
1 lb pork chops, boneless
1/4 cup parmesan cheese, grated
1/3 cup flour
1 tsp paprika
1/2 tsp onion powder
1 tsp creole seasoning
1 tsp garlic powder
Directions:
Add all ingredients except pork chops into the zip-lock bag.
Add pork chops into the bag. Seal bag and shake well.
Place the dehydrating tray in a multi-level air fryer basket and place basket in the instant pot.
Place pork chops on dehydrating tray.
Seal pot with air fryer lid and select air fry mode then set the temperature to 360 F and timer for 12 minutes. Turn pork chops halfway through.
Serve and enjoy.
Nutrition:
Calories 424
Fat 29.6 g
Carbohydrates 9.2 g
Sugar 0.4 g
Protein 28.6 g
Cholesterol 102 mg

Crisp & Tasty Pork Chops

Preparation Time: 10 minutes
Cooking Time: 15 minutes
Serving: 4
Ingredients:
4 pork chops, boneless
1/2 tsp onion powder
1 tsp paprika
1/4 cup parmesan cheese, grated
1 cup pork rind
2 eggs, lightly beaten
1/2 tsp chili powder
1/4 tsp pepper
1/2 tsp salt
Directions:
Season pork chops with pepper and salt.
Add pork rind in food processor and process until crumbs form.
Mix together pork rind crumbs and seasoning in a large bowl.
Place egg in a separate bowl.
Dip pork chops in egg then coat with pork crumb.
Place the dehydrating tray in a multi-level air fryer basket and place basket in the instant pot.
Place coated pork chops on dehydrating tray.
Seal pot with air fryer lid and select air fry mode then set the temperature to 400 F and timer for 15 minutes. Turn pork chops halfway through.
Serve and enjoy.
Nutrition:
Calories 330
Fat 24.7 g
Carbohydrates 1.2 g
Sugar 0.4 g
Protein 25 g
Cholesterol 160 mg

Italian Meatloaf Sliders

Preparation Time: 10 minutes
Cooking Time: 10 minutes
Serving: 8
Ingredients:
1 lb ground beef
1/4 cup coconut flour
1/2 cup almond flour
1 garlic clove, minced
1/4 cup onion, chopped
2 eggs, lightly beaten
1/2 tsp dried tarragon
1 tsp Italian seasoning
1 tbsp Worcestershire sauce
1/4 cup ketchup
1/4 tsp pepper
1/2 tsp sea salt
Directions:
Add all ingredients into the mixing bowl and mix until well combined.

Make patties from meat mixture and place them on a plate. Place in refrigerator for 10 minutes.
Place the dehydrating tray in a multi-level air fryer basket and place basket in the instant pot.
Place patties on dehydrating tray.
Seal pot with air fryer lid and select air fry mode then set the temperature to 360 F and timer for 10 minutes. Turn patties halfway through.
Serve and enjoy.
Nutrition:
Calories 191
Fat 8.5 g
Carbohydrates 7 g
Sugar 2.4 g
Protein 20.8 g
Cholesterol 92 mg

Zaatar Lamb Chops

Preparation Time: 10 minutes
Cooking Time: 10 minutes
Serving: 4
Ingredients:
4 lamb loin chops
1/2 tbsp Zaatar
1 tbsp fresh lemon juice
1 tsp olive oil
2 garlic cloves, minced
Pepper
Salt
Directions:
Coat lamb chops with oil and lemon juice and rubs with zaatar, garlic, pepper, and salt.
Place the dehydrating tray in a multi-level air fryer basket and place basket in the instant pot.
Place lamb chops on dehydrating tray.
Seal pot with air fryer lid and select air fry mode then set the temperature to 400 F and timer for 10 minutes. Turn lamb chops halfway through.
Serve and enjoy.
Nutrition:
Calories 266
Fat 11.2 g
Carbohydrates 0.6 g
Sugar 0.1 g
Protein 38 g
Cholesterol 122 mg

Tasty Southern Pork Chops

Preparation Time: 10 minutes
Cooking Time: 15 minutes
Serving: 2
Ingredients:
2 pork chops, wash and pat dry
2 tbsp flour

1 1/2 tbsp buttermilk
1/2 tsp Montreal chicken seasoning
Salt
Directions:
Season pork chops with pepper and salt.
Coat pork chops with buttermilk.
Place pork chops in a zip-lock bag with flour and shake well to coat. Marinate pork chops for 30 minutes.
Place the dehydrating tray in a multi-level air fryer basket and place basket in the instant pot.
Place marinated pork chops on dehydrating tray.
Seal pot with air fryer lid and select air fry mode then set the temperature to 380 F and timer for 15 minutes. Turn pork chops halfway through.
Serve and enjoy.
Nutrition:
Calories 290
Fat 20.1 g
Carbohydrates 6.7 g
Sugar 0.6 g
Protein 19.2 g
Cholesterol 69 mg

Taco Meatballs

Preparation Time: 10 minutes
Cooking Time: 10 minutes
Serving: 4
Ingredients:
1 egg
1 lb ground beef
2 tbsp taco seasoning
1 tbsp garlic, minced
1/2 cup cheddar cheese, shredded
1/4 cup cilantro, chopped
1/4 cup onion, minced
Pepper
Salt
Directions:
Add all ingredients into the large mixing bowl and mix until well combined.
Place the dehydrating tray in a multi-level air fryer basket and place basket in the instant pot.
Make meatballs meat mixture and place on dehydrating tray.
Seal pot with air fryer lid and select air fry mode then set the temperature to 400 F and timer for 10 minutes. Turn meatballs halfway through.
Serve and enjoy.
Nutrition:
Calories 295
Fat 13.2 g
Carbohydrates 2.1 g
Sugar 0.5 g
Protein 39.9 g
Cholesterol 230 mg

Tasty & Spicy Lamb

Preparation time: 10 minutes
Cooking time: 35 minutes
Servings: 4
Ingredients:
1 lb lamb, cut into pieces
2 tbsp lemon juice
1/2 cup fresh cilantro, chopped
2 onions, chopped
2 cups chicken stock
1 cup of coconut milk
3 tbsp butter
1 cup grape tomatoes, chopped
1/2 tbsp cumin powder
1 1/2 tsp turmeric
2 tsp garam masala
2 1/2 tbsp chili powder
2 tbsp apple cider
1 tsp salt
Directions:
Set instant pot on sauté mode.
Season meat with pepper and salt and place into the pot.
Cook meat for 5 minutes.
Add remaining ingredients and stir well.
Seal pot with lid and cook on manual high pressure for 15 minutes.
Once done then allow to release pressure naturally for 10 minutes then release using the quick-release method.
Open the lid.
Stir and serve.
Nutrition: Calories 487 Fat 32.8 g Carbohydrates 15.2 g Sugar 7.3 g Protein 35.5 g Cholesterol 125 mg

Lamb Shanks

Preparation time: 10 minutes
Cooking time: 35 minutes
Servings: 4
Ingredients:
4 lamb shanks
3 garlic cloves
1 small onion, chopped
1/4 cup apple cider vinegar
3 tbsp olive oil
3 cups chicken broth
7 oz mushrooms, sliced
1/2 tsp dried rosemary
1 tomato, chopped
1/4 cup leeks, chopped
2 celery stalks, chopped
2 tsp sea salt
Directions:
Add all ingredients into the instant pot and stir well.
Seal pot with lid and cook on manual high pressure for 25 minutes.
Once done then allow to release pressure naturally for 10 minutes then release using the quick-release method.
Open the lid.
Serve and enjoy.

Nutrition: Calories 309 Fat 18 g Carbohydrates 6.6 g Sugar 2.9 g Protein 29.7 g Cholesterol 77 mg

Tasty Air Fried Pork Chops

Preparation Time: 10 minutes
Cooking Time: 10 minutes
Serving: 3
Ingredients:
3 pork chops
1/4 tsp garlic powder
2 tsp avocado oil
1/2 tsp smoked paprika
Pepper
Salt
Directions:
Coat pork chops with avocado oil and season with garlic powder, paprika, pepper, and salt.
Place the dehydrating tray in a multi-level air fryer basket and place basket in the instant pot.
Place lamb chops on dehydrating tray.
Seal pot with air fryer lid and select air fry mode then set the temperature to 380 F and timer for 10 minutes. Turn lamb chops halfway through.
Serve and enjoy.
Nutrition:
Calories 262
Fat 20.3 g
Carbohydrates 0.6 g
Sugar 0.1 g
Protein 18.1 g
Cholesterol 69 mg

Lemon Mustard Lamb Chops

Preparation Time: 10 minutes
Cooking Time: 14 minutes
Serving: 4
Ingredients:
4 lamb loin chops
1/2 tbsp lemon juice
1/2 tsp tarragon
1/2 tsp olive oil
1 tbsp Dijon mustard
Pepper
Salt
Directions:
Coat lamb chops with oil and rubs with lemon juice, tarragon, mustard, pepper, and salt.
Place the dehydrating tray in a multi-level air fryer basket and place basket in the instant pot.
Place lamb chops on dehydrating tray.
Seal pot with air fryer lid and select air fry mode then set the temperature to 390 F and timer for 14 minutes. Turn lamb chops halfway through.
Serve and enjoy.
Nutrition:
Calories 260
Fat 10.7 g

Carbohydrates 0.3 g
Sugar 0.1 g
Protein 38.1 g
Cholesterol 122 mg

Pork with Cabbage

Preparation time: 10 minutes
Cooking time: 10 minutes
Servings: 4
Ingredients:
1 1/4 lbs pork loin, boneless and cut into cubes
1/2 tsp pepper
1/4 tsp fennel seeds
1 tbsp vinegar
1 cup chicken stock
1 tsp dried dill weed
1/2 small cabbage, cored and cut into wedges
1 onion, cut into wedges
2 tsp olive oil
Directions:
Add oil into the instant pot and set the pot on sauté mode.
Add onion and sauté for 2 minutes.
Add meat and cook for 3 minutes.
Add cabbage and stir well.
In a small bowl, mix dill weed, pepper, and fennel seeds and sprinkle over cabbage.
Pour vinegar and stock to the pot.
Seal pot with lid and cook on manual high pressure for 5 minutes.
Once done then allow to release pressure naturally then open the lid.
Serve and enjoy.
Nutrition: Calories 382 Fat 22.3 g Carbohydrates 3.8 g Sugar 1.7 g Protein 39.4 g Cholesterol 113 mg

---

Salsa Pork

Preparation time: 10 minutes
Cooking time: 15 minutes
Servings: 4
Ingredients:
2 lbs pork shoulder, boneless and cut into chunks
3 tbsp fresh cilantro, chopped
1/2 cup chicken stock
1/2 tsp ground cumin
1 1/2 tbsp honey
14.5 oz can tomato, drained and diced
14 oz salsa
1/2 tsp dried oregano
Pepper
Salt
Directions:
Season meat with pepper and salt.
Add meat, stock, oregano, cumin, honey, tomatoes, and salsa to the pot.
Seal pot with lid and cook on manual high pressure for 15 minutes.

Once done then allow to release pressure naturally then open the lid.
Shred the meat using a fork.
Garnish with cilantro and serve.
Nutrition: Calories 738 Fat 48.8 g Carbohydrates 18.3 g Sugar 13.1 g Protein 55.5 g Cholesterol 204 mg

---

Pork Fajitas

Preparation time: 10 minutes
Cooking time: 20 minutes
Servings: 6
Ingredients:
1 3/4 lbs. pork loin sirloin chops, cut into strips
1 onion, sliced
2 bell pepper, cut into strips
1 1/2 tbsp Italian seasoning
1/2 cup chicken stock
2 tbsp fresh lime juice
oz salsa
Directions:
Add all ingredients into the instant pot and stir well.
Seal pot with lid and cook on manual high pressure for 1 minute.
Once done then allow to release pressure naturally for 10 minutes then release using the quick-release method.
Open the lid.
Stir and serve.
Nutrition: Calories 369 Fat 19.7 g Carbohydrates 9.2 g Sugar 5.1 g Protein 37.8 g Cholesterol 108 mg

---

Beef Pork Meatballs

Preparation Time: 10 minutes
Cooking Time: 20 minutes
Serving: 4
Ingredients:
8 oz ground pork
8 oz ground beef
1 egg, lightly beaten
1/4 cup parmesan cheese, grated
1/2 cup breadcrumbs
1/4 cup parsley, chopped
1 tsp garlic, minced
1/2 onion, chopped
Pepper
Salt
Directions:
Add all ingredients into the large bowl and mix until well combined.
Place the dehydrating tray in a multi-level air fryer basket and place basket in the instant pot.
Make meatballs meat mixture and place on dehydrating tray.
Seal pot with air fryer lid and select bake mode then set the temperature to 380 F and timer for 20 minutes. Turn meatballs halfway through.
Serve and enjoy.
Nutrition:
Calories 263
Fat 8.6 g
Carbohydrates 11.8 g

Sugar 1.5 g
Protein 37.3 g
Cholesterol 137 mg

Lamb Meatballs

Preparation Time: 10 minutes
Cooking Time: 20 minutes
Serving: 4
Ingredients:
1 lb ground lamb
1/4 tsp red pepper flakes
1 tsp ground cumin
2 tsp oregano, chopped
2 tbsp parsley, chopped
1 tsp garlic, minced
1 egg, lightly beaten
Pepper
Salt
Directions:
Add all ingredients into the mixing bowl and mix until well combined.
Place the dehydrating tray in a multi-level air fryer basket and place basket in the instant pot.
Make meatballs meat mixture and place on dehydrating tray.
Seal pot with air fryer lid and select bake mode then set the temperature to 380 F and timer for 20 minutes. Turn meatballs halfway through.
Serve and enjoy.
Nutrition:
Calories 233
Fat 9.6 g
Carbohydrates 1.2 g
Sugar 0.2 g
Protein 33.5 g
Cholesterol 143 mg

Greek Meatballs

Preparation Time: 10 minutes
Cooking Time: 20 minutes
Serving: 4
Ingredients:
1 lb ground beef
1 egg, lightly beaten
1/4 cup parsley, chopped
4 oz feta cheese, crumbled
1 tbsp garlic, minced
1/4 cup breadcrumbs
1/2 onion, chopped
1/2 lb ground lamb
Pepper
Salt
Directions:

Add all ingredients into the mixing bowl and mix until well combined.
Place the dehydrating tray in a multi-level air fryer basket and place basket in the instant pot.
Make meatballs meat mixture and place on dehydrating tray.
Seal pot with air fryer lid and select bake mode then set the temperature to 380 F and timer for 25 minutes. Turn meatballs halfway through.
Serve and enjoy.
Nutrition:
Calories 443
Fat 18.8 g
Carbohydrates 8.3 g
Sugar 2.3 g
Protein 57 g
Cholesterol 219 mg

Garlicky Lamb Chops

Preparation Time: 10 minutes
Cooking Time: 10 minutes
Serving: 4
Ingredients:
1 lb lamb chops
1 tbsp olive oil
4 garlic cloves, minced
2 tbsp rosemary, chopped
Pepper
Salt
Directions:
Mix together oil, garlic, rosemary, pepper, and salt and rub over lamb chops.
Place the dehydrating tray in a multi-level air fryer basket and place basket in the instant pot.
Place lamb chops on dehydrating tray.
Seal pot with air fryer lid and select air fry mode then set the temperature to 400 F and timer for 10 minutes. Turn lamb chops halfway through.
Serve and enjoy.
Nutrition:
Calories 251
Fat 12.1 g
Carbohydrates 2.1 g
Sugar 0 g
Protein 32.1 g
Cholesterol 102 mg

Mushrooms & Steak Bites

Preparation Time: 10 minutes
Cooking Time: 20 minutes
Serving: 2
Ingredients:
1/2 lb steaks, cut into 1-inch cubes
1/4 tsp garlic powder
1/2 tbsp Worcestershire sauce
1 tbsp butter, melted
4 oz mushrooms, sliced

Pepper
Salt
Directions:
In a mixing bowl, toss together steak cubes, mushrooms, garlic powder, Worcestershire sauce, butter, pepper, and salt.
Spray instant pot multi-level air fryer basket with cooking spray.
Add steak mushroom mixture into the air fryer basket and place basket into the instant pot.
Seal pot with air fryer lid and select air fry mode then set the temperature to 400 F and timer for 20 minutes. mix halfway through.
Serve and enjoy.
Nutrition:
Calories 294
Fat 11.6 g
Carbohydrates 2.9 g
Sugar 1.8 g
Protein 42.9 g
Cholesterol 117 mg

Air Fryer Beef with Homemade Marinade

Preparation: 10 minutes
Cooking time: 45 minutes
Servings: 3
Ingredients:
1-pound beef sirloin
½ cup red onion slices
½ cup green onion slices
1 yellow bell pepper, cut into strips
1 green pepper, cut into strips
1 red bell pepper, cut into strips
1½ pounds broccoli florets
1 tablespoon vegetable oil
For the marinade:
¼ cup of water
1 teaspoon minced ginger
1 tablespoon soy sauce
1 tablespoon sesame oil
2 teaspoons finely grated garlic
¼ cup hoisin sauce
Directions:
Wash and pat dry the beef.
Cut the beef sirloin into 2-inch strips.
For making the marinade, add the hoisin sauce, garlic, sesame oil, soy sauce, finely grated ginger, and water in a bowl and mix thoroughly.
Add the meat in the marinade and mix to coat for perfect seasoning.
Cover the bowl and refrigerate for 20 minutes.
Put all the vegetables in a large bowl and add one teaspoon vegetable oil into it and mix thoroughly for even coating.
Transfer the oil-coated vegetables into the air fryer basket and place it in the inner pot of the instant pot air fryer.
Close the crisp lid.
In the air fry mode, select temperature 200°f and set the timer to 5 minutes.
Press start to begin the cooking.
After the vegetables become soft, transfer it into a bowl.
Now place the marinated meat in the air fryer basket.

Close the crisp cover and set the temperature at 360°f on air fry mod.
Set the timer to 40 minutes.
Press start to begin cooking.
After 20 minutes, open the air fryer and flip the meat.
To resume cooking for the remaining period, close the crisp cover.
Serve it with salad.
Nutrition: Calories: 509, total fat: 28.9g, saturated fat: 8.6g, trans fat: 0g, cholesterol: 110mg, sodium: 585mg, total carbs: 24g, dietary fiber: 8g, sugars: 11g, protein: 41g

---

Bourbon Bacon Burger in The Air Fryer

Preparation: 10 minutes
Cooking time: 25 minutes
Servings: 2
Ingredients:
¾ pound minced beef
3 strips bacon, cut into half
2 kaiser rolls
4 tablespoons barbeque sauce
¼ teaspoon paprika
2 tablespoons mayonnaise
1 teaspoon ground black pepper, fresh
1 tablespoon bourbon
1 tablespoon onion, finely chopped
2 tablespoons brown sugar
½ teaspoon salt
½ lettuce, finely chopped (serving
1 tomato, chopped (serving
Directions:
In a small bowl, combine the bourbon and brown sugar.
Brush this mixture over the bacon strips on both sides.
Place the marinated bacon strips in the air fryer basket.
Put the air fryer basket in the inner pot of the instant pot air fryer.
Close the crisp cover.
In the air fry mode, select the temperature to 390°f and set the timer to 10 minutes.
Press start to begin the cooking.
Halfway through the cooking, open the air fryer, and flip the bacon.
Sprinkle the bourbon mixture on the bacon, if required and cook for the remaining period.
While the cooking in progress, make the burger patties by combining the ground beef, bbq sauce, onion, salt, and pepper in a large bowl.
Combine it thoroughly and make 2 patties out of the mixture.
Remove the cooked bacon into a bowl and start the cooking process for burger patties.
Place the patties in the air fryer basket and put in the inner pot of the instant pot air fryer.
Close the crisp cover.
In the air fry mode, select temperature 370°f and set the timer for 20 minutes.
Press start to begin the cooking process.
Now let us make the burger sauce by mixing bbq sauce, paprika, mayonnaise, and pepper in a bowl.
Once the patties cooked, top it with cheese and air fry for one more minute.
Spread the sauce in the kaiser rolls, place these burgers on rolls and top with the bourbon bacon, tomato, and lettuce.
Serve it with additional sauces if needed.
Nutrition: Calories 1020, carbohydrates: 49g, fat 68g, protein: 44g, cholesterol 175mg, sodium:1750mg, potassium: 695mg, sugars: 26g, saturated fat: 25g, calcium: 31.8mg

Crispy Air Fryer Bacon

Preparation: 5 minutes
Cooking time: 10 minutes
Servings: 8
Ingredients:
¾ pound bacon, thick-cut pieces
Directions:
Place the bacon strips in the air fryer basket, don't overlap them.
Put the air fryer basket in the inner pot of the instant pot air fryer.
Close the crisp lid.
Under the broil mode, set the timer for 10 minutes. The default temperature will read at 400°f.
Press start to begin the cooking.
Check the air fryer halfway to flip the bacon strips.
You can open the crisp lid (this will pause the cooking procedure and close the crisp cover once you have flipped the meat. The cooking will resume as soon as you close the lid.
Once the bacon is ready, serve hot.
Nutrition: Calories: 132, total fat: 12.6g, saturated fat: 2g, trans fat: 0g, cholesterol: 0mg, sodium: 623mg, total carbs: 3g, dietary fiber: 1g, sugars: 0g, protein: 5g

Beef Pie

Preparation time: 10 minutes
Cooking Time: 65 minutes
Serving: 4
Ingredients:
3 tablespoons soy sauce
1 tablespoon Worcestershire sauce
1/4 cup plain flour
1/4 teaspoon salt
1/2 teaspoon pepper
3 bay leaves
3 sprigs thyme
2 lbs. lean beef, cubed
3 garlic cloves
1 carrot, sliced
1 onion, sliced
6 new potatoes, halved
2 celery ribs, sliced
1 cup red wine
1 cup beef stock
2 tablespoons parsley
Directions:
Whisk seasonings with flour, soy, Worcestershire sauce, thyme, and bay leaves in a pot.
Stir cook this sauce for 5 minutes then add carrot, garlic, onion, stock, red wine, and beef.
Mix well, then spread this beef mixture into the Instant Pot Duo.
Put on the Air Fryer lid and seal it.
Hit the "Bake Button" and select 60 minutes of cooking time, then press "Start."
Once the Instant Pot Duo beeps, remove its lid.
Serve
Nutrition:
Calories 535
Total Fat 10.8g
Saturated Fat 4g
Cholesterol 149mg

Sodium 850mg
Total Carbohydrate 43.7g
Dietary Fiber 6.4g
Total Sugars 4.9g
Protein 56.2g

Air Fried Herb Rack of Lamb

Preparation: 5 minutes
Cooking time: 20 minutes
Servings: 2
Ingredients:
1-pound whole rack of lamb
2 tablespoons rosemary, dried
1 tablespoon thyme, dried
2 teaspoons garlic, minced
½ teaspoon salt
½ teaspoon pepper
4 tablespoons olive oil
Directions:
Wash the lamb and pat dry.
In a small bowl, mix all the herbs along with olive oil and keep it aside.
Rub the herb mixture over the lamb rack and coat it thoroughly.
Place the lamb in the air fryer basket and put it in the inner pot of instant pot air fryer.
Close the crisp lid and set the temperature at 360° f in the air fry mode.
Set the timer for 10 minutes.
Press start to begin the cooking.
Halfway through the cooking, open the crisp lid and flip the lamb for even cooking.
After flipping, close the crisp lid, so that the appliance can automatically resume cooking for the remaining period.
Once done, remove it from the air fryer and serve hot.
Nutrition: Calories: 614, total fat: 46.7g, saturated fat: 10.1g, trans fat: 0.7g, cholesterol: 145mg, sodium: 736mg, total carbs: 3g, dietary fiber: 1g, sugars: 1g, protein: 47g

---

Pork Chops with Asparagus

Preparation time:10 minutes
Cooking Time: 25 minutes
Serving: 4
Ingredients:
4 pork chops, bone-in
Salt and Pepper to taste
2 tablespoons canola oil
1 tablespoon creole seasoning
1 1/2 teaspoons minced thyme
1 tablespoon garlic, minced
½ tablespoon Dijon mustard
1 teaspoon Worchester sauce
2-3 tablespoons brown sugar
2 tablespoons parsley, for garnish
1-pound potatoes, cubed
1-pound asparagus, chopped
Directions:

Whisk ½ of the creole seasoning with thyme, garlic, mustard, sugar, oil, and Worcestershire sauce in a bowl.
Season the pork chops with this creole mixture and place them in the Air Fryer Basket.
Season the potatoes with remaining creole seasoning, oil, and salt.
Place these potatoes around the pork chops in the Air Fryer Basket.
Set the Air basket in the Instant Pot Duo.
Put on the Air Fryer lid and seal it.
Hit the "Bake Button" and select 22 minutes of cooking time, then press "Start."
Once the Instant Pot Duo beeps, switch it to Broil mode and cook for 3 minutes.
Garnish with parsley and enjoy.
Nutrition:
Calories 467
Total Fat 27.1g
Saturated Fat 8g
Cholesterol 69mg
Sodium 992mg
Total Carbohydrate 34.8g
Dietary Fiber 5.8g
Total Sugars 11.6g
Protein 21.1g

Tasty Lamb Chops

Preparation Time: 10 minutes
Cooking Time: 10 minutes
Serving: 4
Ingredients:
4 lamb chops
1 garlic clove, minced
1/2 tbsp fresh oregano, chopped
1 tbsp olive oil
Pepper
Salt
Directions:
Coat lamb chops with olive oil and rubs with garlic, oregano, pepper, and salt.
Place the dehydrating tray in a multi-level air fryer basket and place basket in the instant pot.
Place lamb chops on dehydrating tray.
Seal pot with air fryer lid and select air fry mode then set the temperature to 400 F and timer for 10 minutes. Turn lamb chops halfway through.
Serve and enjoy.
Nutrition:
Calories 284
Fat 13.5 g
Carbohydrates 0.6 g
Sugar 0 g
Protein 38 g
Cholesterol 122 mg

Delicious Fajitas

Preparation Time: 10 minutes
Cooking Time: 8 minutes
Serving: 2
Ingredients:
1/2 lb beef, sliced
1/2 tsp garlic powder
1/2 tsp paprika
3/4 tsp cumin
1/4 tbsp chili powder
1 1/2 tbsp olive oil
1/4 onion, sliced
1 bell pepper, sliced
Pepper
Salt
Directions:
Add meat and remaining ingredients into the mixing bowl and toss well.
Spray instant pot multi-level air fryer basket with cooking spray.
Add meat mixture into the air fryer basket and place basket into the instant pot.
Seal pot with air fryer lid and select air fry mode then set the temperature to 390 F and timer for 8 minutes. mix halfway through.
Serve and enjoy.
Nutrition:
Calories 335
Fat 18.2 g
Carbohydrates 7.5 g
Sugar 3.9 g
Protein 35.6 g
Cholesterol 101 mg

Juicy Steak

Preparation Time: 10 minutes
Cooking Time: 20 minutes
Serving: 2
Ingredients:
2 steaks, 3/4-inch thick
1/2 tsp garlic powder
1/4 tsp onion powder
1 tsp olive oil
Pepper
Salt
Directions:
Coat steak with olive oil and season with garlic powder, onion powder, pepper, and salt.
Place the dehydrating tray in a multi-level air fryer basket and place basket in the instant pot.
Place steaks on dehydrating tray.
Seal pot with air fryer lid and select air fry mode then set the temperature to 400 F and timer for 20 minutes. Turn steaks halfway through.
Serve and enjoy.
Nutrition:
Calories 543
Fat 15.4 g
Carbohydrates 0.8 g

Sugar 0.3 g
Protein 94.4 g
Cholesterol 235 mg

Mustard Pork Chops

Preparation time: 30 minutes
Cooking time: 10 minutes
Servings: 4
Ingredients:
4 pork chops
10 oz. Beef stock
2/3 cup cream cheese, soft
1 tbsp. Olive oil
1 tbsp. Mustard
1 tbsp. Parsley; chopped
¼ tsp. Oregano; dried
¼ tsp. Thyme; dried
¼ tsp. Garlic powder
A pinch of salt and black pepper
Directions:
In a baking dish that fits your air fryer, mix all the ingredients, introduce the pan in the fryer and cook at 400°f for 25 minutes
Divide everything between plates and serve.
Nutrition: Calories: 284; Fat: 14g; Fiber: 4g; Carbs: 6g; Protein: 22

Easy Pork Chops

Preparation time: 25 minutes
Cooking time: 10 minutes
Servings: 4
Ingredients:
1½ oz. Pork rinds, finely ground
1 tsp. Chili powder
½ tsp. Garlic powder.
1 tbsp. Coconut oil; melted
4 (4-oz. pork chops
Directions:
Take a large bowl, mix ground pork rinds, chili powder and garlic powder.
Brush each pork chop with coconut oil and then press into the pork rind mixture, coating both sides. Place each coated pork chop into the air fryer basket
Adjust the temperature to 400 degrees f and set the timer for 15 minutes.
Flip each pork chop halfway through the cooking time
When fully cooked the pork chops will be golden on the outside and have an internal temperature of at least 145 degrees f.
Nutrition: Calories: 292; Protein: 29.5g; Fiber: 0.3g; Fat: 18.5g; Carbs: 0.6g

Pork Roast

Preparation time: 35 minutes
Cooking time: 10 minutes
Servings: 4
Ingredients:
1 lb. Pork tenderloin, trimmed
2 tbsp. Balsamic vinegar
3 tbsp. Mustard
2 tbsp. Olive oil
A pinch of salt and black pepper
Directions:
Take a bowl and mix the pork tenderloin with the rest of the ingredients and rub well.
Put the roast in your air fryer's basket and cook at 380°f for 30 minutes. Slice the roast, divide between plates and serve.
Nutrition: Calories: 274; Fat: 13g; Fiber: 4g; Carbs: 7g; Protein: 22

Coconut and Chili Pork

Preparation time: 30 minutes
Cooking time: 10 minutes
Servings: 4
Ingredients:
4 pork chops
2 garlic cloves; minced
1 shallot; chopped
1 ½ cups coconut milk
3 tbsp. Coconut aminos
2 tbsp. Olive oil
2 tsp. Chili paste
Salt and black pepper to taste.
Directions:
In a pan that fits your air fryer, mix the pork the rest of the ingredients, toss, introduce the pan in the fryer and cook at 400°f for 25 minutes, shaking the fryer halfway.
Divide everything into bowls and serve.
Nutrition: Calories: 267; Fat: 12g; Fiber: 4g; Carbs: 6g; Protein: 18g

Herbed Lamb Rack

Preparation time: 5-10 Minutes
Cooking Time: 10 Minutes
Serving: 2
Ingredients: 1-pound whole rack of lamb
2 teaspoons garlic, minced
½ teaspoon salt
2 tablespoons rosemary, dried
1 tablespoon thyme, dried
½ teaspoon pepper
4 tablespoons olive oil
Directions:
In a mixing bowl, add the olive oil and herbs. Combine the ingredients to mix well with each other. Coat the lamb with the herb mixture.

Place Instant Pot Air Fryer Crisp over kitchen platform. Press Air Fry set the temperature to 400°F and set the timer to 5 minutes to preheat. Press "Start" and allow it to preheat for 5 minutes.

In the inner pot, place the Air Fryer basket. In the basket, add the lamb rack.

Close the Crisp Lid and press the "Air Fry" setting. Set temperature to 360°F and set the timer to 10 minutes. Press "Start."

Halfway down, open the Crisp Lid, shake the basket and close the lid to continue cooking for the remaining time.

Open the Crisp Lid after cooking time is over. Serve warm.

Nutrition: Calories: 542
Fat: 37g
Saturated Fat: 9g
Trans Fat: 0.5g
Carbohydrates: 3g
Fiber: 0.5g
Sodium: 693mg
Protein: 45g

Baked Carrot Beef

Preparation time: 5-10 Minutes
Cooking Time: 60 Minutes
Serving: 5-6
Ingredients: 2 carrots, chopped
2 sticks celery, chopped
3 pounds beef
Olive oil to taste
2 medium onions, sliced
Garlic cloves from 1 bunch
1 bunch mixed fresh herbs (thyme, rosemary, bay, sage etc.) Directions:
Grease a baking pan with some cooking spray. Add the vegetables, beef roast, olive oil, and herbs; combine well.

Place Instant Pot Air Fryer Crisp over kitchen platform. Press Air Fry, set the temperature to 400°F and set the timer to 5 minutes to preheat. Press "Start" and allow it to preheat for 5 minutes.

In the inner pot, place the Air Fryer basket. In the basket, add the pan.

Close the Crisp Lid and press the "Bake" setting. Set temperature to 380°F and set the timer to 60 minutes. Press "Start."

Open the Crisp Lid after cooking time is over. Serve warm.

Nutrition: Calories: 306
Fat: 21g
Saturated Fat: 7g
Trans Fat: 0g
Carbohydrates: 10g
Fiber: 3g
Sodium: 324mg
Protein: 32g

Juicy & Crispy Meatballs

Preparation Time: 10 minutes
Cooking Time: 15 minutes
Serving: 4

Ingredients:
1 lb ground beef
1/2 tsp Italian seasoning
2 garlic cloves, minced
1/4 cup milk
1/2 cup parmesan cheese, grated
1/2 cup breadcrumbs
Pepper
Salt
Directions:
Add all ingredients into the mixing bowl and mix until well combined.
Place the dehydrating tray in a multi-level air fryer basket and place basket in the instant pot.
Make small meatballs and place them on a dehydrating tray.
Seal pot with air fryer lid and select air fry mode then set the temperature to 375 F and timer for 15 minutes. Turn meatballs halfway through.
Serve and enjoy.
Nutrition:
Calories 312
Fat 10.7 g
Carbohydrates 11.5 g
Sugar 1.6 g
Protein 40.4 g
Cholesterol 111 mg

BBQ Meatballs

Preparation Time: 10 minutes
Cooking Time: 14 minutes
Serving: 2
Ingredients:
1/2 lb ground beef
2 tbsp BBQ sauce
1/2 tbsp Montreal steak seasoning
1/2 egg whites
1/4 cup cheddar cheese, shredded
1/4 cup parmesan cheese, grated
Pepper
Salt
Directions:
Add all ingredients into the mixing bowl and mix until well combined.
Place the dehydrating tray in a multi-level air fryer basket and place basket in the instant pot.
Make small meatballs and place them on a dehydrating tray.
Seal pot with air fryer lid and select air fry mode then set the temperature to 360 F and timer for 14 minutes. Turn meatballs halfway through.
Serve and enjoy.
Nutrition:
Calories 337
Fat 14.2 g
Carbohydrates 6.3 g
Sugar 4.2 g
Protein 42.5 g
Cholesterol 124 mg

Lamb Roast

Preparation Time: 10 minutes
Cooking Time: 15 minutes
Serving: 2
Ingredients:
10 oz lamb leg roast
1 tsp dried thyme
1 tsp dried rosemary
1 tbsp olive oil
Pepper
Salt
Directions:
Coat lamb roast with olive oil and rub with thyme, rosemary, pepper, and salt.
Place the dehydrating tray in a multi-level air fryer basket and place basket in the instant pot.
Place lamb roast on dehydrating tray.
Seal pot with air fryer lid and select air fry mode then set the temperature to 360 F and timer for 15 minutes.
Serve and enjoy.
Nutrition:
Calories 319
Fat 16.6 g
Carbohydrates 0.7 g
Sugar 0 g
Protein 40 g
Cholesterol 123 mg

Air Fried Spicy Lamb Sirloin Steak

Preparation: 40 minutes
Cooking time: 15 minutes
Servings: 4
Ingredients:
½ onion
4 ginger cubes
5 garlic cloves
1 teaspoon of garam masala
1 teaspoon fennel, ground
1 teaspoon cinnamon, ground
½ teaspoon cayenne powder
1 teaspoon salt
1-pound lamb sirloin, boneless steaks
Directions:
Wash the lamb and pat dry.
Add all the ingredients in a blender except for the lamb chops and blend it into a fine paste.
Make strips over the lamb chops to ensure the margination reaches within the meat.
Rub the paste on to the chops and mix them well.
Let the marinade mixture rest for 30 minutes or overnight in the refrigerator, as preferred.
Place the lamb steaks in the air fryer basket and put it in the inner pot.
Close the crisp lid.
Select the smart option roast under air fry mode for 15 minutes. Select the temperature to 380°f. It will automatically select temperature to 380°f by default.
Press start to begin the cooking.
Halfway through the cooking, open the crisp lid and flip the lamb for even cooking.
Close the crisp lid to resume cooking for the remaining period.

Serve hot.
Nutrition: Calories: 171, saturated fat: 2.1g, trans fat: 0g, cholesterol: 75mg, sodium: 708mg, total carbs: 4g, dietary fiber: 1g, sugars: 1g, protein: 24g

---

Beef & Lemon Schnitzel for One

Preparation time: 5 minutes
Cooking time: 12 minutes
Servings: 1
Ingredients
2 tbsp oil
2–3 oz breadcrumbs
1 whisked egg in a saucer/soup plate
1 beef schnitzel
1 freshly picked lemon
Directions:
Preparing the ingredients. Mix the oil and breadcrumbs together until loose and crumbly.
Dip the meat into the egg, then into the crumbs.
Make sure that it is evenly covered.
Air frying. Gently place in the instant crisp air fryer basket, close air fryer lid and cook at 350° f (preheat if needed until done). The timing will depend on the thickness of the schnitzel, but for a relatively thin one, it should take roughly 12 MinutesServe with a lemon half and a garden salad.

Crispy Beef Schnitzel

Preparation time: 5 minutes
Cooking time: 12 minutes
Servings: 1
Ingredients:
1 beef schnitzel
Salt and ground black pepper, to taste
2 tablespoons olive oil
1/3 cup breadcrumbs
1 egg, whisked
Directions:
Preparing the ingredients. Season the schnitzel with salt and black pepper.
In a mixing bowl, combine the oil and breadcrumbs. In another shallow bowl, beat the egg until frothy.
Dip the schnitzel in the egg; then, dip it in the oil mixture. Close air fryer lid.
Air-fry at 350 degrees f for 12 minutes. Enjoy!

Simple Burger Patties

Preparation Time: 10 minutes
Cooking Time: 12 minutes
Serving: 4
Ingredients:
1 lb ground beef
1/2 tsp garlic powder
1/2 tsp onion powder
1/4 tsp red pepper flakes
Pepper
Salt

Directions:
Add all ingredients into the mixing bowl and mix until well combined.
Place the dehydrating tray in a multi-level air fryer basket and place basket in the instant pot.
Make four patties from meat mixture and place on dehydrating tray.
Seal pot with air fryer lid and select air fry mode then set the temperature to 350 F and timer for 12 minutes. Turn patties halfway through.
Serve and enjoy.
Nutrition:
Calories 213
Fat 7.1 g
Carbohydrates 0.6 g
Sugar 0.2 g
Protein 34.5 g
Cholesterol 101 mg

Herbed Vegetable Beef

Preparation time:10 minutes
Cooking Time: 60 minutes
Serving: 6
Ingredients:
3 lbs. beef
2 medium onions, sliced
2 carrots, chopped
2 sticks celery, chopped
1 bulb. of garlic, peeled cloves
1 bunch mixed fresh herbs (thyme, rosemary, bay, sage)
olive oil
Directions:
Add all the vegetables to the Instant Pot Duo Crisp.
Top the veggies with the beef roast, olive oil, and herbs.
Put on the Air Fryer lid and seal it.
Hit the "Bake Button" and select 60 minutes of cooking time, then press "Start."
Once the Instant Pot Duo beeps, remove its lid.
Serve.
Nutrition:
Calories 338
Total Fat 23.5g
Saturated Fat 8.8g
Cholesterol 335mg
Sodium 286mg
Total Carbohydrate 9.5g
Dietary Fiber 2.3g
Total Sugars 4.1g
Protein 34.8g

Russian Beef Bake

Preparation time:10 minutes
Cooking Time: 60 minutes
Serving: 6

Ingredients:
1 (2 pounds) beef tenderloin
Salt and ground black pepper to taste
2 onions, sliced
1 1/2 cups Cheddar cheese, grated
1 cup milk
3 tablespoons mayonnaise
Directions:
Slice the beef into thick slices and pound them with a mallet.
Place these pounded slices in the Instant Pot Duo's pan.
Top these slices with onion, salt, black pepper, cheese, milk, and mayonnaise.
Put on the Air Fryer lid and seal it.
Hit the "Bake Button" and select 60 minutes of cooking time, then press "Start."
Crush the crackers and mix them well with 4 tablespoons melted butter.
Once the Instant Pot Duo beeps, remove its lid.
Serve.
Nutrition:
Calories 489
Total Fat 26.5g
Saturated Fat 12.1g
Cholesterol 174mg
Sodium 338mg
Total Carbohydrate 7.5g
Dietary Fiber 0.8g
Total Sugars 4g
Protein 52.6g

Beef Pie

Preparation time:10 minutes
Cooking Time: 65 minutes
Serving: 4
Ingredients:
3 tablespoons soy sauce
1 tablespoon Worcestershire sauce
1/4 cup plain flour
1/4 teaspoon salt
1/2 teaspoon pepper
3 bay leaves
3 sprigs thyme
2 lbs. lean beef, cubed
3 garlic cloves
1 carrot, sliced
1 onion, sliced
6 new potatoes, halved
2 celery ribs, sliced
1 cup red wine
1 cup beef stock
2 tablespoons parsley
Directions:
Whisk seasonings with flour, soy, Worcestershire sauce, thyme, and bay leaves in a pot.
Stir cook this sauce for 5 minutes then add carrot, garlic, onion, stock, red wine, and beef.
Mix well, then spread this beef mixture into the Instant Pot Duo.
Put on the Air Fryer lid and seal it.

Hit the "Bake Button" and select 60 minutes of cooking time, then press "Start."
Once the Instant Pot Duo beeps, remove its lid.
Serve
Nutrition:
Calories 535
Total Fat 10.8g
Saturated Fat 4g
Cholesterol 149mg
Sodium 850mg
Total Carbohydrate 43.7g
Dietary Fiber 6.4g
Total Sugars 4.9g
Protein 56.2g

Chapter 8: Vegetable Recipes

Tofu with Capers

Preparation time: 20 minutes
Cooking time: 20 minutes
Servings: 4
Ingredients:
For marinade:
¼ cup fresh lemon juice
2 tablespoons fresh parsley
1 garlic clove, peeled
Salt and ground black pepper, as required
For tofu:
1 (14-oz. block extra-firm tofu, pressed and cut into 8 rectangular cutlets
½ cup mayonnaise
1 cup panko breadcrumbs
For sauce:
1 cup vegetable broth
¼ cup lemon juice
1 garlic clove, peeled
2 tablespoons fresh parsley
2 teaspoons cornstarch
Salt and ground black pepper, as required
2 tablespoons capers
Directions:
For marinade: in a food processor, add all the ingredients and pulse until smooth.
In a bowl, mix together the marinade and tofu.
Set aside for about 15-30 minutes.
In 2 shallow bowls, place the mayonnaise and panko breadcrumbs respectively.
Coat the tofu pieces with mayonnaise and then, roll into the panko.
Press "power button" of air fry oven and turn the dial to select the "air fry" mode.
Press the time button and again turn the dial to set the cooking time to 20 minutes.
Now push the temp button and rotate the dial to set the temperature at 375 degrees f.
Press "start/pause" button to start.
When the unit beeps to show that it is preheated, open the lid.
Arrange the tofu cubes in greased "air fry basket" and insert in the oven.
Flip the tofu cubes once halfway through.
Meanwhile, for the sauce: add broth, lemon juice, garlic, parsley, cornstarch, salt and black pepper in a food processor and pulse until smooth.
Transfer the sauce into a small pan and stir in the capers.
Place the pan over medium heat and bring to a boil.
Reduce the heat to low and simmer for about 5-7 minutes, stirring continuously.
Transfer the tofu cubes onto serving plates.
Top with the sauce and serve.
Nutrition: Calories 327 Total fat 18 g Saturated fat 3 g Cholesterol 8 mg Sodium 540 mg Total carbs 15.7 g Fiber 0.8 g Sugar 3 g Protein 12.4 g

Hasselback Potatoes

Preparation Time: 10 minutes
Cooking Time: 20 minutes
Serving: 2
Ingredients:
2 medium potatoes
2 rosemary springs, diced
1 1/2 tsp garlic, minced
1/4 cup butter, melted
Pepper
Salt
Directions:
Using a sharp knife to cut potato across the potato to make 1/8-inch slices.
In a small bowl, mix together butter, garlic, rosemary, pepper, and salt and brush over potatoes.
Spray instant pot multi-level air fryer basket with cooking spray.
Place potatoes into the air fryer basket and place basket into the instant pot.
Seal pot with air fryer lid and select air fry mode then set the temperature to 375 F and timer for 10 minutes.
Brush potatoes with remaining butter mixture and air fry for 10 minutes more.
Serve and enjoy.
Nutrition:
Calories 356
Fat 23.3 g
Carbohydrates 34.6 g
Sugar 2.5 g
Protein 4 g
Cholesterol 61 mg

Zucchini Fritters

Preparation Time: 10 minutes
Cooking Time: 7 minutes
Serving: 2
Ingredients:
1 egg
1/2 cup breadcrumbs
1 tsp garlic, minced
1/4 cup parmesan cheese, grated
2 cups zucchini, shredded & squeeze out all liquid
Pepper
Salt
Directions:
Add all ingredients into the bowl and mix until well combined.
Place the dehydrating tray in a multi-level air fryer basket and place basket in the instant pot.
Make patties and place on dehydrating tray.
Seal pot with air fryer lid and select air fry mode then set the temperature to 390 F and timer for 7 minutes. Turn patties after 4 minutes.
Serve and enjoy.
Nutrition:
Calories 195
Fat 6.2 g
Carbohydrates 24.3 g
Sugar 3.8 g
Protein 11.5 g

Cholesterol 90 mg

Haloumi Baked Rusti

Preparation time:10 minutes
Cooking Time: 35 minutes
Serving: 4
Ingredients:
Olive oil, to brush
7 oz. sweet potato, coarsely grated
10 oz. potatoes, coarsely grated
10 oz. carrots, coarsely grated
9 oz. halloumi, coarsely grated
1/2 onion, coarsely grated
2 tbsp thyme leaves
2 eggs
1/3 cup plain flour
1/2 cup sour cream, to serve
Fennel Salad
2 celery stalks, thinly sliced
1 fennel, thinly sliced
1/2 cup olives, chopped
Juice of 1 lemon
1 lemon quarter, chopped
1 teaspoon toasted coriander seeds, ground
Directions:
Toss sweet potato, carrot, potato, onion, halloumi, thyme, flour, and eggs in a bowl.
Spread this mixture in the Instant Pot Duo insert.
Put on the Air Fryer lid and seal it.
Hit the "Bake Button" and select 35 minutes of cooking time, then press "Start."
Once the Instant Pot Duo beeps, remove its lid.
Prepare the salad by mixing its Ingredients: in a salad bowl.
Serve the sweet potato rosti with the prepared salad.
Nutrition:
Calories 462
Total Fat 21.1g
Saturated Fat 12.8g
Cholesterol 124mg
Sodium 1064mg
Total Carbohydrate 43.9g
Dietary Fiber 5.9g
Total Sugars 8.9g
Protein 23g

Roasted Broccoli

Preparation Time: 10 minutes
Cooking Time: 8 minutes
Serving: 4
Ingredients:
1 lb broccoli florets

1 tbsp olive oil
Pepper
Salt
Directions:
Add broccoli, oil, pepper, and salt into the mixing bowl and toss well.
Spray instant pot multi-level air fryer basket with cooking spray.
Add broccoli into the air fryer basket and place basket into the instant pot.
Seal pot with air fryer lid and select air fry mode then set the temperature to 350 F and timer for 8 minutes. Stir broccoli halfway through.
Serve and enjoy.
Nutrition:
Calories 69
Fat 3.9 g
Carbohydrates 7.6 g
Sugar 1.9 g
Protein 3.2 g
Cholesterol 0 mg

Garlic Lemon Green Beans

Preparation Time: 10 minutes
Cooking Time: 10 minutes
Serving: 4
Ingredients:
1 lb green beans, Trimmed ends and cut into pieces
2 tbsp butter
1 tbsp parmesan cheese, grated
1/4 cup lemon juice
2 garlic cloves, minced
2 tbsp olive oil
Pepper
Salt
Directions:
Add beans, oil, pepper, and salt into the mixing bowl and toss well.
Spray instant pot multi-level air fryer basket with cooking spray.
Add green beans into the air fryer basket and place basket into the instant pot.
Seal pot with air fryer lid and select air fry mode then set the temperature to 390 F and timer for 10 minutes. Stir beans halfway through.
Meanwhile, in a pan, melt butter. Add garlic and saute for 30 seconds. Add lemon juice and cook for 2 minutes.
Transfer green beans into the mixing bowl. Pour melted butter mixture over green beans and toss well.
Sprinkle with parmesan cheese and serve.
Nutrition:
Calories 157
Fat 13.3 g
Carbohydrates 9 g
Sugar 1.9 g
Protein 2.8 g
Cholesterol 16 mg

Spicy Beans

Preparation Time: 10 minutes
Cooking Time: 6 minutes
Serving: 4
Ingredients:
1 lb green beans, ends trimmed
1 tsp red pepper flakes
2 tbsp garlic, minced
4 tsp red wine vinegar
1 tbsp soy sauce
2 tbsp sesame oil
Directions:
Add green beans into the mixing bowl.
Mix together oil, soy sauce, vinegar, garlic, and red pepper flakes and pour over green beans and toss well.
Spray instant pot multi-level air fryer basket with cooking spray.
Add green beans into the air fryer basket and place basket into the instant pot.
Seal pot with air fryer lid and select air fry mode then set the temperature to 400 F and timer for 6 minutes. Stir beans halfway through.
Serve and enjoy.
Nutrition:
Calories 106
Fat 7 g
Carbohydrates 10.1 g
Sugar 1.8 g
Protein 2.6 g
Cholesterol 0 mg

Delicious Pigeon Pea

Preparation time: 10 minutes
Cooking time: 7 minutes
Servings: 4
Ingredients:
1 cup split pigeon pea, rinsed and drained
1 tbsp ginger, chopped
1 green chili, sliced
1/4 tsp cumin seeds
1 tbsp olive oil
2 cups spinach
1/2 tsp garam masala
3 cups of water
1 large tomato, chopped
1 tbsp garlic, chopped
Spices:
1/4 tsp turmeric
1/2 tsp chili powder
1 tsp salt
Directions:
Add oil into the inner pot of instant pot duo crisp and set pot on sauté mode.
Add cumin seeds, garlic, ginger, and green chili and sauté for 30 seconds.
Add tomatoes and spices and sauté for 1 minute.
Add lentils and water. Stir well.
Seal the pot with pressure cooking lid and cook on high for 3 minutes.

Once done, release pressure using a quick release. Remove lid.
Set pot on sauté mode. Add spinach and garam masala and stir until spinach is wilted.
Serve and enjoy.
Nutrition: Calories 97 Fat 4.3 g Carbohydrates 12.2 g Sugar 1.6 g Protein 3.5 g Cholesterol 0 mg

---

Tofu in Sweet & Sour Sauce

Preparation time: 20 minutes
Cooking time: 20 minutes
Servings: 4
Ingredients:
For tofu:
1 (14-oz. block firm tofu, pressed and cubed
½ cup arrowroot flour
½ teaspoon sesame oil
For sauce:
4 tablespoons low-sodium soy sauce
1½ tablespoons rice vinegar
1½ tablespoons chili sauce
1 tablespoon agave nectar
2 large garlic cloves, minced
1 teaspoon fresh ginger, peeled and grated
2 scallions (green part), chopped
Directions:
In a bowl, mix together the tofu, arrowroot flour, and sesame oil.
Press "power button" of air fry oven and turn the dial to select the "air fry" mode.
Press the time button and again turn the dial to set the cooking time to 20 minutes.
Now push the temp button and rotate the dial to set the temperature at 360 degrees f.
Press "start/pause" button to start.
When the unit beeps to show that it is preheated, open the lid.
Arrange the tofu cubes in greased "air fry basket" and insert in the oven.
Flip the tofu cubes once halfway through.
Meanwhile, for the sauce: in a bowl, add all the ingredients except scallions and beat until well combined.
Transfer the tofu into a skillet with sauce over medium heat and cook for about 3 minutes, stirring occasionally.
Garnish with scallions and serve hot.
Nutrition: Calories 115 Total fat4.8 g Saturated fat 1 g Cholesterol 0 mg Sodium 1000 mg Total carbs 10.2 g Fiber 1.7 g Sugar 5.6 g Protein 10.1 g

---

Pineapple Salsa

Preparation Time: 10 minutes
Cooking Time: 8 minutes
Serving: 2
Ingredients:
1 cup pineapple, diced
1/3 cup cilantro, chopped
1 cup tomatoes, diced
1 cup peppers, diced
4 tbsp lime juice
1/4 cup onion, minced
Pepper
Salt
Directions:

Add all ingredients into the inner pot of instant pot duo crisp and stir well.
Seal the pot with pressure cooking lid and cook on high for 8 minutes.
Once done, release pressure using a quick release. Remove lid.
Stir and serve.
Nutrition:
Calories 137
Fat 1 g
Carbohydrates 35.6 g
Sugar 12.7 g
Protein 3.9 g
Cholesterol 0 mg

Italian Seasoned Cauliflower

Preparation Time: 10 minutes
Cooking Time: 12 minutes
Serving: 4
Ingredients:
1 cauliflower head, cut into florets
1/2 tsp Italian seasoning
1/2 tsp garlic powder
1 lemon zest
3 tbsp olive oil
2 tsp lemon juice
1/4 tsp pepper
1/4 tsp salt
Directions:
In a bowl, mix together olive oil, lemon juice, Italian seasoning, garlic powder, lemon zest, pepper, and salt.
Add cauliflower florets into the bowl and toss well.
Spray instant pot multi-level air fryer basket with cooking spray.
Add cauliflower florets into the air fryer basket and place basket into the instant pot.
Seal pot with air fryer lid and select air fry mode then set the temperature to 400 F and timer for 12 minutes. Stir halfway through.
Serve and enjoy.
Nutrition:
Calories 115
Fat 10.8 g
Carbohydrates 5.3 g
Sugar 2.1 g
Protein 1.6 g
Cholesterol 0 mg

Flavorful Mushroom Rice

Preparation time: 10 minutes
Cooking time: 10 minutes
Servings: 4
Ingredients:
2 cups rice, soak for 30 minutes and drained
1/2-inch cinnamon stick
2 tbsp vegetable oil

1/2 tsp caraway seed
15 oz mushrooms, sliced
2 tbsp cashews
1/4 cup coconut milk
4 cloves
2 cups of water
1/2 tsp garam masala
1 tsp chili powder
1/2 tsp turmeric
4 green cardamom
2-star anise
1 bay leaf
3 garlic cloves
1 tbsp ginger, minced
2 tbsp green chilies
1 onion, chopped
Salt

Directions:
Add oil into the inner pot of instant pot duo crisp and set pot on sauté mode.
Add cashews and sauté for a minute.
Add caraway seeds, green chilies, garlic, ginger, all dry spices and sauté for 1-2 minutes.
Add onion and cook for 2 minutes.
Add remaining ingredients and stir everything well.
Seal the pot with pressure cooking lid and cook on high for 4 minutes.
Once done, allow to release pressure naturally for 10 minutes then release remaining pressure using a quick release.
Remove lid.
Stir and serve.

Nutrition: Calories 530 Fat 14.3 g Carbohydrates 90.5 g Sugar 4.4 g Protein 12.6 g Cholesterol 0 mg

Pumpkin Lasagna

Preparation time:10 minutes
Cooking Time: 60 minutes
Serving: 6
Ingredients:
28 oz. pumpkin, cut into slices
1 bunch sage, chopped
1/2 cup ghee, melted
1 leek, thinly sliced
4 garlic cloves, finely grated
3.5 oz. kale and cavolo Nero leaves shredded
270g semi-dried tomatoes, drained, chopped
17 0z. quark
2 eggs, lightly beaten

Directions:
Mix pumpkin slices with sage leaves, 2 teaspoon salt, 2 tablespoon ghee in a bowl.
Toss leek separately with 2 tablespoon ghee, garlic, and ½ teaspoon salt in another bowl.
Mix kale with 1 teaspoon salt, tomato, and cavolo Nero in a bowl.
Now beat eggs with quark and sage in a bowl.
Take a baking pan that can fit into the Instant Pot Duo.
Add 1/3 of the leek mixture at the base of the baking pan.
Top this mixture with a layer of pumpkin slices.
Add 1/3 of quark mixture on top then add 1/3 of kale mixture over it.
Top it with pumpkin slices and continue repeating the layer while ending at the pumpkin slice layer on top.
Place the baking pan in the Instant Pot duo.

Put on the Air Fryer lid and seal it.
Hit the "Bake Button" and select 60 minutes of cooking time, then press "Start."
Once the Instant Pot Duo beeps, remove its lid.
Serve.
Nutrition:
Calories 491
Total Fat 29.9g
Saturated Fat 16.9g
Cholesterol 147mg
Sodium 1462mg
Total Carbohydrate 52.1g
Dietary Fiber 9.7g
Total Sugars 28g
Protein 14.8g

Haloumi Baked Rusti

Preparation time:10 minutes
Cooking Time: 35 minutes
Serving: 4
Ingredients:
Olive oil, to brush
7 oz. sweet potato, coarsely grated
10 oz. potatoes, coarsely grated
10 oz. carrots, coarsely grated
9 oz. halloumi, coarsely grated
1/2 onion, coarsely grated
2 tbsp thyme leaves
2 eggs
1/3 cup plain flour
1/2 cup sour cream, to serve
Fennel Salad
2 celery stalks, thinly sliced
1 fennel, thinly sliced
1/2 cup olives, chopped
Juice of 1 lemon
1 lemon quarter, chopped
1 teaspoon toasted coriander seeds, ground
Directions:
Toss sweet potato, carrot, potato, onion, halloumi, thyme, flour, and eggs in a bowl.
Spread this mixture in the Instant Pot Duo insert.
Put on the Air Fryer lid and seal it.
Hit the "Bake Button" and select 35 minutes of cooking time, then press "Start."
Once the Instant Pot Duo beeps, remove its lid.
 Prepare the salad by mixing its Ingredients: in a salad bowl.
Serve the sweet potato rosti with the prepared salad.
Nutrition:
Calories 462
Total Fat 21.1g
Saturated Fat 12.8g
Cholesterol 124mg
Sodium 1064mg
Total Carbohydrate 43.9g
Dietary Fiber 5.9g

Total Sugars 8.9g

Wheat Berry Pilaf

Preparation time: 10 minutes
Cooking time: 35 minutes
Servings: 6
Ingredients:
1 1/2 cups wheat berries, rinsed and drained
1/2 cup onion, minced
1 tsp coriander seeds
2 tsp cumin seeds
1 tbsp olive oil
3 cups of water
1 1/2 tsp turmeric
1 tbsp garlic, minced
Salt
Directions:
Add oil into the inner pot of instant pot duo crisp and set pot on sauté mode.
Add onion and cook until softened.
Add turmeric, garlic, coriander, and cumin and sauté for 2 minutes.
Add wheat berries and sauté for 2 minutes.
Add water and stir everything well.
Seal the pot with pressure cooking lid and cook on high for 30 minutes.
Once done, allow to release pressure naturally. Remove lid.
Stir well and serve.
Nutrition: Calories 84 Fat 2.9 g Carbohydrates 13.5 g Sugar 0.5 g Protein 2.4 g Cholesterol 0 mg

---

Spicy Tomato Chutney

Preparation time: 10 minutes
Cooking time: 6 minutes
Servings: 4
Ingredients:
4 green tomatoes, chopped
1/2 tsp mustard seeds
1 tbsp brown sugar
2 jalapeno pepper, chopped
1/2 tsp turmeric
1 tbsp olive oil
1 tsp salt
Directions:
Add oil into the inner pot of instant pot duo crisp and set pot on sauté mode.
Once the oil is hot then add mustard seeds and let them pop.
Add remaining ingredients and stir well.
Seal the pot with pressure cooking lid and cook on high for 5 minutes.
Once done, release pressure using a quick release. Remove lid.
Mash tomatoes mixture using a potato masher until getting the desired consistency.
Serve and enjoy.
Nutrition: Calories 66 Fat 3.9 g Carbohydrates 7.7 g Sugar 5.7 g Protein 1.3 g Cholesterol 0 mg

Simple Green Beans

Preparation Time: 5 minutes
Cooking Time: 10 minutes
Serving: 2
Ingredients:
8 oz green beans, trimmed and cut in half
1 tbsp tamari
1 tsp sesame oil
Directions:
Add all ingredients into the large mixing bowl and toss well.
Spray instant pot multi-level air fryer basket with cooking spray.
Transfer green beans into the air fryer basket and place basket into the instant pot.
Seal pot with air fryer lid and select air fry mode then set the temperature to 400 F and timer for 10 minutes. Stir halfway through.
Serve and enjoy.
Nutrition:
Calories 61
Fat 2.4 g
Carbohydrates 8.6 g
Sugar 1.7 g
Protein 3 g
Cholesterol 0 mg

Kale and Mushrooms

Preparation time: 20 minutes
Servings: 4
Ingredients:
1 lb. Brown mushrooms; sliced
1 lb. Kale, torn
14 oz. Coconut milk
2 tbsp. Olive oil
Salt and black pepper to taste.
Directions:
In a pan that fits your air fryer, mix the kale with the rest of the ingredients and toss
Put the pan in the fryer, cook at 380°f for 15 minutes, divide between plates and serve
Nutrition: Calories: 162; Fat: 4g; Fiber: 1g; Carbs: 3g; Protein: 5g

Parmesan Broccoli and Asparagus

Preparation time: 20 minutes
Servings: 4
Ingredients:
½ lb. Asparagus, trimmed
1 broccoli head, florets separated
Juice of 1 lime
3 tbsp. Parmesan, grated
2 tbsp. Olive oil
Salt and black pepper to taste.
Directions:

Take a bowl and mix the asparagus with the broccoli and all the other ingredients except the parmesan, toss, transfer to your air fryer's basket and cook at 400°f for 15 minutes
Divide between plates, sprinkle the parmesan on top and serve.
Nutrition: calories: 172; fat: 5g; fiber: 2g; carbs: 4g; protein: 9g

---

Beans & Veggie Burgers

Preparation time: 20 minutes
Cooking time: 22 minutes
Servings: 4
Ingredients:
1 cup cooked black beans
2 cups boiled potatoes, peeled and mashed
1 cup fresh spinach, chopped
1 cup fresh mushrooms, chopped
2 teaspoons chile lime seasoning
Olive oil cooking spray

Directions:
In a large bowl, add the beans, potatoes, spinach, mushrooms, and seasoning and with your hands, mix until well combined.
Make 4 equal-sized patties from the mixture.
Spray the patties with cooking spray evenly.
Press "power button" of air fry oven and turn the dial to select the "air fry" mode.
Press the time button and again turn the dial to set the cooking time to 22 minutes.
Now push the temp button and rotate the dial to set the temperature at 370 degrees f.
Press "start/pause" button to start.
When the unit beeps to show that it is preheated, open the lid.
Arrange the skewers in greased "air fry basket" and insert in the oven.
Flip the patties once after 12 minutes.
Nutrition: Calories 113 Total fat 0.4 g Saturated fat 0 g Cholesterol 0 mg Sodium 166 mg Total carbs 23.1 g Fiber 6.2 g Sugar 1.7 g Protein 6 g

---

Marinated Tofu

Preparation time: 15 minutes
Cooking time: 25 minutes
Servings: 4
Ingredients:
2 tablespoon low-sodium soy sauce
2 tablespoon fish sauce
1 teaspoon olive oil
12 oz. Extra-firm tofu, drained and cubed into 1-inch size
1 teaspoon butter, melted
Directions:
In a large bowl, add the soy sauce, fish sauce and oil and mix until well combined.
Add the tofu cubes and toss to coat well.
Set aside to marinate for about 30 minutes, tossing occasionally.
Press "power button" of air fry oven and turn the dial to select the "air fry" mode.
Press the time button and again turn the dial to set the cooking time to 25 minutes.
Now push the temp button and rotate the dial to set the temperature at 355 degrees f.
Press "start/pause" button to start.
When the unit beeps to show that it is preheated, open the lid.

Arrange the tofu cubes in greased "air fry basket" and insert in the oven.
Flip the tofu after every 10 minutes during the cooking.
Serve hot.
Nutrition: Calories 102 Total fat 7.1 g Saturated fat 1.2 g Cholesterol 3 mg Sodium 1100 mg Total carbs 2.5 g Fiber 0.3 g Sugar 1.3 g Protein 9.4 g

---

Crusted Tofu

Preparation time: 15 minutes
Cooking time: 28 minutes
Servings: 3
Ingredients:
1 (14-oz. block firm tofu, pressed and cubed into ½-inch size
2 tablespoons cornstarch
¼ cup rice flour
Salt and ground black pepper, as required
2 tablespoons olive oil
Directions:
In a bowl, mix together the cornstarch, rice flour, salt, and black pepper.
Coat the tofu with flour mixture evenly.
Then, drizzle the tofu with oil.
Press "power button" of air fry oven and turn the dial to select the "air fry" mode.
Press the time button and again turn the dial to set the cooking time to 28 minutes.
Now push the temp button and rotate the dial to set the temperature at 360 degrees f.
Press "start/pause" button to start.
When the unit beeps to show that it is preheated, open the lid.
Arrange the tofu cubes in greased "air fry basket" and insert in the oven.
Flip the tofu cubes once halfway through.
Serve hot.
Nutrition: Calories 241 Total fat 15 g Saturated fat 2.5 g Cholesterol 0 mg Sodium 67 mg Total carbs 17.7 g Fiber 1.6 g Sugar 0.8 g Protein 11.6 g

---

Turmeric Cabbage

Preparation time: 20 minutes
Servings: 4
Ingredients:
1 green cabbage head, shredded
¼ cup ghee; melted
1 tbsp. Dill; chopped.
2 tsp. Turmeric powder
Directions:
In a pan that fits your air fryer, mix the cabbage with the rest of the ingredients except the dill, toss, put the pan in the fryer and cook at 370°f for 15 minutes
Divide everything between plates and serve with dill sprinkled on top.
Nutrition: Calories: 173; Fat: 5g; Fiber: 3g; Carbs: 6g; Protein: 7g

---

Flavors Eggplant

Preparation Time: 10 minutes
Cooking Time: 12 minutes
Serving: 2

Ingredients:
1 eggplant, washed and cubed
1/4 tsp oregano
1 tbsp olive oil
1/2 tsp garlic powder
1/4 tsp marjoram
Directions:
Add all ingredients into the mixing bowl and toss well.
Spray instant pot multi-level air fryer basket with cooking spray.
Transfer eggplant into the air fryer basket and place basket into the instant pot.
Seal pot with air fryer lid and select air fry mode then set the temperature to 390 F and timer for 12 minutes. Stir halfway through.
Serve and enjoy.
Nutrition:
Calories 120
Fat 7.5 g
Carbohydrates 14.2 g
Sugar 7.1 g
Protein 2.4 g
Cholesterol 0 mg

Air-fried Avocado

Preparation Time: 10 minutes
Cooking Time: 10 minutes
Servings: 2
Ingredients
½ cup all-purpose flour
2 avocados
2 large eggs
2 tbsps. canola mayonnaise
1 tbsp. apple cider vinegar
1 tbsp. Sriracha chili sauce
1½ tsps. black pepper
¼ tsp. Kosher salt
½ cup Panko bread crumbs
¼ cup no-salt-added ketchup
1 tbsp. water
Cooking spray
Directions
Cut avocados into 4 wedges each. Prepare 3 shallow dishes.
In the first shallow dish, combine avocado wedges with flour and pepper.
In another dish, lightly beat eggs.
Place breadcrumbs in the third dish.
First, dredge avocado wedges in the flour mixture, one after the other. After coating with flour, shake lightly to remove excess flour and dip the avocado to the egg mixture, likewise shaking lightly to drip off excess liquid.
Finally, dip each wedge to the breadcrumbs coating them evenly on all sides and spray with cooking oil.
Arrange avocado wedges in the instant pot duo air fryer basket, place inside the pot, and cover with the air fryer lid. Set to air fry at 400 degrees F until wedges turn golden brown, turning them over halfway through cooking.
Remove avocado wedges from the fryer and sprinkle them with salt.
Meanwhile, while waiting for the avocado wedges to get cooked, mix mayonnaise, ketchup, apple cider vinegar, water and Sriracha sauce in a small bowl.
Serve the prepared sauce with the avocado wedges while still warm.
Nutrition: Calories – 274 kcal; Fat – 18g; Carbohydrates – 23g; Protein –5g; sugar –5g; Fiber – 7g; Sodium – 306mg

Mediterranean Veggies

Preparation Time: 5 minutes
Cooking Time: 20 minutes
Servings: 4
Ingredients
1 large courgetti
2 oz. cherry tomatoes
1 green pepper
1 medium carrot
1 large parsnip
1 tsp. mixed herbs
2 tbsps. honey
3 tbsps. olive oil
2 tsps. garlic puree
1 tsp. mustard
Salt and pepper to taste
Directions
Slice up the courgette and the green pepper.
Peel and dice the carrot and the parsnip.
Add them all altogether in the air fryer basket of the instant pot duo along with raw cherry tomatoes, herbs, garlic puree, mustard, salt and pepper. Drizzle with three tablespoons of olive oil.
Place the air fryer in the pot and air fry for 15 minutes at 356 degrees F using the instant pot duo crisp air fryer.
Sprinkle with more salt if needed and serve.
Nutrition: Calories – 281 kcal; Fat – 21g; Carbohydrates – 21g; Protein –2g; sugar –13g; Fiber – 3g; Sodium – 36mg

Air Fried Bell Peppers

Preparation Time: 5 minutes
Cooking Time: 8 minutes
Serving: 3
Ingredients:
3 cups bell peppers, cut into chunks
1/4 tsp garlic powder
1 tsp olive oil
Pepper
Salt
Directions:
Add all ingredients into the mixing bowl and toss well.
Spray instant pot multi-level air fryer basket with cooking spray.
Transfer bell peppers into the air fryer basket and place basket into the instant pot.
Seal pot with air fryer lid and select air fry mode then set the temperature to 360 F and timer for 8 minutes. Stir halfway through.
Serve and enjoy.
Nutrition:
Calories 52
Fat 1.9 g
Carbohydrates 9.2 g
Sugar 6.1 g
Protein 1.2 g

Cholesterol 0 mg

Tasty Cauliflower & Broccoli

Preparation Time: 10 minutes
Cooking Time: 12 minutes
Serving: 6
Ingredients:
3 cups cauliflower florets
1/2 tsp garlic powder
2 tbsp olive oil
1/4 tsp onion powder
3 cups broccoli florets
1/4 tsp paprika
1/8 tsp pepper
1/4 tsp sea salt
Directions:
Add cauliflower and broccoli into the large bowl. Add remaining ingredients and toss well.
Spray instant pot multi-level air fryer basket with cooking spray.
Transfer broccoli and cauliflower mixture into the air fryer basket and place basket into the instant pot.
Seal pot with air fryer lid and select air fry mode then set the temperature to 380 F and timer for 12 minutes. Stir halfway through.
Serve and enjoy.
Nutrition:
Calories 69
Fat 4.9 g
Carbohydrates 6 g
Sugar 2.1 g
Protein 2.3 g
Cholesterol 0 mg

Brussels Pancetta Pizza

Preparation time:5-10 Minutes
Cooking Time: 20 Minutes
Serving: 4-6
Ingredients:
2 cloves garlic, minced
Brussels sprouts, trimmed and thinly sliced, to taste 1 (1 1/2-inch thick) medium-size pizza crust
9 slices pancetta
2 teaspoons extra-virgin olive oil
1/2 teaspoon fennel seeds

Directions:
Place Instant Pot Air Fryer Crisp over kitchen platform. Press "Sauté," select "Hi" setting and press "Start." In the inner pot, add 1 tablespoon oil and allow it to heat.
Add the pancetta and stir-cook until it becomes softened for 4-5 minutes. Drain over paper towels.
Add remaining oil and garlic and stir-cook until it becomes fragrant for 20-30 seconds. Mix in the sprouts and stir-cook until softened 5-10 minutes.
Add the sprouts and garlic to a bowl; add the pancetta, cheese, and fennel seed. Toss well.

Place Instant Pot Air Fryer Crisp over kitchen platform. Press Air Fry, set the temperature to 400°F and set the timer to 5 minutes to preheat. Press "Start" and allow it to preheat for 5 minutes.

In the inner pot, place the Air Fryer basket. Line it with a parchment paper and arrange the pizza crust over. On top, add the prepared mixture.

Close the Crisp Lid and press the "Bake" setting. Set temperature to 450°F and set the timer to 12-15 minutes. Press "Start." Cook until the crust becomes golden brown.

Open the Crisp Lid after cooking time is over. Slice and serve warm.

Nutrition: **Calories: 356**
Fat: 22g
Saturated Fat: 5g
Trans Fat: 0g
Carbohydrates: 39g
Fiber: 5g
Sodium: 972mg
Protein: 26.5g

Cheesy Brussels Sprouts

Preparation time: 5-10 Minutes
Cooking Time: 16 Minutes
Serving: 2-3

Ingredients:
 1 tablespoon extra-virgin olive oil
1 teaspoon garlic powder
2 tablespoon parmesan cheese, grated
1/2-pound Brussels sprouts, thinly sliced
Caesar dressing for dipping
Black pepper, ground and Kosher salt to taste

Directions:
In a mixing bowl, add the oil, Brussels sprouts, garlic powder, and Parmesan cheese. Combine the ingredients to mix well with each other. Season with black pepper and salt to taste.

Place Instant Pot Air Fryer Crisp over kitchen platform. Press Air Fry set the temperature to 400°F and set the timer to 5 minutes to preheat. Press "Start" and allow it to preheat for 5 minutes.

In the inner pot, place the Air Fryer basket. In the basket, add the Brussels sprouts.

Close the Crisp Lid and press the "Air Fry" setting. Set temperature to 350°F and set the timer to 16 minutes. Press "Start."

Halfway down, open the Crisp Lid, shake the basket and close the lid to continue cooking for the remaining time until becoming crisp and golden brown.

Open the Crisp Lid after cooking time is over. Serve warm with the Parmesan cheese on top.

Nutrition: **Calories: 198**
Fat: 11g
Saturated Fat: 4g
Trans Fat: 0g
Carbohydrates: 17g
Fiber: 5g
Sodium: 346mg
Protein: 7g

Veggie Kabobs

Preparation time: 20 minutes
Cooking time: 10 minutes

Servings: 6
Ingredients:
¼ cup carrots, peeled and chopped
¼ cup French beans
½ cup green peas
1 teaspoon ginger
3 garlic cloves, peeled
3 green chilies
¼ cup fresh mint leaves
½ cup cottage cheese
2 medium boiled potatoes, mashed
½ teaspoon five spice powder
Salt, to taste
2 tablespoons corn flour
Olive oil cooking spray
Directions:
In a food processor, add the carrot, beans, peas, ginger, garlic, mint, cheese and pulse until smooth.
Transfer the mixture into a bowl.
Add the potato, five spice powder, salt and corn flour and mix until well combined.
Divide the mixture into equal sized small balls.
Press each ball around a skewer in a sausage shape.
Spray the skewers with cooking spray.
Press "power button" of air fry oven and turn the dial to select the "air fry" mode.
Press the time button and again turn the dial to set the cooking time to 10 minutes.
Now push the temp button and rotate the dial to set the temperature at 390 degrees f.
Press "start/pause" button to start.
When the unit beeps to show that it is preheated, open the lid.
Arrange the skewers in greased "air fry basket" and insert in the oven.
Serve warm.
Nutrition: Calories 120 Total fat 0.8 g Saturated fat 0.3 g Cholesterol 2 mg Sodium 115 mg Total carbs 21.9 g Fiber 4.9 g Sugar 1.8 g Protein 6.3 g

Roasted Squash

Preparation Time: 10 minutes
Cooking Time: 12 minutes
Serving: 4
Ingredients:
1 lb butternut squash, peeled and cut into chunks
1 tsp thyme
1 tbsp sage
1 tbsp olive oil
Pepper
Salt
Directions:
Add squash and remaining ingredients into the large bowl and toss well.
Line instant pot multi-level air fryer basket with foil.
Add squash mixture into the air fryer basket and place basket into the instant pot.
Seal pot with air fryer lid and select air fry mode then set the temperature to 390 F and timer for 12 minutes. Stir after 10 minutes.
Serve and enjoy.
Nutrition:
Calories 83
Fat 3.7 g
Carbohydrates 13.7 g

Sugar 2.5 g
Protein 1.2 g
Cholesterol 0 mg

Air Fried Ratatouille

Preparation Time: 10 minutes
Cooking Time: 15 minutes
Serving: 6
Ingredients:
1 eggplant, diced
2 bell peppers, diced
1 tbsp vinegar
1 1/2 tbsp olive oil
2 tbsp herb de Provence
3 garlic cloves, chopped
1 onion, diced
3 tomatoes, diced
Pepper
Salt
Directions:
Line instant pot multi-level air fryer basket with foil.
Add all ingredients into the bowl and toss well and transfer into the air fryer basket and place basket into the instant pot.
Seal pot with air fryer lid and select air fry mode then set the temperature to 400 F and timer for 15 minutes. Stir halfway through.
Serve and enjoy.
Nutrition:
Calories 91
Fat 4.3 g
Carbohydrates 12.1 g
Sugar 6.7 g
Protein 2.9 g
Cholesterol 0 mg

Asian Cauliflower

Preparation Time: 10 minutes
Cooking Time: 10 minutes
Serving: 2
Ingredients:
1/2 cauliflower head, cut into florets
1/2 tbsp vinegar
3/4 tbsp tamari
2 garlic cloves, sliced
1/4 cup onion, sliced
1 green onion, sliced
1/2 tbsp hot sauce
1/4 tsp coconut sugar
Directions:
Line instant pot multi-level air fryer basket with foil.

Add cauliflower florets into the air fryer basket and place basket into the instant pot.

Seal pot with air fryer lid and select air fry mode then set the temperature to 400 F and timer for 10 minutes. Stir halfway through.

Transfer cauliflower into the mixing bowl. Add remaining ingredients and toss well.

Serve and enjoy.

Nutrition:
Calories 46
Fat 0.1 g
Carbohydrates 9.2 g
Sugar 2.6 g
Protein 2.7 g
Cholesterol 0 mg

Veggie Ratatouille

Preparation time: 15 minutes
Cooking time: 15 minutes
Servings: 4
Ingredients:
1 green bell pepper, seeded and chopped
1 yellow bell pepper, seeded and chopped
1 eggplant, chopped
1 zucchini, chopped
3 tomatoes, chopped
2 small onions, chopped
2 garlic cloves, minced
2 tablespoons herbs de provence
1 tablespoon olive oil
1 tablespoon balsamic vinegar
Salt and ground black pepper, as required
Directions:
In a large bowl, add the vegetables, garlic, herbs de provence, oil, vinegar, salt, and black pepper and toss to coat well.
Transfer vegetable mixture into a greased baking pan.
Press "power button" of air fry oven and turn the dial to select the "air fry" mode.
Press the time button and again turn the dial to set the cooking time to 15 minutes.
Now push the temp button and rotate the dial to set the temperature at 355 degrees f.
Press "start/pause" button to start.
When the unit beeps to show that it is preheated, open the lid.
Arrange the pan over the "wire rack" and insert in the oven.
Serve hot.
Nutrition: Calories 119 Total fat 4.2 g Saturated fat 0.6 g Cholesterol 0 mg Sodium 54 mg Total carbs 20.3 g Fiber 7.3 g Sugar 11.2 g Protein 3.6 g

Glazed Veggies

Preparation time: 015 minutes
Cooking time: 20 minutes
Servings: 4
Ingredients:
2 oz. Cherry tomatoes
2 large zucchinis, chopped

2 green bell peppers, seeded and chopped
6 tablespoons olive oil, divided
2 tablespoons honey
1 teaspoon dijon mustard
1 teaspoon dried herbs
1 teaspoon garlic paste
Salt, as required

Directions:
In a parchment paper-lined baking pan, place the vegetables and drizzle with 3 tablespoons of oil.
Press "power button" of air fry oven and turn the dial to select the "air fry" mode.
Press the time button and again turn the dial to set the cooking time to 15 minutes.
Now push the temp button and rotate the dial to set the temperature at 355 degrees f.
Press "start/pause" button to start.
When the unit beeps to show that it is preheated, open the lid.
Arrange the pan over the "wire rack" and insert in the oven.
Meanwhile, in a bowl, add the remaining oil, honey, mustard, herbs, garlic, salt, and black pepper and mix well.
After 15 minutes of cooking, add the honey mixture into vegetable mixture and mix well.
Now, set the temperature to 392 degrees f for 5 minutes.
Serve immediately.
Nutrition: Calories 262 Total fat 21.5 g Saturated fat 3.1 g Cholesterol 0 mg Sodium 72 mg Total carbs 19.5 g Fiber 2.9 g Sugar 14.8 g Protein 2.8 g

Parmesan Mixed Veggies

Preparation time: 15 minutes
Cooking time: 18 minutes
Servings: 5
Ingredients:
1 tablespoon olive oil
1 tablespoon garlic, minced
1 cup cauliflower florets
1 cup broccoli florets
1 cup zucchini, sliced
½ cup yellow squash, sliced
½ cup fresh mushrooms, sliced
1 small onion, sliced
¼ cup balsamic vinegar
1 teaspoon red pepper flakes
Salt and ground black pepper, as required
¼ cup parmesan cheese, grated
Directions:
In a large bowl, add all the ingredients except cheese and toss to coat well.
Press "power button" of air fry oven and turn the dial to select the "air fry" mode.
Press the time button and again turn the dial to set the cooking time to 18 minutes.
Now push the temp button and rotate the dial to set the temperature at 400 degrees f.
Press "start/pause" button to start.
When the unit beeps to show that it is preheated, open the lid.
Arrange the vegetables in greased "air fry basket" and insert in the oven.
After 8 minutes of cooking, flip the vegetables.
After 16 minutes of cooking, sprinkle the vegetables with cheese evenly.
Serve hot.
Nutrition: Calories 102 Total fat 6.2 g Saturated fat 2.4 g Cholesterol 12 mg Sodium 352 mg Total carbs 6.6 g Fiber 1.9 g Sugar 2.2 g Protein 6.6 g

Roasted Beans

Preparation time: 10 minutes
Cooking time: 30 minutes
Servings: 4
Ingredients:
1 lb green beans
1/2 tsp onion powder
2 tbsp olive oil
3/4 tsp garlic powder
1/2 tsp pepper
1/2 tsp salt
Directions:
In a large bowl, add all ingredients and toss well.
Arrange green beans into the instant pot air fryer basket and place basket in the pot.
Seal the pot with air fryer lid and select bake mode and cook at 400 f for 25-30 minutes.
Serve and enjoy.
Nutrition: Calories 99 Fat 7.2 g Carbohydrates 8.9 g Sugar 1.8 g Protein 2.2 g Cholesterol 0 mg

Parmesan Zucchini & Eggplant

Preparation time: 10 minutes
Cooking time: 35 minutes
Servings: 6
Ingredients:
1 eggplant, sliced
1 tbsp olive oil
1 tbsp garlic, minced
1 cup cherry tomatoes, halved
3 medium zucchinis, sliced
1/4 cup basil, chopped
3 oz parmesan cheese, grated
1/4 cup parsley, chopped
1/4 tsp pepper
1/4 tsp salt
Directions:
Line instant pot air fryer basket with parchment paper or foil.
In a mixing bowl, add cherry tomatoes, eggplant, zucchini, olive oil, garlic, cheese, basil, pepper, and salt toss well.
Transfer vegetable mixture into the air fryer basket and place basket in the pot.
Seal the pot with air fryer basket and select bake mode and cook at 350 f for 35 minutes.
Garnish with parsley and serve.
Nutrition: Calories 109 Fat 5.8 g Carbohydrates 10.2 g Sugar 4.8 g Protein 7 g Cholesterol 10 mg

Roasted Carrots & Potatoes

Preparation Time: 10 minutes
Cooking Time: 14 minutes
Serving: 4
Ingredients:
1/2 lb baby carrots, diced
1/2 lb baby potatoes, diced
1 tbsp dried parsley
1 tbsp dried thyme

1 tbsp dried rosemary
2 tbsp olive oil
Pepper
Salt
Directions:
Add carrots and potatoes into the mixing bowl. Add remaining ingredients and toss well.
Spray instant pot multi-level air fryer basket with cooking spray.
Add potatoes and carrots into the air fryer basket and place basket into the instant pot.
Seal pot with air fryer lid and select air fry mode then set the temperature to 370 F and timer for 14 minutes. Stir halfway through.
Serve and enjoy.
Nutrition:
Calories 118
Fat 7.3 g
Carbohydrates 12.8 g
Sugar 2.7 g
Protein 2 g
Cholesterol 0 mg

Air Fried Mushrooms

Preparation Time: 5 minutes
Cooking Time: 8 minutes
Serving: 2
Ingredients:
12 button mushrooms, cleaned
1 tsp olive oil
1/4 tsp Pepper
1/4 tsp garlic salt
Directions:
Add all ingredients into the bowl and toss well.
Spray instant pot multi-level air fryer basket with cooking spray.
Transfer mushrooms into the air fryer basket and place basket into the instant pot.
Seal pot with air fryer lid and select air fry mode then set the temperature to 380 F and timer for 8 minutes. Stir halfway through.
Serve and enjoy.
Nutrition:
Calories 45
Fat 2.7 g
Carbohydrates 4 g
Sugar 1.9 g
Protein 3.5 g
Cholesterol 0 mg

Indian Potato Curry

Preparation time: 10 minutes
Cooking time: 7 minutes
Servings: 4
Ingredients:
2 medium potatoes, peeled and chopped

1/2 tsp garam masala
1 serrano, minced
1/2 cup onion masala
1 tsp cumin seeds
1 1/2 cups water
2 cups fresh peas
2 tbsp olive oil
1/4 tsp pepper
1 tsp salt

Directions:

Add oil into the inner pot of instant pot duo crisp and set pot on sauté mode.
Add serrano pepper and cumin seeds and sauté for 1-2 minutes.
Add remaining ingredients and stir well.
Seal the pot with pressure cooking lid and cook on high for 5 minutes.
Once done, release pressure using a quick release. Remove lid.
Serve and enjoy.

Nutrition: Calories 244 Fat 9.5 g Carbohydrates 33.4 g Sugar 6.2 g Protein 7.7 g Cholesterol 2 mg

Veggie Quinoa

Preparation time: 10 minutes
Cooking time: 7 minutes
Servings: 4
Ingredients:
1 1/2 cups quinoa, rinsed and drained
1 carrot, chopped
1 cup green beans, chopped
1 potato, cubed
1 tomato, chopped
1 small onion, chopped
2 tsp ginger paste
1 garlic clove, minced
1/4 cup cilantro, chopped
1 1/2 cups water
1/4 cup coconut milk
1 tsp garam masala
1/2 tsp chili powder
1/2 tsp black pepper
1/4 tsp turmeric
1 bay leaf
4 cloves
1 tsp cumin seeds
2-star anise
2 tbsp olive oil
Salt

Directions:

Add oil into the inner pot of instant pot duo crisp and set pot on sauté mode.
Add cumin seeds, cloves, and star anise and sauté for 30 seconds.
Add ginger and garlic and sauté for 1 minute.
Add tomatoes, onions, and dry spices and sauté for 1-2 minutes.
Add all the vegetables, salt, and coconut milk, water, and quinoa. Stir well.
Seal the pot with pressure cooking lid and cook on high for 4 minutes.
Once done, allow to release pressure naturally for 10 minutes then release remaining pressure using a quick release.
Remove lid.
Serve and enjoy.

Nutrition: Calories 404 Fat 15.2 g Carbohydrates 58 g Sugar 3.2 g Protein 11.8 g Cholesterol 0 mg

---

Healthy Quinoa Black Bean Chili

Preparation time: 10 minutes
Cooking time: 12 minutes
Servings: 6
Ingredients:
1/2 cup quinoa, rinsed and drained
14 oz can black beans, rinsed and drained
14 oz can tomato, diced
2 tbsp tomato paste
4 cups vegetable broth
2 celery stalks, diced
1 tsp garlic, minced
1 onion, chopped
1 tsp chili powder
1 tsp ground coriander
2 tsp ground cumin
2 tsp paprika
3 sweet potatoes, peeled and diced
1 bell pepper, diced
1 tsp salt
Directions:
Add all ingredients into the inner pot of instant pot duo crisp and stir well.
Seal the pot with pressure cooking lid and cook on high for 12 minutes.
Once done, release pressure using a quick release. Remove lid.
Stir and serve.
Nutrition: Calories 267 Fat 2.6 g Carbohydrates 51.2 g Sugar 6.2 g Protein 11.5 g Cholesterol 0 mg

---

Garlic Basil Carrots

Preparation Time: 10 minutes
Cooking Time: 20 minutes
Serving: 4
Ingredients:
15 baby carrots
6 garlic cloves, minced
4 tbsp olive oil
1 tbsp fresh parsley, chopped
1 tbsp dried basil
1 1/2 tsp salt
Directions:
In a bowl, toss together with oil, carrots, basil, garlic, and salt.
Spray instant pot multi-level air fryer basket with cooking spray.
Transfer carrots into the air fryer basket and place basket into the instant pot.
Seal pot with air fryer lid and select air fry mode then set the temperature to 350 F and timer for 20 minutes. Stir halfway through.
Garnish with parsley and serve.
Nutrition:
Calories 140
Fat 14.1 g
Carbohydrates 4.7 g

Sugar 1.9 g
Protein 0.6 g
Cholesterol 0 mg

Toasted Coco Flakes

Preparation time: 8 minutes
Cooking Time: 20 minutes
Servings: 4
Ingredients:
1 cup unsweetened coconut flakes
¼ cup granular erythritol.
2 tsp. Coconut oil
⅛ tsp. Salt
Directions:
Toss coconut flakes and oil in a large bowl until coated.
Sprinkle with erythritol and salt.
Place coconut flakes into the air fryer basket.
Adjust the temperature to 300 degrees f and set the timer for 3 minutes.
Toss the flakes when 1-minute remains.
Add an extra minute if you would like a more golden coconut flake.
Store in an airtight container up to 3 days.
Nutrition: Calories: 165; Protein: 1.3g; Fiber: 2.7g; Fat: 15.5g; Carbs: 20.3g

Celeriac Potato Gratin

Preparation time: 10 minutes
Cooking Time: 63 minutes
Serving: 6
Ingredients:
2 cups cream
1 teaspoon caraway seeds, toasted
1 garlic clove, crushed
1 teaspoon fennel seeds, toasted
2 bay leaves
1/4 teaspoon ground cloves
Zest of 1/2 a lemon
2 teaspoon melted butter
1kg potatoes, peeled
1 cup celeriac, peeled and minced
6 slices prosciutto, torn
3/4 cup fresh ricotta
¼ cup fontina cheese, grated
Directions:
Add cream, garlic, caraway seeds, cloves, bay leaves, fennel, zest, and cloves to a saucepan.
Stir cook this mixture for 3 minutes then remove from the heat.
Thinly slices potato by passing through the mandolin and spread the potatoes in the insert of Instant Pot Duo.
Top the potato with celeriac, prepared white sauce, prosciutto, and ricotta.
Put on the Air Fryer lid and seal it.
Hit the "Bake Button" and select 60 minutes of cooking time, then press "Start."
Once the Instant Pot Duo beeps, remove its lid.
Serve.
Nutrition:

Calories 399
Total Fat 20.3g
Saturated Fat 10.9g
Cholesterol 99mg
Sodium 1484mg
Total Carbohydrate 23.6g
Dietary Fiber 3.8g
Total Sugars 4.8g
Protein 31.3g

Eggplant Pine Nut Roast

Preparation time: 10 minutes
Cooking Time: 66 minutes
Serving: 6
Ingredients:
6 Japanese eggplants
2/3 cup olive oil
1 onion, finely chopped
4 garlic cloves, crushed
1 1/2 tbsp sundried tomato pesto
1 teaspoon smoked paprika
14 oz. can cherry tomatoes
1 teaspoon zaatar, plus extra to serve
2/3 cup vegetable stock
1/2 bunch mint, chopped
2 tbsp toasted pine nuts, roughly crushed
1/4 cup Greek yogurt
Juice of 1 lemon
Directions:
Add eggplants to the Air Fryer Basket and pour 2 tablespoon oil over them.
Set the Air Fryer Basket in the Instant Pot Duo.
Put on the Air Fryer lid and seal it.
Hit the "Bake Button" and select 30 minutes of cooking time, then press "Start."
Once the Instant Pot Duo beeps, remove its lid.
Meanwhile, prepare the sauce by sautéing onion with remaining oil in a pan.
After 4 minutes, add garlic to sauté for 2 minutes.
Add tomato, stock, zaatar, paprika and tomato pesto.
Cook this sauce for 10 minutes until it thickens.
Pour this sauce over the eggplant and continue baking it for another 20 minutes.
Mix yogurt with lemon juice, mint, and pine nuts.
Serve the baked eggplants with yogurt.
Nutrition:
Calories 413
Total Fat 25g
Saturated Fat 3.7g
Cholesterol 0mg
Sodium 85mg
Total Carbohydrate 45g
Dietary Fiber 22.1g
Total Sugars 27.2g
Protein 9.2g

Roasted Veggie Casserole

Preparation time: 10 minutes
Cooking Time: 50 minutes
Serving: 6
Ingredients:
½ head cauliflower, cut into chunks
1 sweet potato, peeled and cubed
2 red bell peppers, cubed
1 yellow onion, sliced
3 tablespoons olive oil
1 teaspoon ground cumin
Salt
Freshly ground black pepper
2 ¼ cups red salsa
½ cup chopped fresh cilantro
9 corn tortillas cut in half
1 can (15 oz.) black beans, drained
2 big handfuls (about 2 oz.) baby spinach leaves
2 cups Monterey Jack cheese, shredded
Directions:
Toss the vegetables with olive oil, salt, black pepper, and cumin in a large bowl.
Add these vegetables to the Air Fryer Basket and set it inside the Instant Pot Duo.
Put on the Air Fryer lid and seal it.
Hit the "Bake Button" and select 30 minutes of cooking time, then press "Start."
Once the Instant Pot Duo beeps, remove its lid.
Transfer the veggies to a baking pan and top it with salsa, tortilla, beans, spinach, and cheese.
Place this pan in the Instant Pot Duo.
Put on the Air Fryer lid and seal it.
Hit the "Bake Button" and select 20 minutes of cooking time, then press "Start."
Once the Instant Pot Duo beeps, remove its lid.
Serve.
Nutrition:
Calories 390
Total Fat 20.5g
Saturated Fat 8.4g
Cholesterol 34mg
Sodium 686mg
Total Carbohydrate 38.7g
Dietary Fiber 7.4g
Total Sugars 9.6g
Protein 15.8g

Chapter 9: Dehydrator and Casserole Recipes

Eggplant Jerky

Preparation Time: 10 minutes
Cooking Time: 12 hours
Serving: 4

Ingredients:
1 eggplant, sliced
1 tsp paprika
1/2 tsp black pepper
1 garlic clove, minced
1/2 cup vinegar
1/2 cup olive oil
1/2 tsp sea salt
Directions:
Add eggplant slices into the large bowl.
Add remaining ingredients and toss well. Cover and set aside for 2 hours.
Place the dehydrating tray in a multi-level air fryer basket and place basket in the instant pot.
Arrange marinated eggplant slices on dehydrating tray.
Seal pot with air fryer lid and select dehydrate mode then set temperature to 115 F and timer for 12 hours.
Serve and enjoy.
Nutrition:
Calories 254
Fat 25.5 g
Carbohydrates 7.7 g
Sugar 3.6 g
Protein 1.3 g
Cholesterol 0 mg

Dehydrated Pear Slices

Preparation Time: 10 minutes
Cooking Time: 5 hours
Serving: 3
Ingredients:
2 pears, cut into 1/4-inch thick slices
1 tbsp lemon juice
Directions:
In a large bowl, mix lemon juice and 2 cups of water.
Add pear slices into the lemon water and soak for 10 minutes.
Place the dehydrating tray in a multi-level air fryer basket and place basket in the instant pot.
Place pear slices on the dehydrating tray.
Seal pot with air fryer lid and select dehydrate mode then set temperature to 160 F and timer for 5 hours.
Serve and enjoy.
Nutrition:
Calories 82
Fat 0.2 g
Carbohydrates 21.3 g
Sugar 13.7 g
Protein 0.5 g
Cholesterol 0 mg

Sausage Casserole

Preparation Time: 10 minutes
Cooking Time: 30 minutes
Serving: 8

Ingredients:
1 lb ground sausage
1/2 tsp garlic powder
8 oz Velveeta cheese
1 cup milk
10 oz cream of mushroom soup
10 oz cream of chicken soup
2 cups cooked macaroni
Pepper

Directions:
Add sausage into the instant pot and saute until browned. Turn off the saute mode.
Add remaining ingredients and stir everything well.
Seal pot with air fryer lid and select bake mode then set the temperature to 350 F and timer for 30 minutes.
Serve and enjoy.

Nutrition:
Calories 414
Fat 26.2 g
Carbohydrates 24.1 g
Sugar 4.4 g
Protein 21 g
Cholesterol 73 mg

Squash Casserole

Preparation Time: 10 minutes
Cooking Time: 35 minutes
Serving: 8

Ingredients:
4 1/2 lbs yellow squash, cut into bite-size pieces
2 tbsp mayonnaise
1 1/2 cups cheddar cheese, shredded
1 egg, lightly beaten
10 oz cream of celery soup
1 cup onion, chopped
Pepper
Salt

For topping:
1/2 cup butter, melted
1 cup crushed crackers

Directions:
Add squash pieces into the boiling water and boil until tender. Drain well and set aside.
Mix together squash, onion, celery soup, egg, mayonnaise, pepper, and salt and pour into the instant pot.
Sprinkle cheddar cheese on top.
Seal pot with air fryer lid and select bake mode then set the temperature to 350 F and timer for 20 minutes.
Mix together butter and crushed crackers and sprinkle on top.
Seal pot with air fryer lid and select bake mode then set the temperature to 350 F and timer for 15 minutes.
Serve and enjoy.

Nutrition:
Calories 281
Fat 22.4 g
Carbohydrates 13.6 g
Sugar 5.9 g
Protein 9.8 g

Cholesterol 78 mg

Apple Chips

Preparation Time: 10 minutes
Cooking Time: 8 hours
Serving: 2
Ingredients:
1 apple, cut into 1/8-inch thick slices
1/4 tbsp ground cinnamon
1/4 tbsp granulated sugar
Directions:
Add apple slices, cinnamon, and sugar into the large bowl and mix well.
Place the dehydrating tray in a multi-level air fryer basket and place basket in the instant pot.
Arrange apple slices on dehydrating tray.
Seal pot with air fryer lid and select dehydrate mode then set temperature to 130 F and timer for 8 hours.
Serve and enjoy.
Nutrition:
Calories 66
Fat 0.2 g
Carbohydrates 17.6 g
Sugar 13.1 g
Protein 0.3 g
Cholesterol 0 mg

Apple Sweet Potato Fruit Leather

Preparation Time: 10 minutes
Cooking Time: 4 hours
Serving: 2
Ingredients:
1/2 cup mashed sweet potatoes
1/4 tsp cinnamon
1 tbsp honey
1/2 cup applesauce
Directions:
Add all ingredients into the blender and blend until smooth.
Place the dehydrating tray in a multi-level air fryer basket and place basket in the instant pot.
Line dehydrating tray with parchment paper.
Spread blended mixture on dehydrating tray.
Seal pot with air fryer lid and select dehydrate mode then set temperature to 110 F and timer for 4 hours or until leathery.
Serve and enjoy.
Nutrition:
Calories 123
Fat 0.2 g
Carbohydrates 30.6 g
Sugar 18.3 g
Protein 1.4 g
Cholesterol 0 mg

Dehydrated Mango

Preparation Time: 10 minutes
Cooking Time: 14 hours
Serving: 3
Ingredients:
1 mango, peel and sliced 1/4-inch thick
Directions:
Place the dehydrating tray in a multi-level air fryer basket and place basket in the instant pot.
Arrange mango slices on dehydrating tray.
Seal pot with air fryer lid and select dehydrate mode then set temperature to 135 F and timer for 14 hours.
Serve and enjoy.
Nutrition:
Calories 67
Fat 0.4 g
Carbohydrates 16.8 g
Sugar 15.3 g
Protein 0.9 g
Cholesterol 0 mg

Sausage Zucchini Casserole

Preparation Time: 10 minutes
Cooking Time: 45 minutes
Serving: 8
Ingredients:
12 eggs
2 small zucchinis, shredded
1 lb ground Italian sausage
3 tomatoes, sliced
3 tbsp coconut flour
1/4 cup coconut milk
Pepper
Salt
Directions:
Spray instant pot from inside with cooking spray.
Add sausage into the instant pot and cook on saute mode until browned.
Spread shredded zucchini and sliced tomatoes on top of sausage.
In a bowl, whisk eggs, coconut flour, milk, pepper, and salt and pour over sausage mixture.
Seal pot with air fryer lid and select bake mode then set the temperature to 350 F and timer for 45 minutes.
Serve and enjoy.
Nutrition:
Calories 306
Fat 21.8 g
Carbohydrates 6.6 g
Sugar 3.5 g
Protein 19.6 g
Cholesterol 286 mg

Broccoli Rice Casserole

Preparation Time: 10 minutes
Cooking Time: 20 minutes
Serving: 8
Ingredients:
2 cups cooked rice
10 oz cream of chicken soup
1 cup Velveeta cheese, diced
3 tbsp butter
1/2 cup onion, chopped
16 oz broccoli, steam & chopped
Directions:
Add butter into the instant pot and set the pot on saute mode.
Add onion and saute until softened. Turn off the saute mode.
Add broccoli, soup, cheese, and rice and stir well.
Seal pot with air fryer lid and select bake mode then set the temperature to 350 F and timer for 20 minutes.
Serve and enjoy.
Nutrition:
Calories 293
Fat 9.3 g
Carbohydrates 45.2 g
Sugar 2.3 g
Protein 7.9 g
Cholesterol 22 mg

Cheesy Mashed Potato Casserole

Preparation Time: 10 minutes
Cooking Time: 20 minutes
Serving: 8
Ingredients:
4 cups mashed potatoes
3/4 cup cheddar cheese, shredded
1 cup french onion rings
1 tsp dried parsley
1 tsp dried chives
3/4 cup sour cream
Directions:
Spray instant pot from inside with cooking spray.
Add mashed potatoes, sour cream, chives, and parsley into the instant pot stir well.
Sprinkle cheese and onion rings on top.
Seal pot with air fryer lid and select bake mode then set the temperature to 350 F and timer for 20 minutes.
Serve and enjoy.
Nutrition:
Calories 204
Fat 10.2 g
Carbohydrates 22.4 g
Sugar 0.2 g
Protein 6.3 g
Cholesterol 23 mg

Corn Gratin

Preparation Time: 10 minutes
Cooking Time: 30 minutes
Serving: 8
Ingredients:
2 cups corn
1 cup cheddar cheese, shredded
1 cup milk
1 tbsp flour
1 tbsp butter
1 cup crushed crackers
Directions:
Add butter into the instant pot and set the pot on saute mode.
Add flour and milk and stir until smooth. Turn off the saute mode.
Add corn and cup cheese and stir well.
Sprinkle remaining cheese and crushed crackers on top.
Seal pot with air fryer lid and select bake mode then set the temperature to 350 F and timer for 15 minutes.
Serve and enjoy.
Nutrition:
Calories 137
Fat 8 g
Carbohydrates 11.6 g
Sugar 3.1 g
Protein 6.1 g
Cholesterol 21 mg

Flavors Crab Casserole

Preparation Time: 10 minutes
Cooking Time: 30 minutes
Serving: 5
Ingredients:
8 oz crabmeat
1 onion, sliced
1/4 tsp garlic powder
1/4 tsp onion powder
1 tsp Worcestershire sauce
1 cup Swiss cheese, shredded
1 cup cheddar cheese, shredded
1/4 cup sour cream
5 oz cream cheese
Directions:
Spray instant pot from inside with cooking spray.
Add all ingredients except cheddar cheese into the instant pot and stir well.
Sprinkle cheddar cheese on top.
Seal pot with air fryer lid and select bake mode then set the temperature to 350 F and timer for 30 minutes.
Serve and enjoy.
Nutrition:
Calories 350
Fat 26 g
Carbohydrates 11.9 g
Sugar 4.5 g
Protein 17.7 g

Cholesterol 89 mg

Broccoli Chicken Casserole

Preparation Time: 10 minutes
Cooking Time: 25 minutes
Serving: 6
Ingredients:
3 chicken breasts, boneless, cooked and diced
1/2 cup breadcrumbs
1 cup cheddar cheese, shredded
2 tbsp parmesan cheese, grated
1 tsp lemon juice
3/4 cup milk
10 oz broccoli florets, cooked and drained
10 oz cream of chicken soup
Directions:
Spray instant pot from inside with cooking spray.
Add chicken, lemon juice, milk, broccoli, and soup into the instant pot and stir well.
Sprinkle cheddar cheese, parmesan cheese, and breadcrumbs on top.
Seal pot with air fryer lid and select bake mode then set the temperature to 350 F and timer for 25 minutes.
Serve and enjoy.
Nutrition:
Calories 330
Fat 16.1 g
Carbohydrates 14.8 g
Sugar 3.1 g
Protein 31.1 g
Cholesterol 92 mg

Asian Mushroom Jerky

Preparation Time: 10 minutes
Cooking Time: 12 hours
Serving: 4
Ingredients:
2 large portabella mushroom caps, sliced into 1/8-inch thick pieces
1 tsp ginger, grated
1 garlic clove, grated
1 tsp sriracha
1 1/2 tsp sesame oil
2 tbsp brown sugar
3 tbsp vinegar
1/4 cup soy sauce, low-sodium
Directions:
Add mushrooms sliced into the large bowl.
Add remaining ingredients and mix well and marinate for 8 hours.
Place the dehydrating tray in a multi-level air fryer basket and place basket in the instant pot.
Arrange marinated mushroom pieces on dehydrating tray.
Seal pot with air fryer lid and select dehydrate mode then set temperature to 125 F and timer for 12 hours.
Serve and enjoy.

Nutrition:
Calories 60
Fat 1.8 g
Carbohydrates 9.1 g
Sugar 5.6 g
Protein 2.3 g
Cholesterol 0 mg

Banana Fruit Leather

Preparation Time: 10 minutes
Cooking Time: 4 hours
Serving: 2
Ingredients:
1 small banana
1 tbsp Nutella
Directions:
Add banana and Nutella into the blender and blend until smooth.
Place the dehydrating tray in a multi-level air fryer basket and place basket in the instant pot.
Line dehydrating tray with parchment paper.
Spread banana mixture on dehydrating tray.
Seal pot with air fryer lid and select dehydrate mode then set temperature to 125 F and timer for 4 hours.
Serve and enjoy.
Nutrition:
Calories 94
Fat 2.9 g
Carbohydrates 17.1 g
Sugar 11 g
Protein 1 g
Cholesterol 0 mg

Cauliflower Casserole

Preparation Time: 10 minutes
Cooking Time: 25 minutes
Serving: 6
Ingredients:
1 cauliflower head, cut into florets
1 1/2 cups cheddar cheese, shredded
3/4 cup heavy cream
Pepper
Salt
Directions:
Spray instant pot from inside with cooking spray.
Add cauliflower florets into the boiling water and cook for 6 minutes. Drain well.
Add cauliflower florets, 1/2 cup cheddar cheese, heavy cream, pepper, and salt into the instant pot and stir well.
Sprinkle remaining cheddar cheese on top.
Seal pot with air fryer lid and select bake mode then set the temperature to 350 F and timer for 20 minutes.
Serve and enjoy.
Nutrition:
Calories 177

Fat 15 g
Carbohydrates 3.1 g
Sugar 1.2 g
Protein 8.2 g
Cholesterol 50 mg

Buffalo Chicken Casserole

Preparation Time: 10 minutes
Cooking Time: 30 minutes
Serving: 8
Ingredients:
18 oz cauliflower florets
1 cup celery, chopped
12 oz chicken, cooked and diced
8 oz cheddar cheese, shredded
2 eggs, lightly beaten
1/4 cup ranch dressing
1/3 cup hot sauce
8 oz cream cheese
Directions:
Spray instant pot from inside with cooking spray.
Add cauliflower florets into the boiling water and cook for 6 minutes. Drain well and set aside.
Add cauliflower florets, chicken, and celery into the instant pot.
In a bowl, mix together cream cheese, hot sauce, ranch dressing, eggs, and 4 oz cheddar cheese and pour over cauliflower mixture.
Sprinkle remaining cheddar cheese on top.
Seal pot with air fryer lid and select bake mode then set the temperature to 350 F and timer for 30 minutes.
Serve and enjoy.
Nutrition:
Calories 314
Fat 21.8 g
Carbohydrates 5.5 g
Sugar 2.3 g
Protein 24.4 g
Cholesterol 135 mg

Turkey Stroganoff

Preparation Time: 10 minutes
Cooking Time: 34 minutes
Serving: 8
Ingredients:
12 oz egg noodles, cooked and drained
1/4 cup parmesan cheese, grated
2 cups cooked turkey, diced
1 cup sour cream
2 cups chicken broth
1/4 cup all-purpose flour
1 tbsp parsley, chopped
8 oz mushrooms, sliced

2 tbsp butter
Directions:
Add butter into the instant pot and set the pot on saute mode.
Add mushrooms and saute for 3-4 minutes. remove mushrooms from pot and set aside.
Add flour, sour cream, and broth and stir until smooth. Turn off the saute mode.
Add noodles, turkey, mushrooms, and parsley and stir well.
Sprinkle parmesan cheese on top.
Seal pot with air fryer lid and select bake mode then set the temperature to 350 F and timer for 30 minutes.
Serve and enjoy.
Nutrition:
Calories 244
Fat 12.6 g
Carbohydrates 16.2 g
Sugar 0.9 g
Protein 16.5 g
Cholesterol 61 mg

Parmesan Zucchini Chips

Preparation Time: 10 minutes
Cooking Time: 5 hours
Serving: 2
Ingredients:
1 cup zucchini slices
1/2 tsp apple cider vinegar
1/8 tsp garlic powder
1 tbsp parmesan cheese, grated
Salt
Directions:
In a bowl, toss zucchini, cheese, garlic powder, vinegar, and salt.
Place the dehydrating tray in a multi-level air fryer basket and place basket in the instant pot.
Arrange zucchini slices on dehydrating tray.
Seal pot with air fryer lid and select dehydrate mode then set temperature to 135 F and timer for 5 hours.
Serve and enjoy.
Nutrition:
Calories 141
Fat 8.5 g
Carbohydrates 10.1 g
Sugar 1.1 g
Protein 5.5 g
Cholesterol 10 mg

Peanut Butter Banana Chips

Preparation Time: 10 minutes
Cooking Time: 8 hours
Serving: 2
Ingredients:
1 banana, cut into 1/4-inch thick slices
1 tbsp creamy peanut butter
Directions:
In a bowl, mix together peanut butter and banana slices.

Place the dehydrating tray in a multi-level air fryer basket and place basket in the instant pot.
Arrange banana slices on dehydrating tray.
Seal pot with air fryer lid and select dehydrate mode then set temperature to 160 F and timer for 8 hours.
Serve and enjoy.
Nutrition:
Calories 100
Fat 4.2 g
Carbohydrates 15.1 g
Sugar 8 g
Protein 2.6 g
Cholesterol 0 mg

Corn Chips

Preparation Time: 10 minutes
Cooking Time: 8 hours
Serving: 2
Ingredients:
1 cup sweet corn
Pepper
Salt
Directions:
Add corn, pepper, and salt into the blender and blend until creamy.
Place the dehydrating tray in a multi-level air fryer basket and place basket in the instant pot.
Line dehydrating tray with parchment paper.
Spread corn mixture on dehydrating tray.
Seal pot with air fryer lid and select dehydrate mode then set temperature to 115 F and timer for 8 hours.
Serve and enjoy.
Nutrition:
Calories 66
Fat 0.9 g
Carbohydrates 14.5 g
Sugar 2.5 g
Protein 2.5 g
Cholesterol 0 mg

Strawberry Mango Fruit Leather

Preparation Time: 10 minutes
Cooking Time: 4 hours
Serving: 2
Ingredients:
1/4 cup fresh strawberries
1/2 mango, peel and chopped
Directions:
Add strawberries and mango into the blender and blend until smooth.
Place the dehydrating tray in a multi-level air fryer basket and place basket in the instant pot.
Line dehydrating tray with parchment paper.
Spread blended fruit mixture on dehydrating tray.
Seal pot with air fryer lid and select dehydrate mode then set temperature to 160 F and timer for 4 hours.
Serve and enjoy.

Nutrition:
Calories 56
Fat 0.4 g
Carbohydrates 14 g
Sugar 12.4 g
Protein 0.8 g
Cholesterol 0 mg

Noodle Ham Casserole

Preparation Time: 10 minutes
Cooking Time: 25 minutes
Serving: 8
Ingredients:
10.5 oz cream of chicken soup
3 cups ham, cooked & diced
12 oz egg noodles, cooked and drained
2 cups Monterey jack cheese, shredded
1/2 tsp garlic powder
1 1/2 cups milk
1 cup sour cream
Pepper
Salt
Directions:
Spray instant pot from inside with cooking spray.
Add chicken soup, garlic powder, milk, sour cream, pepper, and salt into the instant pot and stir well.
Add ham and cooked noodles and stir well.
Sprinkle shredded cheese on top.
Seal pot with air fryer lid and select bake mode then set the temperature to 350 F and timer for 25 minutes.
Serve and enjoy.
Nutrition:
Calories 365
Fat 22.9 g
Carbohydrates 19.1 g
Sugar 2.7 g
Protein 20.6 g
Cholesterol 86 mg

Banana Chocolate Fruit Leather

Preparation Time: 10 minutes
Cooking Time: 10 hours
Serving: 2
Ingredients:
1 banana
1/4 tbsp brown sugar
1/2 tbsp cocoa powder
Directions:
Add banana, brown sugar, and cocoa powder into the blender and blend until smooth.
Place the dehydrating tray in a multi-level air fryer basket and place basket in the instant pot.
Line dehydrating tray with parchment paper.
Spread banana mixture on dehydrating tray.

Seal pot with air fryer lid and select dehydrate mode then set temperature to 130 F and timer for 10 hours. Serve and enjoy.

Nutrition:
Calories 60
Fat 0.4 g
Carbohydrates 15.3 g
Sugar 8.3 g
Protein 0.9 g
Cholesterol 0 mg

Spicy Chickpeas

Preparation Time: 10 minutes
Cooking Time: 10 hours
Serving: 2
Ingredients:
10 oz can chickpeas, drained and rinsed
1/2 tbsp sugar
1 1/2 tbsp sriracha
Salt
Directions:
In a bowl, mix together chickpeas, sugar, sriracha, and salt.
Place the dehydrating tray in a multi-level air fryer basket and place basket in the instant pot.
Arrange chickpeas on dehydrating tray.
Seal pot with air fryer lid and select dehydrate mode then set temperature to 130 F and timer for 10 hours.
Serve and enjoy.
Nutrition:
Calories 191
Fat 1.6 g
Carbohydrates 37.3 g
Sugar 3 g
Protein 7 g
Cholesterol 0 mg

Delicious Nacho Zucchini Chips

Preparation Time: 10 minutes
Cooking Time: 6 hours
Serving: 2
Ingredients:
1 yellow squash, sliced thinly
1/2 tsp tomato powder
1/4 tsp paprika
1/2 tsp chili powder
1/4 tsp onion powder
1/4 tsp garlic powder
1 tbsp cheddar cheese, grated
Salt
Directions:
Add squash slices into the mixing bowl. Add remaining ingredients and toss well.
Place the dehydrating tray in a multi-level air fryer basket and place basket in the instant pot.

Arrange squash slices on the dehydrating tray.
Seal pot with air fryer lid and select dehydrate mode then set temperature to 135 F and timer for 6 hours.
Serve and enjoy.
Nutrition:
Calories 110
Fat 1.6 g
Carbohydrates 23 g
Sugar 13 g
Protein 5.5 g
Cholesterol 4 mg

Banana Peanut Butter Roll

Preparation Time: 10 minutes
Cooking Time: 4 hours
Serving: 2
Ingredients:
1 banana, peeled and sliced
1 tbsp peanut butter
Directions:
Add banana and peanut butter into the blender and blend until smooth.
Place the dehydrating tray in a multi-level air fryer basket and place basket in the instant pot.
Line dehydrating tray with parchment paper.
Spread banana mixture on dehydrating tray.
Seal pot with air fryer lid and select dehydrate mode then set temperature to 135 F and timer for 4 hours.
Serve and enjoy.
Nutrition:
Calories 100
Fat 4.2 g
Carbohydrates 15.1 g
Sugar 8 g
Protein 2.6 g
Cholesterol 0 mg

Pumpkin Fruit Leather

Preparation Time: 10 minutes
Cooking Time: 8 hours
Serving: 2
Ingredients:
1/2 cup pumpkin puree
1/8 tsp ground allspice
1/8 tsp ground nutmeg
1/4 tsp cinnamon
1 tbsp shredded coconut
1 tbsp honey
1/2 cup applesauce
1/4 cup coconut milk
Directions:
Place the dehydrating tray in a multi-level air fryer basket and place basket in the instant pot.
Line dehydrating tray with parchment paper.

Add all ingredients into the bowl and mix until well combined and spread mixture on dehydrating tray.
Seal pot with air fryer lid and select dehydrate mode then set temperature to 135 F and timer for 8 hours.
Serve and enjoy.
Nutrition:
Calories 159
Fat 8.3 g
Carbohydrates 22.9 g
Sugar 18 g
Protein 1.6 g
Cholesterol 0 mg

Dried Lemon Slices

Preparation Time: 10 minutes
Cooking Time: 10 hours
Serving: 4
Ingredients:
2 lemons, wash and cut into 1/4-inch thick slices
Directions:
Place the dehydrating tray in a multi-level air fryer basket and place basket in the instant pot.
Arrange lemon slices on dehydrating tray.
Seal pot with air fryer lid and select dehydrate mode then set temperature to 125 F and timer for 10 hours.
Serve and enjoy.
Nutrition:
Calories 8
Fat 0.1 g
Carbohydrates 2.7 g
Sugar 0.7 g
Protein 0.3 g
Cholesterol 0 mg

Banana Jerky

Preparation Time: 10 minutes
Cooking Time: 8 hours
Serving: 2
Ingredients:
2 bananas, cut into 1/4-inch thick slices
1 tbsp fresh lemon juice
Directions:
Add banana slices and lemon juice in a bowl and toss well.
Place the dehydrating tray in a multi-level air fryer basket and place basket in the instant pot.
Arrange banana slices on dehydrating tray.
Seal pot with air fryer lid and select dehydrate mode then set temperature to 135 F and timer for 8 hours.
Serve and enjoy.
Nutrition:
Calories 107
Fat 0.5 g
Carbohydrates 27.1 g
Sugar 14.6 g
Protein 1.4 g

Cholesterol 0 mg

Parsnips Chips

Preparation Time: 10 minutes
Cooking Time: 6 hours
Serving: 2
Ingredients:
1 parsnip, cut into 1/4-inch thick slices
Pepper
Salt
Directions:
Add parsnip slices, pepper, and salt into the bowl and toss well.
Place the dehydrating tray in a multi-level air fryer basket and place basket in the instant pot.
Arrange parsnip slices on dehydrating tray.
Seal pot with air fryer lid and select dehydrate mode then set temperature to 125 F and timer for 6 hours.
Serve and enjoy.
Nutrition:
Calories 50
Fat 0.2 g
Carbohydrates 12 g
Sugar 3.2 g
Protein 0.8 g
Cholesterol 0 mg

Cauliflower Popcorn

Preparation Time: 10 minutes
Cooking Time: 8 hours
Serving: 2
Ingredients:
2 cups cauliflower florets, chopped
1/4 tsp ground cumin
1/2 tsp cayenne
1/2 tbsp paprika
2 tbsp hot sauce
1 1/2 tbsp olive oil
Directions:
Add cauliflower into the large bowl.
Add remaining ingredients over the cauliflower and toss well.
Place the dehydrating tray in a multi-level air fryer basket and place basket in the instant pot.
Place cauliflower pieces on dehydrating tray.
Seal pot with air fryer lid and select dehydrate mode then set temperature to 130 F and timer for 8 hours.
Serve and enjoy.
Nutrition:
Calories 124
Fat 11 g
Carbohydrates 6.9 g
Sugar 2.8 g
Protein 2.4 g

Cholesterol 0 mg

Spaghetti Casserole

Preparation Time: 10 minutes
Cooking Time: 30 minutes
Serving: 6
Ingredients:
12 oz spaghetti, cooked and drained
1/2 cup parmesan cheese, grated
8 oz cream cheese
1 garlic clove, minced
1 tsp Italian seasoning
1 lb ground beef
26 oz jar spaghetti sauce
Directions:
Add ground beef into the instant pot and set the pot on saute mode and cook until meat is browned.
Add spaghetti sauce and stir well.
Add cream cheese, garlic, Italian seasoning, and cooked spaghetti and stir well.
Sprinkle parmesan cheese on top.
Seal pot with air fryer lid and select bake mode then set the temperature to 350 F and timer for 30 minutes.
Serve and enjoy.
Nutrition:
Calories 539
Fat 23.9 g
Carbohydrates 44.9 g
Sugar 10.6 g
Protein 36.5 g
Cholesterol 156 mg

Tater Tot Casserole

Preparation Time: 10 minutes
Cooking Time: 30 minutes
Serving: 8
Ingredients:
1 lb ground beef
2 lbs tater tots
1 1/2 cups cheddar cheese, shredded
1/2 cup milk
10 oz cream of chicken soup
2 cups hash browns, shredded
1 tsp onion powder
1 tsp garlic powder
2 tbsp Italian seasoning
3 tbsp onion, chopped
Directions:
Spray instant pot from inside with cooking spray.
Add meat, onion, garlic powder, Italian seasoning, and onion powder into the instant pot and saute until meat is browned.
Add remaining ingredients except for tater tots and stir well.

Spread tater tots on top.
Seal pot with air fryer lid and select bake mode then set the temperature to 350 F and timer for 30 minutes.
Serve and enjoy.
Nutrition:
Calories 564
Fat 28.6 g
Carbohydrates 49.9 g
Sugar 2.5 g
Protein 27.5 g
Cholesterol 79 mg

Dehydrated Okra

Preparation Time: 10 minutes
Cooking Time: 24 hours
Serving: 2
Ingredients:
6 pods okra, slice into rounds
Directions:
Place the dehydrating tray in a multi-level air fryer basket and place basket in the instant pot.
Arrange sliced okra on dehydrating tray.
Seal pot with air fryer lid and select dehydrate mode then set temperature to 130 F and timer for 24 hours.
Serve and enjoy.
Nutrition:
Calories 26
Fat 0.8 g
Carbohydrates 2.5 g
Sugar 0 g
Protein 1.7 g
Cholesterol 0 mg

Cucumber Chips

Preparation Time: 10 minutes
Cooking Time: 10 hours
Serving: 2
Ingredients:
1 cucumber, sliced thinly
1 tsp apple cider vinegar
1/2 tbsp olive oil
Salt
Directions:
Toss cucumber slices with vinegar, oil, and salt.
Place the dehydrating tray in a multi-level air fryer basket and place basket in the instant pot.
Arrange cucumber slices on dehydrating tray.
Seal pot with air fryer lid and select dehydrate mode then set temperature to 135 F and timer for 10 hours.
Serve and enjoy.
Nutrition:
Calories 53
Fat 3.7 g
Carbohydrates 5.5 g

Sugar 2.5 g
Protein 1 g
Cholesterol 0 mg

Chapter 10: Snacks and desserts

Cheese Zucchini Bites

Preparation Time: 10 minutes
Cooking Time: 10 minutes
Serving: 4
Ingredients:
4 zucchinis, grated and squeeze out all liquid
1 cup breadcrumbs
1 egg, lightly beaten
1 tsp Italian seasoning
1/2 cup parmesan cheese, grated
Directions:
Add all ingredients into the bowl and mix until well combined.
Place the dehydrating tray in a multi-level air fryer basket and place basket in the instant pot.
Make small balls from the zucchini mixture and place it on a dehydrating tray.
Seal pot with air fryer lid and select air fry mode then set the temperature to 400 F and timer for 10 minutes. Turn halfway through.
Serve and enjoy.
Nutrition:
Calories 193
Fat 5.6 g
Carbohydrates 26.6 g
Sugar 5.2 g
Protein 11 g
Cholesterol 50 mg

Potato Chips

Preparation time: 15 minutes
Cooking time: 30 minutes
Servings: 6
Ingredients:
4 small russet potatoes, thinly sliced
2 tablespoons fresh rosemary, finely chopped
1 tablespoon olive oil
¼ teaspoon salt
Directions:
Preheat the air fryer to 350 o f and grease an air fryer basket.
Mix together the potato slices, olive oil, rosemary and salt in a bowl.
Arrange the potato chips in the air fryer basket and cook for about 30 minutes.
Dish out and serve warm.
Nutrition: Calories: 87, fat: 0.4g, carbohydrates: 15.9g, sugar: 1.1g, protein: 1.7g, sodium: 88mg

Tortilla Chips

Preparation time: 10 minutes
Cooking time: 6 minutes
Servings: 6
Ingredients:
8 corn tortillas, cut into triangles
1 tablespoon olive oil
Salt, to taste
Directions:
Preheat the air fryer to 390 o f and grease an air fryer basket.
Drizzle the tortilla chips with olive oil and season with salt.
Arrange half of the tortilla chips in the air fryer basket and cook for about 3 minutes, flipping in between.
Repeat with the remaining tortilla chips and dish out to serve warm.
Nutrition: Calories: 90, fat: 3.2g, carbohydrates: 14.3g, sugar: 0.3g, protein: 1.8g, sodium: 42mg

Beet chips

Preparation time: 10 minutes
Cooking time: 15 minutes
Servings: 6
Ingredients:
4 medium beetroots, peeled and thinly sliced
¼ teaspoon smoked paprika
½ teaspoon salt
2 tablespoons olive oil
Directions:
Preheat the air fryer to 325 o f and grease an air fryer basket.
Mix together all the ingredients in a bowl until well combined.
Arrange the beet slices in the air fryer basket and cook for about 15 minutes.
Dish out and serve warm.
Nutrition: Calories: 60, fat: 4.8g, carbohydrates: 5.3g, sugar: 3.7g, protein: 0.9g, sodium: 236mg

Avocado Fries

Preparation time: 20 minutes
Cooking Time: 20 minutes
Servings: 4
Ingredients:
1 oz. Pork rinds, finely ground
2 medium avocados
Directions:
Cut each avocado in half. Remove the pit.
Carefully remove the peel and then slice the flesh into ¼-inch-thick slices.
Place the pork rinds into a medium bowl and press each piece of avocado into the pork rinds to coat completely.
Place the avocado pieces into the air fryer basket.
Adjust the temperature to 350 degrees f and set the timer for 5 minutes.
Serve immediately
Nutrition: Calories: 153; Protein: 5.4g; Fiber: 4.6g; Fat: 11.9g; Carbs: 5.9g

Onion Rings

Preparation time:10 minutes
Cooking Time: 10 minutes
Serving: 4
Ingredients:
3/4 cup flour
1 large yellow onion, sliced and rings separated
¼ tsp garlic powder
¼ tsp paprika
1 cup almond milk
1 large egg
1/2 cup cornstarch
1 ½ teaspoons of baking powder
1 teaspoon salt
1 cup bread crumbs
cooking spray
Directions:
Whisk flour with baking powder, salt, and cornstarch in a bowl.
Coat the onion rings with this dry flour mixture and keep them aside.
Beat egg with milk in a bowl and dip the rings in this mixture.
Place the coated rings in the Air Fryer Basket and set it inside the Instant Pot Duo.
Spray the onion rings with cooking oil. Put on the Air Fryer lid and seal it.
Hit the "Air fry Button" and select 10 minutes of cooking time, then press "Start."
Flip the rings when cooked halfway through.
Once the Instant Pot Duo beeps, remove its lid.
Serve.
Nutrition:
Calories 319
Total Fat 4.2g
Saturated Fat 1.5g
Cholesterol 46mg
Sodium 829mg
Total Carbohydrate 59.9g
Dietary Fiber 2.9g
Total Sugars 6.2g
Protein 9.9g

Chocolate Smarties Cookies

Preparation time:10 minutes
Cooking Time: 15 minutes
Serving: 6
Ingredients:
3.5 oz. butter
3.5 oz. caster sugar
8 oz. self-rising flour
1 teaspoon vanilla essence
5 tablespoon milk
3 tablespoon cocoa powder
2 oz. nestle smarties
Directions:
Whisk cocoa powder with caster sugar and self-rising flour in a bowl.
Stir in butter and mix well to form a crumbly mixture.

Stir in milk and vanilla essence, then mix well to form a smooth dough.
Add the smarties and knead the dough well.
Roll this cookie dough into a 1-inch thick layer.
Use a cookies cutter to cut maximum cookies out of it.
Roll the remaining dough again to carve out more cookies.
Place half of the cookies in the Air Fryer Basket.
Set the Air Fryer Basket in the Instant Pot Duo.
Put on the Air Fryer lid and seal it.
Hit the "Bake Button" and select 10 minutes of cooking time, then press "Start."
Flip the cookies after 5 minutes then resume cooking.
Once the Instant Pot Duo beeps, remove its lid.
Bake the remaining cookies in a similar way.
Enjoy.
Nutrition:
Calories 372
Total Fat 16g
Saturated Fat 9.8g
Cholesterol 38mg
Sodium 108mg
Total Carbohydrate 53.3g
Dietary Fiber 2.1g
Total Sugars 23.3g
Protein 5.3g

Strawberry Cupcakes

Preparation time:10 minutes
Cooking Time: 8 minutes
Serving: 6
Ingredients:
3.5 oz. butter
3.5 oz. caster sugar
2 medium eggs
3.5 oz. self-rising flour
½ teaspoon vanilla essence
Topping
2 oz. butter
3.5 oz. icing sugar
½ teaspoon pink food coloring
1 tablespoon whipped cream
1 oz. fresh strawberries blended
Directions:
Beat butter with sugar in a mixer until fluffy.
Stir in eggs, and vanilla then beat well.
Slowly add flour while mixing the batter.
Divide this mixture into a mini muffin tray, greased with cooking spray.
Place the muffin tray in the Instant Pot Duo.
Put on the Air Fryer lid and seal it.
Hit the "Bake Button" and select 8 minutes of cooking time, then press "Start."
Once the Instant Pot Duo beeps, remove its lid.
Meanwhile, beat the cream with the rest of the Ingredients: in a beater until fluffy.
 Add this topping to a piping bag and pipe the topping on top of the baked cupcakes.
Serve.
Nutrition:

Calories 337
Total Fat 15.9g
Saturated Fat 9.5g
Cholesterol 93mg
Sodium 118mg
Total Carbohydrate 46.3g
Dietary Fiber 0.5g
Total Sugars 33.2g
Protein 3.8g

Lava Cakes

Preparation Time: 10 minutes
Cooking Time: 10 minutes
Serving: 4
Ingredients:
2 eggs
3.5 oz dark chocolate, melted
1 1/2 tbsp self-rising flour
3 tbsp sugar
3.5 oz butter, melted
Directions:
Spray four ramekins with cooking spray and set aside.
In a bowl, beat eggs and sugar until frothy.
Add melted chocolate, flour, and butter and fold well.
Pour batter into the prepared ramekins.
Place the dehydrating tray in a multi-level air fryer basket and place basket in the instant pot.
Place ramekins on a dehydrating tray.
Seal pot with air fryer lid and select air fry mode then set the temperature to 375 F and timer for 10 minutes.
Serve and enjoy.
Nutrition:
Calories 387
Fat 29.7 g
Carbohydrates 26.2 g
Sugar 22 g
Protein 5.2 g
Cholesterol 141 mg

Chocolate Strawberry Cups

Preparation time: 15 minutes
Cooking Time: 20 minutes
Servings: 8
Ingredients:
16 strawberries; halved
2 cups chocolate chips; melted
2 tbsp. Coconut oil
Directions:
In a pan that fits your air fryer, mix the strawberries with the oil and the melted chocolate chips, toss gently, put the pan in the air fryer and cook at 340°f for 10 minutes.
Divide into cups and serve cold

Nutrition: Calories: 162; Fat: 5g; Fiber: 3g; Carbs: 5g; Protein: 6g

---

Sweet Potato Tots

Preparation time:10 minutes
Cooking Time: 16 minutes
Serving: 4
Ingredients:
2 sweet potatoes, peeled
1/2 teaspoon Cajun seasoning
olive oil cooking spray
sea salt to taste
Directions:
Add sweet potatoes to boiling water in a pot and cook for 15 minutes until soft.
Drain the boiled sweet potatoes and allow them to cool down.
Grate the potatoes into a bowl and stir in Cajun seasoning and salt.
Mix well and make small tater tots out of this mixture.
Place these tater tots in the Air Fryer Basket and spray them with cooking oil.
Set the Air Fryer Basket in the Instant Pot Duo.
Put on the Air Fryer lid and seal it.
Hit the "Air fry Button" and select 16 minutes of cooking time, then press "Start."
After 8 minutes, flip all the tots and spray them again with cooking oil then resume cooking.
Once the Instant Pot Duo beeps, remove its lid.
Serve fresh.
Nutrition:
Calories 89
Total Fat 0.1g
Saturated Fat 0g
Cholesterol 0mg
Sodium 72mg
Total Carbohydrate 20.9g
Dietary Fiber 3.1g
Total Sugars 0.4g
Protein 1.2g

Corn Nuts

Preparation time:10 minutes
Cooking Time: 20 minutes
Serving: 6
Ingredients:
14 oz. giant white corn
3 tablespoons vegetable oil
1 1/2 teaspoons salt
Directions:
Soak white corn in a bowl filled with water and leave it for 8 hours.
Drain the soaked corns and spread them in the Air Fryer Basket.
Leave to dry for 20 minutes after patting them dry with a paper towel.
Add oil and salt on top of the corns and toss them well.
Set the Air Fryer Basket in the Instant Pot.
Put on the Air Fryer lid and seal it.
Hit the "Air fry Button" and select 20 minutes of cooking time, then press "Start."

Shake the corns after every 5 minutes of cooking, then resume the function.
Once the Instant Pot Duo beeps, remove its lid.
Serve.
Nutrition:
Calories 128
Total Fat 7.8g
Saturated Fat 1.3g
Cholesterol 0mg
Sodium 581mg
Total Carbohydrate 14.3g
Dietary Fiber 1.4g
Total Sugars 2.1g
Protein 2.1g

Chocolate Souffle

Preparation Time: 10 minutes
Cooking Time: 15 minutes
Serving: 2
Ingredients:
2 egg whites
2 egg yolks
1/2 tsp vanilla
3 oz chocolate, melted
3 tbsp sugar
2 tbsp flour
1/4 cup butter, melted
Directions:
Spray two ramekins with cooking spray and set aside.
In a bowl, beat egg yolks with vanilla and sugar. Stir in flour, melted chocolate, and butter.
In a separate bowl, beat egg whites and until stiff peak forms.
Slowly fold egg white mixture into the egg yolk mixture.
Pour batter into the prepared ramekins.
Place the dehydrating tray in a multi-level air fryer basket and place basket in the instant pot.
Place ramekins on a dehydrating tray.
Seal pot with air fryer lid and select bake mode then set the temperature to 330 F and timer for 15 minutes.
Serve and enjoy.
Nutrition:
Calories 601
Fat 40.3 g
Carbohydrates 50.2 g
Sugar 40.4 g
Protein 10.6 g
Cholesterol 281 mg

Lemon Muffins

Preparation Time: 10 minutes
Cooking Time: 15 minutes
Serving: 6
Ingredients:

1 egg
1/2 tsp vanilla
1/2 cup milk
2 tbsp olive oil
1/4 tsp baking soda
3/4 tsp baking powder
1 tsp lemon zest, grated
1/2 cup sugar
1 cup flour
1/2 tsp salt

Directions:
In a mixing bowl, mix together all dry ingredients.
In a medium bowl, whisk all wet ingredients until well mixed.
Pour wet ingredients mixture into the dry mixture and mix until well combined.
Pour batter into the 6 silicone muffin molds.
Place the dehydrating tray in a multi-level air fryer basket and place basket in the instant pot.
Place muffin molds on dehydrating tray.
Seal pot with air fryer lid and select bake mode then set the temperature to 350 F and timer for 15 minutes.
Serve and enjoy.

Nutrition:
Calories 201
Fat 6 g
Carbohydrates 34 g
Sugar 17.8 g
Protein 3.8 g
Cholesterol 29 mg

Corn on The Cob

Preparation time: 10 minutes
Cooking time: 4 minutes
Servings: 8
Ingredients:
8 ears corn on the cob, remove husk and silk
4 tbsp butter
Pepper
Salt

Directions:
Pour 2 cups of water into the instant pot then place rack in the pot.
Place corn on the rack. Seal pot with lid and cook on manual high pressure for 4 minutes.
Once done then allow to release pressure naturally then open the lid.
Remove corn from pot and season with pepper and salt.
Top with butter and serve.

Nutrition: Calories 110 Fat 6.2 g Carbohydrates 14.1 g Sugar 2.3 g Protein 2 g Cholesterol 15 mg

Stuffed Bell Peppers

Preparation time: 10 minutes
Cooking time: 36 minutes
Servings: 4
Ingredients:
4 large bell peppers, cut in half

1/4 cup feta cheese, crumbled
2 tsp dried oregano
2 cups of water
3 tbsp pine nuts, roasted
1 cup couscous
1/4 tsp pepper
1 tsp salt
Directions:
Add water and couscous into the instant pot and stir well.
Seal pot with lid and cook on manual high pressure for 3 minutes.
Once done then allow to release pressure naturally then open the lid.
Add remaining ingredients except for bell peppers to the pot and cook on sauté mode for 3 minutes.
Stuff couscous mixture into the bell peppers and place on a baking tray.
Bake at 375 f for 30 minutes.
Serve and enjoy.
Nutrition: Calories 271 Fat 7.1 g Carbohydrates 44.3 g Sugar 6.6 g Protein 9 g Cholesterol 8 mg

Healthy Steamed Vegetables

Preparation time: 10 minutes
Cooking time: 2 minutes
Servings: 6
Ingredients:
1/2 lb. yellow beans, cut into pieces
1/2 lb. green beans, cut into pieces
1 tbsp butter
1 tsp garlic powder
1/4 cup water
1 cauliflower head, cut into florets
Pepper
Salt
Directions:
Add all ingredients into the instant pot and stir well.
Seal pot with lid and cook on manual high pressure for 2 minutes.
Once done then release pressure using the quick-release method than open the lid.
Stir well and serve with your favorite dip.
Nutrition: Calories 96 Fat 2.4 g Carbohydrates 14.9 g Sugar 1.7 g Protein 5.1 g Cholesterol 5 mg

Simple Pepper & Salt Baby Potatoes

Preparation time: 10 minutes
Cooking time: 10 minutes
Servings: 4
Ingredients:
1 lb. baby potatoes
1 1/2 cup water
Pepper
Salt
Directions:
Pour water into the instant pot the place trivet in the pot.
Arrange baby potatoes on top of the trivet.
Seal pot with lid and cook on manual high pressure for 10 minutes.
Once done then allow to release pressure naturally then open the lid.

Season potatoes with pepper and salt and serve.
Nutrition: Calories 1985 Fat 0 g Carbohydrates 453.6 g Sugar 85.1 g Protein 56.7 g Cholesterol 0 mg

---

Mini Coffee Cake

Preparation Time: 10 minutes
Cooking Time: 15 minutes
Serving: 2
Ingredients:
1 egg
1 tsp cocoa powder
1/4 cup flour
1/4 cup sugar
1 tbsp black coffee
1/2 tsp instant coffee
1/4 cup butter
Directions:
Spray a mini baking dish with cooking spray and set aside.
In a bowl, beat egg, butter, and sugar. Add black coffee, instant coffee, and cocoa powder and beat well.
Add flour and stir to combine.
Pour batter into the prepared baking dish.
Place steam rack into the instant pot then place baking dish on top of the rack.
Seal pot with air fryer lid and select bake mode then set the temperature to 330 F and timer for 15 minutes.
Serve and enjoy.
Nutrition:
Calories 388
Fat 25.5 g
Carbohydrates 37.6 g
Sugar 25.3 g
Protein 4.8 g
Cholesterol 143 mg

Strawberry Muffins

Preparation Time: 10 minutes
Cooking Time: 14 minutes
Serving: 12
Ingredients:
1 egg
1 cup strawberries, diced
1/2 cup milk
1/3 cup olive oil
2 tsp baking powder
3/4 cup sugar
1 1/2 cups all-purpose flour
1/2 tsp salt
Directions:
In a large bowl, mix together flour, baking powder, sugar, and salt and set aside.
In a small bowl, whisk together egg, milk, and oil.
Pour egg mixture into the flour mixture and mix until well combined. Add strawberries and fold well.
Pour batter into the 12 silicone muffin molds.

Place the dehydrating tray in a multi-level air fryer basket and place basket in the instant pot.
Place 6 silicone muffin molds on dehydrating tray.
Seal pot with air fryer lid and select bake mode then set the temperature to 380 F and timer for 14 minutes.
Bake remaining muffins using the same method.
Serve and enjoy.
Nutrition:
Calories 167
Fat 6.4 g
Carbohydrates 26.3 g
Sugar 13.6 g
Protein 2.5 g
Cholesterol 14 mg

Banana Muffins

Preparation Time: 10 minutes
Cooking Time: 15 minutes
Serving: 12
Ingredients:
2 eggs
1 1/2 cups flour
1 tsp baking soda
1 1/2 tsp cinnamon
1 tsp vanilla
1/4 cup milk
1 cup mashed banana
1/3 cup maple syrup
4 tbsp butter, melted
1/2 tsp salt
Directions:
In a medium bowl, whisk eggs with vanilla, mashed banana, maple, syrup, and butter until well combined.
Mix together flour, baking soda, cinnamon, and salt in a mixing bowl.
Add egg mixture into the flour mixture and mix until well combined.
Pour batter into the 12 silicone muffin molds.
Place the dehydrating tray in a multi-level air fryer basket and place basket in the instant pot.
Place 6 silicone muffin molds on dehydrating tray.
Seal pot with air fryer lid and select bake mode then set the temperature to 350 F and timer for 15 minutes.
Bake remaining muffins using the same method.
Serve and enjoy.
Nutrition:
Calories 140
Fat 4.9 g
Carbohydrates 21.2 g
Sugar 7.1 g
Protein 2.9 g
Cholesterol 38 mg

Peanut Butter Muffins

Preparation Time: 10 minutes
Cooking Time: 20 minutes
Serving: 12
Ingredients:
1 egg
1 1/2 tsp vanilla
1/4 cup oil
2/3 cup peanut butter
3/4 cup milk
2 1/2 tsp baking powder
2/3 cup brown sugar
1 3/4 cups flour
1/4 tsp salt
Directions:
In a mixing bowl, mix together flour, baking powder, brown sugar, and salt.
In a small bowl, whisk egg, vanilla, oil, peanut butter, and milk.
Pour egg mixture into the flour mixture and mix until well combined.
Pour batter into the 12 silicone muffin molds.
Place the dehydrating tray in a multi-level air fryer basket and place basket in the instant pot.
Place 6 silicone muffin molds on dehydrating tray.
Seal pot with air fryer lid and select bake mode then set the temperature to 350 F and timer for 20 minutes.
Bake remaining muffins using the same method.
Serve and enjoy.
Nutrition:
Calories 237
Fat 12.6 g
Carbohydrates 26 g
Sugar 10 g
Protein 6.4 g
Cholesterol 15 mg

Parmesan Carrot Fries

Preparation Time: 10 minutes
Cooking Time: 15 minutes
Serving: 4
Ingredients:
4 carrots, peeled and cut into fries
2 tbsp parmesan cheese, grated
1 1/2 tbsp garlic, minced
2 tbsp olive oil
Pepper
Salt
Directions:
Add carrots and remaining ingredients into the mixing bowl and toss well.
Spray instant pot multi-level air fryer basket with cooking spray.
Add carrots fries into the air fryer basket and place basket into the instant pot.
Seal pot with air fryer lid and select air fry mode then set the temperature to 350 F and timer for 15 minutes. Stir halfway through.
Serve and enjoy.
Nutrition:
Calories 99

Fat 7.6 g
Carbohydrates 7.2 g
Sugar 3 g
Protein 1.6 g
Cholesterol 2 mg

Tater Tots

Preparation Time: 10 minutes
Cooking Time: 10 minutes
Serving: 2
Ingredients:
16 oz frozen tater tots
1 tbsp olive oil
Salt
Directions:
Drizzle tater tots with olive oil and season with salt.
Spray instant pot multi-level air fryer basket with cooking spray.
Add tater tots into the air fryer basket and place basket into the instant pot.
Seal pot with air fryer lid and select air fry mode then set the temperature to 400 F and timer for 10 minutes. Stir halfway through.
Serve and enjoy.
Nutrition:
Calories 492
Fat 28.6 g
Carbohydrates 54 g
Sugar 1.4 g
Protein 5.4 g
Cholesterol 0 mg

Air Fried Cauliflower Bites

Preparation Time: 10 minutes
Cooking Time: 14 minutes
Serving: 4
Ingredients:
1 lb cauliflower florets
1 1/2 tsp garlic powder
1 tbsp olive oil
1 tsp ground coriander
1 tsp dried rosemary
Pepper
Salt
Directions:
Add cauliflower florets into the large bowl. Add remaining ingredients and toss well.
Spray instant pot multi-level air fryer basket with cooking spray.
Add cauliflower florets into the air fryer basket and place basket into the instant pot.
Seal pot with air fryer lid and select air fry mode then set the temperature to 400 F and timer for 14 minutes. Stir halfway through.
Serve and enjoy.
Nutrition:

Calories 63
Fat 3.7 g
Carbohydrates 7 g
Sugar 3 g
Protein 2.4 g
Cholesterol 0 mg

Potato Wedges

Preparation Time: 10 minutes
Cooking Time: 24 minutes
Serving: 2
Ingredients:
1/2 lb potatoes, cut into wedges
1 tbsp olive oil
Pepper
Salt
Directions:
In a bowl, toss potato wedges with oil, pepper, and salt.
Spray instant pot multi-level air fryer basket with cooking spray.
Potato wedges into the air fryer basket and place basket into the instant pot.
Seal pot with air fryer lid and select air fry mode then set the temperature to 390 F and timer for 24 minutes. Stir halfway through.
Serve and enjoy.
Nutrition:
Calories 138
Fat 7.1 g
Carbohydrates 17.9 g
Sugar 1.3 g
Protein 1.9 g
Cholesterol 0 mg

Ranch Chickpeas

Preparation Time: 10 minutes
Cooking Time: 12 minutes
Serving: 4
Ingredients:
14 oz can chickpeas, rinsed, drained and pat dry
1 1/2 tsp ranch seasoning mix
Pepper
Salt
Directions:
Add chickpeas, ranch seasoning, pepper, and salt into the mixing bowl and toss well.
Place the dehydrating tray in a multi-level air fryer basket and place basket in the instant pot.
Spread chickpeas on dehydrating tray.
Seal pot with air fryer lid and select air fry mode then set the temperature to 375 F and timer for 12 minutes. Stir halfway through.
Serve and enjoy.
Nutrition:

Calories 120
Fat 1.1 g
Carbohydrates 22.5 g
Sugar 0 g
Protein 4.9 g
Cholesterol 0 mg

Crunchy Zucchini Chips

Preparation time:5 Minutes
Cooking Time: 12 Minutes
Serving: 4
Ingredients: 1 medium zucchini, thinly sliced
3/4 cup Parmesan cheese, grated
1 cup Panko breadcrumbs
1 large egg, beaten
Directions:
In a mixing bowl, add the Parmesan cheese and panko breadcrumbs. Combine the ingredients to mix well with each other.
In a mixing bowl, beat the eggs. Coat the zucchini slices with the eggs and then with the crumb mixture. Spray the slices with some cooking spray.
Place Instant Pot Air Fryer Crisp over kitchen platform. Press Air Fry, set the temperature to 400°F and set the timer to 5 minutes to preheat. Press "Start" and allow it to preheat for 5 minutes.
In the inner pot, place the Air Fryer basket. Line it with a parchment paper, add the zucchini slices.
Close the Crisp Lid and press the "Air Fry" setting. Set temperature to 350°F and set the timer to 10-12 minutes. Press "Start."
Halfway down, open the Crisp Lid, shake the basket and close the lid to continue cooking for the remaining time.
Open the Crisp Lid after cooking time is over. Serve warm.

Nutrition: **Calories:**
Fat: g
Saturated Fat: g
Trans Fat: 0g
Carbohydrates: g
Fiber: g
Sodium: mg
Protein: g

Cauliflower Fritters

Preparation time:5-10 Minutes
Cooking Time: 8 Minutes
Serving: 6-8
Ingredients: 1/3 cup shredded mozzarella cheese
1/3 cup shredded sharp cheddar cheese
½ cup chopped parsley
1 cup Italian breadcrumbs
3 chopped scallions
1 head of cauliflower, cut into florets
1 egg

2 minced garlic cloves
Directions:
Blend the florets into a blender to make the rice like structure. Add in a bowl. Mix in the pepper, salt, egg, cheeses, breadcrumbs, garlic, and scallions. Prepare 15 patties from the mixture. Coat them with some cooking spray.
Place Instant Pot Air Fryer Crisp over kitchen platform. Press Air Fry, set the temperature to 400°F and set the timer to 5 minutes to preheat. Press "Start" and allow it to preheat for 5 minutes.
In the inner pot, place the Air Fryer basket. In the basket, add the patties.
Close the Crisp Lid and press the "Air Fry" setting. Set temperature to 390°F and set the timer to 8 minutes. Press "Start."
Halfway down, open the Crisp Lid, shake the basket and close the lid to continue cooking for the remaining time. Open the Crisp Lid after cooking time is over. Serve warm.

Nutrition: **Calories: 235**
Fat: 19g
Saturated Fat: 8g
Trans Fat: 0g
Carbohydrates: 31g
Fiber: 5g
Sodium: 542mg
Protein: 6g

Cinnamon Fried Bananas

Preparation time: 5 minutes
Cooking time: 10 minutes
Servings: 2-3
Ingredients:
1 c. Panko breadcrumbs
3 tbsp. Cinnamon
½ c. Almond flour
3 egg whites
8 ripe bananas
3 tbsp. Vegan coconut oil
Directions:
Preparing the ingredients. Heat coconut oil and add breadcrumbs.
Mix around 2-3 minutes until golden.
Pour into bowl.
Peel and cut bananas in half.
Roll each bananas half into flour, eggs, and crumb mixture.
Air frying. Place into the instant crisp air fryer.
Close the air fryer lid. Select bake, and cook 10 minutes at 280 degrees.
A great addition to a healthy banana split!
Nutrition: Calories: 219; Fat:10g; Protein:3g; Sugar:5g

Cinnamon Bread Pudding

Preparation Time: 10 minutes
Cooking Time: 15 minutes
Serving: 2
Ingredients:
3 eggs, beaten
4 cups bread cube
3 tbsp raisins

1 cup almond milk
1/2 tsp cinnamon
1/2 tsp vanilla
1 tsp olive oil
Pinch of salt
Directions:
Place bread cubes in the oven-safe casserole dish.
In a bowl, mix remaining ingredients and pour over bread cubes. Cover dish with foil.
Pour 2 cups of water into the inner pot of instant pot duo crisp than place steamer rack in the pot.
Place casserole dish on top of the steamer rack.
Seal the pot with pressure cooking lid and cook on high for 15 minutes.
Once done, allow to release pressure naturally for 10 minutes then release remaining pressure using a quick release. Remove lid.
Serve and enjoy.
Nutrition:
Calories 635
Fat 37.6 g
Carbohydrates 58.5 g
Sugar 12.7 g
Protein 11.5 g
Cholesterol 246 mg

Cranberry Coconut Pudding

Preparation Time: 10 minutes
Cooking Time: 20 minutes
Serving: 6
Ingredients:
1 cup brown rice, rinsed and drained
1/2 cup coconut milk
1 1/2 cups milk
1 cup cranberries
1/4 cup sugar
1/2 tsp cinnamon
1/2 cup water
Directions:
Add all ingredients into the inner pot instant pot duo crisp and stir well.
Seal the pot with pressure cooking lid and cook on high for 20 minutes.
Once done, allow to release pressure naturally. Remove lid.
Stir and serve.
Nutrition:
Calories 233
Fat 6.9 g
Carbohydrates 38.4 g
Sugar 12.4 g
Protein 4.9 g
Cholesterol 5 mg

Raspberry Cake

Preparation Time: 10 minutes
Cooking Time: 10 minutes
Serving: 8
Ingredients:
1/2 cup raspberries
5 egg yolks
1/4 cup heavy cream
1/2 cup coconut flour
1 tsp baking powder
3 tsp liquid stevia
1/4 cup butter
1/4 cup coconut oil
1/2 tsp vanilla
Directions:
Add all dry ingredients except raspberries in a large bowl and mix well.
Add all wet ingredients and beat using a blender until well combined.
Spray 6-inch spring-form baking dish with cooking spray.
Pour batter in the prepared baking dish and top with raspberries.
Pour 2 cups of water into the inner pot of instant pot duo crisp then place steamer rack in the pot.
Place baking dish on top of the steamer rack.
Seal the pot with pressure cooking lid and cook on high for 10 minutes.
Once done, release pressure using a quick release. Remove lid.
Serve and enjoy.
Nutrition:
Calories 192
Fat 17.6 g
Carbohydrates 6.7 g
Sugar 0.4 g
Protein 2.9 g
Cholesterol 152 mg

Coconutty Lemon Bars

Preparation time: 5 minutes
Cooking time: 25 minutes
Servings: 12
Ingredients:
¼ cup cashew
¼ cup fresh lemon juice, freshly squeezed
¾ cup coconut milk
¾ cup erythritol
1 cup desiccated coconut
1 teaspoon baking powder
2 eggs, beaten
2 tablespoons coconut oil
An instant crisp air fryer of salt
Directions:
Preparing the ingredients. Preheat the instant crisp air fryer for 5 minutes.
In a mixing bowl, combine all ingredients.
Use a hand mixer to mix everything.
Pour into a baking dish that will fit in the instant crisp air fryer.
Air frying: Close the air fryer lid.

Select bake and cook for 25 minutes at 350°f or until a toothpick inserted in the middle comes out clean.
Nutrition: Calories: 118; Fat:10g; Protein:2.6g; Sugar:5g

Instant Pot Duo Crisp Crisp-Fried Cheeseburgers

Preparation time: 10 minutes
Cooking time: 8 minutes
Servings: 4
Ingredients:
4 hamburger buns
1 lb. Ground beef
1 tbsp. Low-sodium soy sauce
2 cloves garlic, minced
4 slices American cheese
Freshly ground black pepper
Red onion (thinly sliced
Lettuce
Mayonnaise
Sliced tomatoes
Kosher salt
Directions:
Combine beef with soy sauce and garlic in a large mixing bowl.
Mix thoroughly so the mixture can seep through the beef.
Shape marinated ground beef into patties and arrange in a single layer in the air fryer basket.
If there's not enough space to accommodate all patties, cook in batches.
Put the air fryer basket on top of the metal trivet inside the instant pot.
Attach the air fryer lid and cook at 375 degrees Fahrenheit for about 4 minutes.
Turn it over for even cooking and cook for another 4 minutes.
Once done, remove the burgers quickly and top every burger with a slice of cheese.
Cook the remaining patties using the same procedure.
Spread mayo on hamburger buns and then arrange its filling using lettuce as the base followed by a burger with cheese, tomatoes, and onions on top.
Serve immediately while warm.
Nutrition: calories – kcal; carbohydrates – 41.55 g; fat – 41.24 g; protein – 52.09 g; sugar – 11.22 g; sodium – 1327 mg

---

Cream Cheese and Zucchinis Bars

Preparation time: 25 minutes
Cooking Time: 20 minutes
Servings: 12
Ingredients:
3 oz. Zucchini, shredded
4 oz. Cream cheese
6 eggs
2 tbsp. Erythritol
3 tbsp. Coconut oil; melted
2 tsp. Vanilla extract
½ tsp. Baking powder
Directions:
In a bowl, combine all the ingredients and whisk well.
Pour this into a baking dish that fits your air fryer lined with parchment paper, introduce in the fryer and cook at 320°f, bake for 15 minutes.
Slice and serve cold

Nutrition: Calories: 178; Fat: 8g; Fiber: 3g; Carbs: 4g; Protein: 5g

---

Air Fried Zucchini Fried

Preparation: 10 minutes
Cooking: 15 minutes
Servings: 4
Ingredients:
10 ounces (2 Nos.) zucchinis, medium size.
½ teaspoon Italian seasoning
1 teaspoon onion powder
1 teaspoon garlic powder
1 tablespoon yeast
¼ cup coconut flour
¼ teaspoon pepper
½ teaspoon salt
Directions:
Wash, dry and cut the zucchinis into ½ inch thick wedges.
In a large mixing bowl, combine the coconut flour, garlic powder, yeast, onion powder, salt, and pepper with Italian seasoning.
Toss the zucchini pieces in the flour mix to coat them evenly.
Transfer the zucchini in the air fryer basket and place them in a layer without overlapping.
Place the air fryer basket in the inner pot of the Instant Pot Air Fryer.
Close the crisp lid.
Set the air fryer at 400°F for 15 minutes, under the AIR FRY mode.
Press START to begin the cooking.
Halfway through the cooking, open the crisp lid, and shake the basket for even cooking.
After shaking, close the crisp lid to resume the cooking for the remaining period.
Once the cooking is over, serve it hot.
Nutrition: Calories: 33, Calories from fat: 3, Total fat: 0.4g, Saturated fat: 0.1g, Trans fat: 0g, Cholesterol: 0mg, Sodium: 468mg, Total carbs: 5g, Dietary fiber: 2g, Sugars: 1g, Protein: 3g

---

Apple Chips in Instant Pot Air Fryer

Preparation: 5 minutes
Cooking: 20 minutes
Servings: 2
Ingredients:
16 ounces (2 Nos.) apple, large
2 teaspoons sugar
½ teaspoon ground cinnamon

Directions:
Wash, dry apple, and thinly slice.
Mix the apple pieces with sugar and cinnamon in a large bowl.
Place the coated apple slices in the air fryer basket without overlapping.
Put the air fryer basket in the inner pot of the Instant Pot Air Fryer.
Close the crisp lid.
Set the temperature at 350°F and timer for 12 minutes in the ROAST mode.
Press START to begin the roasting.
Halfway through the roasting, open the crisp lid and shake the air fryer basket for even cooking.
Close the crisp lid to resume the roasting.
Keep checking in between to confirm the desired crisp.

Note – the apple slices will continue to crisp as they cool down.
Nutrition: Calories: 129, Calories from fat: 3, Total fat: 0.4g, Saturated fat: 0.1g, Trans fat: 0g, Trans fat: 0g, Cholesterol: 0mg, Sodium: 2mg, Total carbs: 34g, Dietary fiber: 6g, Sugars: 26g, Protein: 1g

---

Beef Olive Balls

Preparation Time: 10 minutes
Cooking Time: 14 minutes
Serving: 4
Ingredients:
1 lb ground beef
1 tbsp oregano, chopped
1 tbsp breadcrumbs
1 tbsp chives, chopped
1 cup olives, pitted and chopped
Pepper
Salt
Directions:
Add all ingredients into the mixing bowl and mix until well combined.
Place the dehydrating tray in a multi-level air fryer basket and place basket in the instant pot.
Make small balls from meat mixture and place on dehydrating tray.
Seal pot with air fryer lid and select air fry mode then set the temperature to 400 F and timer for 14 minutes. Turn meatballs halfway through.
Serve and enjoy.
Nutrition:
Calories 260
Fat 10.9 g
Carbohydrates 4.1 g
Sugar 0.2 g
Protein 35.1 g
Cholesterol 101 mg

Yummy Broccoli Popcorn

Preparation Time: 10 minutes
Cooking Time: 6 minutes
Serving: 4
Ingredients:
2 cups broccoli florets
4 eggs yolks
2 cups coconut flour
Pepper
Salt
Directions:
In a small bowl, whisk eggs with pepper and salt.
In a shallow dish, add coconut flour.
Spray instant pot multi-level air fryer basket with cooking spray.
Dip broccoli floret with egg and coat with coconut flour and place it into the air fryer basket and place basket into the instant pot.
Seal pot with air fryer lid and select air fry mode then set the temperature to 400 F and timer for 6 minutes.
Serve and enjoy.

Nutrition:
Calories 310
Fat 10.8 g
Carbohydrates 43.3 g
Sugar 0.9 g
Protein 12.1 g
Cholesterol 194 mg

Avocado Fries

Preparation time: 20 minutes
Cooking time: 7 minutes
Servings: 2
Ingredients:
¼ cup all-purpose flour
1 egg
1 teaspoon water
½ cup panko breadcrumbs
1 avocado, peeled, pitted and sliced into 8 pieces
Salt and black pepper, to taste
Directions:
Preheat the air fryer to 400 o f and grease an air fryer basket.
Place flour, salt and black pepper in a shallow dish and whisk the egg with water in a second dish.
Place the breadcrumbs in a third shallow dish.
Coat the avocado slices evenly in flour and dip in the egg mixture.
Roll into the breadcrumbs evenly and arrange the avocado slices in an air fryer basket.
Cook for about 7 minutes, flipping once in between and dish out to serve warm.
Nutrition: Calories: 363, fat: 22.4g, carbohydrates: 35.7g, sugar: 1.2g, protein: 8.3g, sodium:

Strawberry Cupcakes

Preparation time:10 minutes
Cooking Time: 8 minutes
Serving: 6
Ingredients:
3.5 oz. butter
3.5 oz. caster sugar
2 medium eggs
3.5 oz. self-rising flour
½ teaspoon vanilla essence
Topping
2 oz. butter
3.5 oz. icing sugar
½ teaspoon pink food coloring
1 tablespoon whipped cream
1 oz. fresh strawberries blended
Directions:
Beat butter with sugar in a mixer until fluffy.
Stir in eggs, and vanilla then beat well.
Slowly add flour while mixing the batter.
Divide this mixture into a mini muffin tray, greased with cooking spray.
Place the muffin tray in the Instant Pot Duo.

Put on the Air Fryer lid and seal it.
Hit the "Bake Button" and select 8 minutes of cooking time, then press "Start."
Once the Instant Pot Duo beeps, remove its lid.
Meanwhile, beat the cream with the rest of the Ingredients: in a beater until fluffy.
 Add this topping to a piping bag and pipe the topping on top of the baked cupcakes.
Serve.
Nutrition:
Calories 337
Total Fat 15.9g
Saturated Fat 9.5g
Cholesterol 93mg
Sodium 118mg
Total Carbohydrate 46.3g
Dietary Fiber 0.5g
Total Sugars 33.2g
Protein 3.8g

Coconut bars

Preparation time: 45 minutes
Cooking Time: 20 minutes
Servings: 12
Ingredients:
1 ¼ cups almond flour
½ cup coconut cream
1 ½ cups coconut, flaked
1 egg yolk
¾ cup walnuts; chopped.
1 cup swerve
1 cup butter; melted
½ tsp. Vanilla extract
Directions:
Take a bowl and mix the flour with half of the swerve and half of the butter, stir well and press this on the bottom of a baking pan that fits the air fryer.
Introduce this in the air fryer and cook at 350°f for 15 minutes
Meanwhile, heat up a pan with the rest of the butter over medium heat, add the remaining swerve and the rest of the ingredients, whisk, cook for 1-2 minutes, take off the heat and cool down
Spread this well over the crust, put the pan in the air fryer again and cook at 350°f for 25 minutes.
Cool down; cut into bars and serve.
Nutrition: Calories: 182; Fat: 12g; Fiber: 2g; Carbs: 4g; Protein: 4g

Air-fried Kale Chips

Preparation Time: 10 minutes
Cooking Time: 5 minutes
Servings: 2-4
Ingredients
2 tbsps. olive oil
1 bunch of Tuscan kale, stems removed, and leaves cut into 2-inch pieces
½ tsp. ground pepper
½ tsp. Kosher salt
Directions
Toss altogether olive oil, kale leaves, salt and pepper.

Place kale in the air fryer basket and insert into the instant pot duo crisp. Attach the air fryer lid to cover and air fry for about 5 minutes at 390 degrees F, shaking air fryer basket halfway through cooking.
Once done, transfer chips to a platter, taste and adjust seasonings.
Serve warm.
Nutrition: Calories – 74 kcal; Carbohydrates – 2 g; Fat – 6.92 g; Protein – 0.83 g; Fiber - 0.07 g; Sugar – 0.67 g; Sodium – 298 mg

Instant Pot Duo Crisp - Crisp Air-Fried Pickles

Preparation time: 10 minutes
Cooking time: 10 minutes
Servings: 3
Ingredients:
1/4 cup parmesan (freshly grated
1 tsp. Garlic powder
2 cups dill pickle slices
1/2 cup bread crumbs
1 large egg (whisked with a tablespoon of water
1 tsp. Dried oregano
Ranch for dipping
Directions:
Pat pickle chips dry using paper towels.
In a medium-size mixing bowl, add parmesan, bread crumbs, garlic powder, and oregano.
Stir to mix.
One by one, dredge pickle chips in egg and then in the bread crumb mixture.
Work in batches to avoid overcrowding in the air fryer basket.
Arrange chips in a single layer.
Place air fryer basket inside the instant pot and attach the crisp air fryer.
Cook at 400 degrees Fahrenheit and cook for 10 minutes.
Serve while warm with ranch for the dip.
Nutrition: calories – 63 kcal; carbohydrates –6.85 g; fat – 2.07 g; protein – 4.31 g; fiber - 0.4g; sugar – 0.55 g; sodium – 146 mg

Broccoli Tots

Preparation Time: 10 minutes
Cooking Time: 25 minutes
Serving: 4
Ingredients:
1 lb broccoli, chopped
1/4 cup ground flaxseed
1/2 tsp garlic powder
1/2 cup flour
1 tsp salt
Directions:
Add broccoli into the microwave-safe bowl and microwave for 3 minutes.
Transfer steamed broccoli into the food processor and process until it looks like rice.
Transfer broccoli to a large bowl.
Add remaining ingredients into the bowl and mix until well combined.
Place the dehydrating tray in a multi-level air fryer basket and place basket in the instant pot.
Make small tots from broccoli mixture and place on dehydrating tray.
Seal pot with air fryer lid and select air fry mode then set the temperature to 375 F and timer for 12 minutes. Turn halfway through.

Serve and enjoy.
Nutrition:
Calories 134
Fat 2.7 g
Carbohydrates 21.7 g
Sugar 2.2 g
Protein 6.2 g
Cholesterol 0 mg

Air Fried Bananas

Preparation time: 5-10 Minutes
Cooking Time: 10 Minutes
Serving: 2-3
Ingredients: ½ cup all-purpose flour
3 egg whites
1 cup panko breadcrumbs
3 tablespoon cinnamon
8 ripe bananas, peeled and halved
3 tablespoon canola oil
Directions:
Place Instant Pot Air Fryer Crisp over kitchen platform. Press "Sauté," select "Hi" setting and press "Start." In the inner pot, add the oil and allow it to heat.
Add the breadcrumbs and stir-cook for 2-3 minutes until evenly golden. Set aside in a bowl. Take two bowls, in one bowl beat the egg whites and in another, add the flour.
Coat the bananas with egg mixture, flour mixture, and then with the crumbs.
In the inner pot, place the Air Fryer basket. In the basket, add the bananas.
Close the Crisp Lid and press the "Bake" setting. Set temperature to 280°F and set the timer to 10 minutes. Press "Start."
Open the Crisp Lid after cooking time is over. Serve warm.
Nutrition: **Calories: 198**
Fat: 9g
Saturated Fat: 3g
Trans Fat: 0g
Carbohydrates: 14g
Fiber: 2g
Sodium: 358mg
Protein: 3.5g

Curried Fries

Preparation Time: 10 minutes
Cooking Time: 20 minutes
Serving: 3
Ingredients:
2 small sweet potatoes, peel and cut into fry's shape
1/2 tsp curry powder
2 tbsp olive oil
1/4 tsp coriander
1/4 tsp sea salt
Directions:
Add all ingredients into the large mixing bowl and toss well.

Spray instant pot multi-level air fryer basket with cooking spray.
Transfer sweet potato fries into the air fryer basket and place basket into the instant pot.
Seal pot with air fryer lid and select air fry mode then set the temperature to 370 F and timer for 20 minutes. Stir halfway through.
Serve and enjoy.
Nutrition:
Calories 140
Fat 9.5 g
Carbohydrates 14.1 g
Sugar 0.3 g
Protein 0.8 g
Cholesterol 0 mg

Easy Salmon Bites

Preparation Time: 10 minutes
Cooking Time: 12 minutes
Serving: 4
Ingredients:
1 lb salmon fillets, boneless and cut into chunks
2 tsp olive oil
1/4 tsp cayenne
1/2 tsp chili powder
1 tsp dried dill
Pepper
Salt
Directions:
Add salmon and remaining ingredients into the large bowl and toss well.
Spray instant pot multi-level air fryer basket with cooking spray.
Add salmon chunks into the air fryer basket and place basket into the instant pot.
Seal pot with air fryer lid and select air fry mode then set the temperature to 350 F and timer for 12 minutes. Turn salmon chunks halfway through.
Serve and enjoy.
Nutrition:
Calories 172
Fat 9.4 g
Carbohydrates 0.4 g
Sugar 0 g
Protein 22.1 g
Cholesterol 50 mg

Blueberry Cream

Preparation time: 24 minutes
Cooking Time: 20 minutes
Servings: 6
Ingredients:
2 cups blueberries
2 tbsp. Swerve
2 tbsp. Water
1 tsp. Vanilla extract

Juice of ½ lemon
Directions:
Take a bowl and mix all the ingredients and whisk well.
Divide this into 6 ramekins, put them in the air fryer and cook at 340°f for 20 minutes.
Cool down and serve
Nutrition: Calories: 123; Fat: 2g; Fiber: 2g; Carbs: 4g; Protein: 3g

Coconut Donuts

Preparation time: 20 minutes
Cooking Time: 20 minutes
Servings: 4
Ingredients:
8 oz. Coconut flour
4 oz. Coconut milk
1 egg, whisked
2 tbsp. Stevia
2 ½ tbsp. Butter; melted
1 tsp. Baking powder
Directions:
Take a bowl and mix all the ingredients and whisk well.
Shape donuts from this mix and place them in your air fryer's basket and cook at 370°f for 15 minutes.
Serve warm
Nutrition: Calories: 190; Fat: 12g; Fiber: 1g; Carbs: 4g; Protein: 6g

Cocoa and Nuts Bombs

Preparation time: 13 minutes
Cooking Time: 20 minutes
Servings: 12
Ingredients:
2 cups macadamia nuts; chopped.
¼ cup cocoa powder
1/3 cup swerve
4 tbsp. Coconut oil; melted
1 tsp. Vanilla extract
Directions:
Take a bowl and mix all the ingredients and whisk well.
Shape medium balls out of this mix, place them in your air fryer and cook at 300°f for 8 minutes.
Serve cold
Nutrition: Calories: 120; Fat: 12g; Fiber: 1g; Carbs: 2g; Protein: 1g

Vanilla Pumpkin Pudding

Preparation Time: 10 minutes
Cooking Time: 20 minutes
Serving: 6
Ingredients:
2 eggs
1/2 cup almond milk
1/2 tsp vanilla
1/2 tsp pumpkin pie spice

14 oz pumpkin puree
1/4 cup sugar
Directions:
Grease 6-inch baking dish with cooking spray and set aside.
In a large bowl, whisk eggs with remaining ingredients.
Pour mixture into the prepared dish and cover with foil.
Pour 1 1/2 cups of water into the inner pot of instant pot duo crisp then place a steamer rack in the pot.
Place dish on top of the steamer rack.
Seal the pot with pressure cooking lid and cook on high for 20 minutes.
Once done, allow to release pressure naturally for 10 minutes then release remaining pressure using a quick release. Remove lid.
Carefully remove dish from the pot and let it cool completely then place in the refrigerator for 5 hours before serving.
Serve and enjoy.
Nutrition:
Calories 122
Fat 6.4 g
Carbohydrates 15 g
Sugar 11.3 g
Protein 3.1 g
Cholesterol 55 mg

Chocolate Rice Pudding

Preparation Time: 10 minutes
Cooking Time: 15 minutes
Serving: 6
Ingredients:
2 eggs, beaten
1 cup rice, rinsed
2 tbsp cocoa powder
1/2 tsp vanilla
5 cups of coconut milk
1 tbsp coconut oil
1/2 cup sugar
Directions:
Add all ingredients into the inner pot of instant pot duo crisp and set pot on sauté mode. Stir constantly and bring to boil.
Seal the pot with pressure cooking lid and cook on high for 15 minutes.
Once done, allow to release pressure naturally. Remove lid.
Stir well and serve.
Nutrition:
Calories 681
Fat 51.9 g
Carbohydrates 53.5 g
Sugar 23.6 g
Protein 9 g
Cholesterol 55 mg

Choco Fudge

Preparation Time: 10 minutes
Cooking Time: 15 minutes
Serving: 8
Ingredients:
5 eggs
1/2 cup cocoa powder
1/2 cup dark chocolate, chopped
2 cups almond flour
1 tsp baking soda
1/2 tsp vanilla
2 tbsp erythritol
3/4 tsp baking powder
1/2 cup almond milk
Pinch of salt
Directions:
Add all dry ingredients into the large bowl and mix to combine.
Add remaining ingredients and beat using a blender until well combined.
Pour 2 cups of water into the inner pot of instant pot duo crisp then place steamer rack in the pot.
Pour batter in the oven-safe baking dish and place on top of the steamer rack.
Seal the pot with pressure cooking lid and cook on high for 15 minutes.
Once done, release pressure using a quick release. Remove lid.
Serve and enjoy.
Nutrition:
Calories 311
Fat 23.4 g
Carbohydrates 17.7 g
Sugar 7.5 g
Protein 11.6 g
Cholesterol 105 mg

Delicious Lime Pudding

Preparation Time: 10 minutes
Cooking Time: 3 minutes
Serving: 4
Ingredients:
1/4 cup coconut milk
3/4 tsp lime zest, grated
1/2 tsp orange extract
1 tbsp swerve
1/4 cup heavy whipping cream
1/4 cup coconut cream
1 tsp agar powder
1 tbsp coconut oil
Directions:
Add coconut oil into the inner pot of instant pot duo crisp and set the pot on sauté mode.
Add coconut milk, whipping cream, and coconut cream to the pot and stir constantly.
Add orange extract, swerve and agar powder. Stir constantly and cook for 2-3 minutes.
Turn off the pot and pour pot mixture into the ramekins.
Sprinkle lime zest on top of each ramekin.
Place ramekins in the fridge for 1-2 hours.
Serve and enjoy.

Nutrition:
Calories 159
Fat 12.8 g
Carbohydrates 11.6 g
Sugar 10.1 g
Protein 0.7 g
Cholesterol 10 mg

Buckwheat Cobbler

Preparation Time: 10 minutes
Cooking Time: 12 minutes
Serving: 6
Ingredients:
1/2 cup dry buckwheat
2 1/2 lbs apples, cut into chunks
1/4 tsp nutmeg
1/4 tsp ground ginger
1 1/2 tsp cinnamon
1 1/2 cups water
1/4 cup dates, chopped
Directions:
Add all ingredients into the inner pot instant pot duo crisp and stir well.
Seal the pot with pressure cooking lid and cook on high for 12 minutes.
Once done, release pressure using a quick release. Remove lid.
Stir well and serve.
Nutrition:
Calories 119
Fat 0.6 g
Carbohydrates 29.2 g
Sugar 14.4 g
Protein 2.1 g

Baked Plums

Preparation time: 25 minutes
Cooking Time: 20 minutes
Servings: 6
Ingredients:
6 plums; cut into wedges
10 drops stevia
Zest of 1 lemon, grated
2 tbsp. Water
1 tsp. Ginger, ground
½ tsp. Cinnamon powder
Directions:
In a pan that fits the air fryer, combine the plums with the rest of the ingredients, toss gently.
Put the pan in the air fryer and cook at 360°f for 20 minutes.
Serve cold
Nutrition: Calories: 170; Fat: 5g; Fiber: 1g; Carbs: 3g; Protein: 5g

Crispy Potatoes in Instant Pot Duo Crisp+ Crisp Air Fryer

Preparation time: 10 minutes
Cooking time: 20 minutes
Servings: 4
Ingredients:
1 tbsp. Extra-virgin olive oil
1 lb. Of baby potatoes (halved
1 tsp. Garlic powder
1 tsp. Cajun seasoning (optional
1 tsp. Italian seasoning
Freshly chopped parsley, for garnish
Salt to taste
Black pepper (freshly ground
Lemon wedge for garnish
Directions:
Toss potatoes in oil in a large bowl with garlic powder, cajun and Italian seasonings.
Add salt and pepper to taste
Place potatoes in the air fryer basket of your instant pot duo crisp and attach the crisp air fryer lid. Cook for 10 minutes at 400 degrees Fahrenheit.
Shake the air fryer basket to stir potatoes and cook for another 10 minutes until golden brown.
Remove from the instant pot and serve on a plate.
Squeeze lemon juice over potatoes and garnish with parsley to serve.
Nutrition: calories – 116 kcal; carbohydrates –22.17 g; fat – 1.73 g; protein – 2.94 g; fiber - 3.3 g; sugar – 1.19 g; sodium – 150 mg

Dill Pickle Fries

Preparation time: 15 minutes
Cooking time: 28 minutes
Servings: 12
Ingredients:
1½ (16-ouncesjars spicy dill pickle spears, drained and pat dried
1 cup all-purpose flour
1 egg, beaten
¼ cup milk
1 cup panko breadcrumbs
½ teaspoon paprika
Directions:
Preheat the air fryer to 440 o f and grease an air fryer basket.
Place flour and paprika in a shallow dish and whisk the egg with milk in a second dish.
Place the breadcrumbs in a third shallow dish.
Coat the pickle spears evenly in flour and dip in the egg mixture.
Roll into the breadcrumbs evenly and arrange half of the pickle spears in an air fryer basket.
Cook for about 14 minutes, flipping once in between.
Repeat with the remaining pickle spears and dish out to serve warm.
Nutrition: Calories: 76, fat: 0.8g, carbohydrates: 14.8g, sugar: 1.2g, protein: 2.7g, sodium: 550mg

Broccoli Nuggets

Preparation Time: 10 minutes
Cooking Time: 15 minutes
Serving: 4
Ingredients:
2 cups broccoli florets, cooked until soft
1 cup cheddar cheese, shredded
1/4 cup almond flour
2 egg whites
1/8 tsp salt
Directions:
Add cooked broccoli into the bowl and using masher mash broccoli into the small pieces.
Add remaining ingredients to the bowl and stir to combine.
Place the dehydrating tray in a multi-level air fryer basket and place basket in the instant pot.
Make nuggets from broccoli mixture and place on dehydrating tray.
Seal pot with air fryer lid and select air fry mode then set the temperature to 425 F and timer for 15 minutes. Turn halfway through.
Serve and enjoy.
Nutrition:
Calories 180
Fat 12.9 g
Carbohydrates 5 g
Sugar 1 g
Protein 11.6 g
Cholesterol 30 mg

Simple Shrimp Kabobs

Preparation Time: 10 minutes
Cooking Time: 8 minutes
Serving: 2
Ingredients:
1 cup shrimp
1 lemon juice
1 garlic clove, minced
Pepper
Salt
Directions:
Add shrimp, lemon juice, garlic, pepper, and salt into the bowl and toss well.
Spray instant pot multi-level air fryer basket with cooking spray.
Thread shrimp onto the soaked wooden skewers and place them into the air fryer basket and place basket into the instant pot.
Seal pot with air fryer lid and select air fry mode then set the temperature to 350 F and timer for 8 minutes. Stir halfway through.
Serve and enjoy.
Nutrition:
Calories 201
Fat 3 g
Carbohydrates 3.5 g
Sugar 0.5 g
Protein 37.3 g
Cholesterol 342 mg

French Fries in Instant Pot Air Fryer

Preparation: 5 minutes
Cooking time: 12 minutes
Servings: 4
Ingredients:
2 pounds (6 nos.parsnips
¼ cup olive oil
¼ cup of water
¼ cup almond flour
1 teaspoon salt
Olive oil cooking spray
Directions:
Wash, peel the parsnips and pat dry before you chop them into ½ inch sizes
In a large bowl to mix the almond flour, water, salt, and olive oil.
Combine it well until there are no lumps at all.
Add the parsnips to this mix and stir it well until everything gets a proper coating.
Place the coated parsnips in the air fryer basket and put the basket in the inner pot of the instant pot air fryer.
Close the crisp cover.
Now in the air fry mode and set the temperature at 390° f and keep the timer for 12 minutes.
Press start to begin the frying.
It is a good habit if you can open the crisp lid and shake the basket for even cooking.
Spritz some cooking spray while shaking the basket, which can help to improve the crispness.
Keep cooking 2 more minutes if you don't find it crispy enough.
Serve it hot.
Nutrition: Calories 281, total fat: 14.2g, saturated fat: 2g, trans fat: 0g, cholesterol: 0mg, sodium: 605mg, total carbs: 39g, dietary fiber: 8g, protein: 3g, sugars: 11g

Radish Chips

Preparation Time: 10 minutes
Cooking Time: 12 minutes
Serving: 2
Ingredients:
1/2 lb radishes, sliced thinly
1/2 tsp red pepper flakes, crushed
1/2 tbsp olive oil
1/2 tbsp lime juice
Pepper
Salt
Directions:
Add radish slices and remaining ingredients into the mixing bowl and toss well.
Spray instant pot multi-level air fryer basket with cooking spray.
Add radish slices into the air fryer basket and place basket into the instant pot.
Seal pot with air fryer lid and select air fry mode then set the temperature to 380 F and timer for 12 minutes. Stir halfway through.
Serve and enjoy.
Nutrition:
Calories 52
Fat 3.7 g
Carbohydrates 5.1 g
Sugar 2.4 g
Protein 0.9 g
Cholesterol 0 mg

Lemon Cupcakes

Preparation Time: 10 minutes
Cooking Time: 15 minutes
Serving: 12
Ingredients:
2 eggs
1 tbsp fresh lemon juice
1 tbsp lemon zest, grated
1/4 cup milk
1 tsp vanilla
3/4 cup sugar
1/4 cup butter
1 1/2 tsp baking powder
1 1/4 cups all-purpose flour
1/4 tsp salt
Directions:
In a small bowl, mix together flour, baking powder, and salt and set aside.
In a mixing bowl, beat together sugar and butter until well combined.
Add eggs, lemon juice, lemon zest, milk, and vanilla and beat until combined.
Add flour mixture and stir to combine.
Pour batter into the 12 silicone muffin molds.
Place the dehydrating tray in a multi-level air fryer basket and place basket in the instant pot.
Place 6 silicone muffin molds on dehydrating tray.
Seal pot with air fryer lid and select bake mode then set the temperature to 350 F and timer for 15 minutes.
Bake remaining cupcakes using the same method.
Serve and enjoy.
Nutrition:
Calories 143
Fat 4.8 g
Carbohydrates 23.2 g
Sugar 12.9 g
Protein 2.5 g
Cholesterol 38 mg

Apple Crisp

Preparation Time: 10 minutes
Cooking Time: 9 minutes
Serving: 3
Ingredients:
4 large apples, cored and sliced
1/4 cup water
For topping:
1/4 cup butter, melted
1/2 tsp nutmeg
1 1/2 tsp ground cinnamon
1/2 cup all-purpose flour
1/2 cup brown sugar
1 cup old fashioned oats
1/2 tsp salt
Directions:
Add water and apple slices into the instant pot.
Mix together all topping ingredients and sprinkle over apple mixture.

Seal the pot with pressure cooking lid and cook on high pressure for 5 minutes.
Once done, allow to release pressure naturally for 5 minutes then release remaining pressure using quick release. Remove lid.
Seal pot with air fryer lid and select broil mode and set timer for 4 minutes.
Serve and enjoy.
Nutrition:
Calories 671
Fat 19.7 g
Carbohydrates 117.6 g
Sugar 56 g
Protein 9.9 g
Cholesterol 41 mg

Parmesan Truffle Fries

Preparation time:10 minutes
Cooking time: 15 minutes
Serving 2
7 Ingredients
2 large gold potatoes, peeled
1 tablespoon parsley flakes
1/2 teaspoon garlic powder
1 teaspoon black pepper, crushed
1/2 teaspoon truffle salt
olive oil spray
2 tablespoons parmesan cheese
Directions
1. Use a mandoline with a French fry setting, slice the whole potato using the spring-form handle to slice into French fries.
2. Place sliced potatoes in a bowl and spray with olive spray for about 3 seconds. Add garlic powder, black pepper, and parsley flakes.
3. Place all of them into the Instant Pot Duo Crisp Air Fryer Basket.
4. Close the Air Fryer lid and cook for about 5 minutes at 390°F.
5. Take out the basket and flip fries in order to evenly cook the fries. Cook another 8 minutes and remove from the Air Fryer and add to a bowl. Sprinkle with truffle salt and parmesan cheese.
Nutrition: Calories 188, Total Fat 10g, Total Carbs 14.3g, Protein 10.3g

Moist Chocolate Cake

Preparation Time: 10 minutes
Cooking Time: 25 minutes
Serving: 8
Ingredients:
1 egg
1 tsp baking soda
1 tsp baking powder
3 tbsp cocoa powder
1 cup of sugar
1 cup all-purpose flour
1 tsp vanilla
1/4 cup butter
1 cup boiling water

1/4 tsp salt
Directions:
Spray a baking dish with cooking spray and set aside.
Add butter and boiling water in a mixing bowl and beat until butter is melted.
Add vanilla and egg and beat until well combined.
In a medium bowl, mix together flour, baking soda, baking powder, cocoa powder, sugar, and salt.
Add egg mixture into the flour mixture and beat until well combined.
Pour batter in prepared baking dish.
Place steam rack in the instant pot then places a baking dish on top of the rack.
Seal pot with air fryer lid and select bake mode then set the temperature to 350 F and timer for 25 minutes.
Serve and enjoy.
Nutrition:
Calories 216
Fat 6.7 g
Carbohydrates 38.5 g
Sugar 25.2 g
Protein 2.7 g
Cholesterol 36 mg

Raspberry Bites

Preparation time: 37 minutes
Cooking Time: 5 minutes
Servings: 10
Ingredients:
2 oz. Full-fat cream cheese; softened.
1 large egg.
1 cup blanched finely ground almond flour.
3 tbsp. Granular swerve.
1 tsp. Baking powder.
10 tsp. Sugar-free raspberry preserves.
Directions:
Mix all ingredients except preServing in a large bowl until a wet dough form.
Place the bowl in the freezer for 20 minutes until dough is cool and able to roll into a ball.
Roll dough into ten balls and press gently in the center of each ball. Place 1 tsp. PreServing in the center of each ball.
Cut a piece of parchment to fit your air fryer basket. Place each danish bite on the parchment, pressing down gently to flatten the bottom.
Adjust the temperature to 400 degrees f and set the timer for 7 minutes. Allow to cool completely before moving, or they will crumble.
Nutrition: Calories: 96; Protein: 3.4g; Fiber: 1.3g; Fat: 7.7g

Endives and Walnuts

Preparation time: 20 minutes
Cooking Time: 5 minutes
Servings: 4
Ingredients:
4 endives, trimmed
½ cup walnuts; chopped.
3 tbsp. Olive oil
2 tbsp. White vinegar
1 tsp. Mustard

A pinch of salt and black pepper
Directions:
Take a bowl and mix the oil with salt, pepper, mustard and vinegar and whisk really well.
Add the endives, toss and transfer them to your air fryer's basket. Cook at 350°f for 15 minutes, divide between plates and serve with walnuts sprinkled on top
Nutrition: Calories: 154; Fat: 4g; Fiber: 3g; Carbs: 6g; Protein: 7g

Air-fried Toasted Sticks

Preparation Time: 5 minutes
Cooking Time: 8 minutes
Servings: 6
Ingredients
⅓ cup heavy cream
2 large eggs
⅓ cup whole milk
¼ tsp. ground cinnamon
1 tsp. maple syrup
3 tbsps. granulated sugar
6 thick pullman slices, cut into 3 parts (alternative: brioche or white loaf)
½ tsp. pure vanilla extract
Kosher salt to taste
Directions
Beat eggs and add sugar, milk, cream, vanilla, cinnamon with salt in a large shallow baking dish. Coat bread with the mixture, turning for even coating at all sides.
Line air fryer basket with parchment paper before arranging French toasts sticks inside. Avoid overcrowding and work in batches when necessary.
Place the basket inside the instant pot, attach the air fryer lid to the pressure cooker and set to cook at 370 degrees F for 8 minutes, tossing halfway through for even cooking.
Drizzle maple syrup over toast and serve warm.
Nutrition: Calories – 132 kcal; Carbohydrates – 18.37 g; Fat – 5.03 g; Protein – 3.21 g; Sugar – 7.05 g; Sodium – 110 mg

Currant Cream

Preparation time: 35 minutes
Cooking Time: 8 minutes
Servings: 4
Ingredients:
7 cups red currants
6 sage leaves
1 cup water
1 cup swerve
Directions:
In a pan that fits your air fryer, mix all the ingredients, toss, put the pan in the fryer and cook at 330°f for 30 minutes
Discard sage leaves.
Divide into cups and serve cold.
Nutrition: Calories: 171; Fat: 4g; Fiber: 2g; Carbs: 3g; Protein: 6g

Plum Cake

Preparation time: 40 minutes
Cooking Time: 8 minutes
Servings: 8
Ingredients:
4 plums, pitted and chopped.
1 ½ cups almond flour
½ cup coconut flour
¾ cup almond milk
½ cup butter, soft
3 eggs
½ cup swerve
1 tbsp. Vanilla extract
2 tsp. Baking powder
¼ tsp. Almond extract
Directions:
Take a bowl and mix all the ingredients and whisk well.
Pour this into a cake pan that fits the air fryer after you've lined it with parchment paper, put the pan in the machine and cook at 370°f for 30 minutes.
Cool the cake down, slice and serve
Nutrition: Calories: 183; Fat: 4g; Fiber: 3g; Carbs: 4g; Protein: 7g

Crumbly Fruit Cakes

Preparation time:10 minutes
Cooking Time: 15 minutes
Serving: 4
Ingredients:
4 oz. plain flour
2 oz. butter
1 oz. caster sugar
1 oz. gluten-free oats
1 oz. brown sugar
4 plums, cored and chopped
1 small apple, cored and chopped
1 small pear, cored and chopped
1 small peach, cored and chopped
handful blueberries, quartered
1 tablespoon honey
Directions:
Add all the fruits to a bowl and divide them into 4 ramekins.
Drizzle honey and brown sugar over the fruits in each ramekin.
Whisk flour with caster sugar and butter in a mixing bowl to get a crumbly mixture.
Divide this crumble into the ramekins then place these ramekins in the Instant Pot Duo.
Put on the Air Fryer lid and seal it.
Hit the "Air fry Button" and select 10 minutes of cooking time, then press "Start."
Once the Instant Pot Duo beeps, switch it Broil mode and broil for 5 minutes.
Remove the lid and serve.
Nutrition:
Calories 388
Total Fat 11.4g
Saturated Fat 6.5g
Cholesterol 27mg
Sodium 75mg

Total Carbohydrate 70.9g
Dietary Fiber 6.2g
Total Sugars 39.4g

Breaded Avocado Fries

Preparation time:10 minutes
Cooking Time: 7 minutes
Serving: 4
Ingredients:
1/4 cup all-purpose flour
1/2 teaspoon ground black pepper
1/4 teaspoon salt
1 egg
1 teaspoon water
1 ripe avocado, peeled, pitted and sliced
1/2 cup panko breadcrumbs
cooking spray
Directions:
Whisk flour with salt and black pepper in one bowl.
Beat egg with water in another and spread the crumbs in a shallow tray.
First coat the avocado slices with the flour mixture then dip them into the egg.
Drop off the excess and coat the avocado with panko crumbs liberally.
Place all the coated slices in the Air Fryer Basket and spray them with cooking oil.
Set the Air Fryer Basket inside the Instant Pot Duo.
Put on the Air Fryer lid and seal it.
Hit the "Air fry Button" and select 7 minutes of cooking time, then press "Start."
Flip the fries after 4 minutes of cooking and resume cooking.
Once the Instant Pot Duo beeps, remove its lid.
Serve fresh.
Nutrition:
Calories 201
Total Fat 11.7g
Saturated Fat 2.6g
Cholesterol 41mg
Sodium 265mg
Total Carbohydrate 20.3g
Dietary Fiber 4.3g
Total Sugars 1.2g
Protein 5g

Cinnamon Maple Chickpeas

Preparation Time: 10 minutes
Cooking Time: 12 minutes
Serving: 4
Ingredients:
14 oz can chickpeas, rinsed, drained and pat dry
1 tsp ground cinnamon
1 tbsp brown sugar
1 tbsp maple syrup
1 tbsp olive oil

Pepper
Salt
Directions:
Place the dehydrating tray in a multi-level air fryer basket and place basket in the instant pot.
Spread chickpeas on dehydrating tray.
Seal pot with air fryer lid and select air fry mode then set the temperature to 375 F and timer for 12 minutes. Stir halfway through.
In a mixing bowl, mix together cinnamon, brown sugar, maple syrup, oil, pepper, and salt. Add chickpeas and toss well to coat.
Serve and enjoy.
Nutrition:
Calories 171
Fat 4.7 g
Carbohydrates 28.5 g
Sugar 5.2 g
Protein 4.9 g
Cholesterol 0 mg

Fluffy Baked Donuts

Preparation Time: 10 minutes
Cooking Time: 8 minutes
Serving: 6
Ingredients:
2 eggs
2 tbsp butter, melted
1 tsp vanilla
3/4 cup buttermilk
1/4 tsp cinnamon
1/4 tsp nutmeg
2 tsp baking powder
3/4 cup sugar
2 cups flour
1 tsp salt
Directions:
In a mixing bowl, whisk eggs, butter, vanilla, and buttermilk until well combined.
In a large bowl, mix together flour, cinnamon, nutmeg, baking powder, sugar, and salt.
Pour egg mixture into the flour mixture and mix until well combined.
Pour batter into the 6 silicone donut molds.
Place the dehydrating tray in a multi-level air fryer basket and place basket in the instant pot.
Place 4 silicone donut molds on dehydrating tray.
Seal pot with air fryer lid and select bake mode then set the temperature to 325 F and timer for 8 minutes.
Bake remaining donut using the same method.
Serve and enjoy.
Nutrition:
Calories 317
Fat 6 g
Carbohydrates 59.4 g
Sugar 26.8 g
Protein 7.2 g
Cholesterol 66 mg

Healthy Eggplant Chips

Preparation Time: 10 minutes
Cooking Time: 30 minutes
Serving: 2
Ingredients:
1 eggplant, sliced 1/4-inch thick
2 tbsp rosemary, chopped
1/2 cup parmesan cheese, grated
Pepper
Salt
Directions:
Add eggplant slices, cheese, rosemary, pepper, and salt into the mixing bowl and toss well.
Place the dehydrating tray in a multi-level air fryer basket and place basket in the instant pot.
Arrange eggplant slices on the dehydrating tray.
Seal pot with air fryer lid and select air fry mode then set the temperature to 400 F and timer for 30 minutes. Turn eggplant slices halfway through.
Serve and enjoy.
Nutrition:
Calories 141
Fat 5.7 g
Carbohydrates 16.4 g
Sugar 6.9 g
Protein 9.6 g
Cholesterol 16 mg

Crispy Roasted Cashews

Preparation Time: 10 minutes
Cooking Time: 6 minutes
Serving: 3
Ingredients:
1 cup cashews
1/4 tsp onion powder
1/4 tsp garlic powder
1/2 tsp nutritional yeast
1 tbsp rice flour
1 tbsp olive oil
Pepper
Salt
Directions:
Add cashews and remaining ingredients into the large bowl and toss well.
Place the dehydrating tray in a multi-level air fryer basket and place basket in the instant pot.
Spread cashews on dehydrating tray.
Seal pot with air fryer lid and select air fry mode then set the temperature to 350 F and timer for 6 minutes. Stir halfway through.
Serve and enjoy.
Nutrition:
Calories 318
Fat 25.9 g
Carbohydrates 18.2 g
Sugar 2.4 g
Protein 7.5 g

Cholesterol 0 mg

Vanilla Brownie

Preparation Time: 10 minutes
Cooking Time: 20 minutes
Serving: 4
Ingredients:
1 egg
1/4 cup cocoa powder
1 tsp vanilla
2 tbsp olive oil
1/3 cup flour
2 tbsp sugar
1/4 cup chocolate chips
Directions:
Spray a baking dish with cooking spray and set aside.
In a bowl, whisk egg, vanilla, oil, and sugar.
In a mixing bowl, mix together flour and cocoa powder.
Add egg mixture into the flour mixture and mix until well combined.
Pour batter into the prepared baking dish.
Place steam rack in the instant pot then place baking dish on top of the rack.
Seal pot with air fryer lid and select bake mode then set the temperature to 320 F and timer for 20 minutes.
Serve and enjoy.
Nutrition:
Calories 207
Fat 12 g
Carbohydrates 23.4 g
Sugar 11.7 g
Protein 4.2 g
Cholesterol 43 mg

Crunchy Zucchini Chips

Preparation time:5 Minutes
Cooking Time: 12 Minutes
Serving: 4
Ingredients:
1 medium zucchini, thinly sliced
3/4 cup Parmesan cheese, grated
1 cup Panko breadcrumbs
1 large egg, beaten
Directions:
In a mixing bowl, add the Parmesan cheese and panko breadcrumbs. Combine the ingredients to mix well with each other.
In a mixing bowl, beat the eggs. Coat the zucchini slices with the eggs and then with the crumb mixture. Spray the slices with some cooking spray.
Place Instant Pot Air Fryer Crisp over kitchen platform. Press Air Fry set the temperature to 400°F and set the timer to 5 minutes to preheat. Press "Start" and allow it to preheat for 5 minutes.
In the inner pot, place the Air Fryer basket. Line it with a parchment paper, add the zucchini slices.

Close the Crisp Lid and press the "Air Fry" setting. Set temperature to 350°F and set the timer to 10-12 minutes. Press "Start."
Halfway down, open the Crisp Lid, shake the basket and close the lid to continue cooking for the remaining time.
Open the Crisp Lid after cooking time is over. Serve warm.
Nutrition: Calories:
Fat: g
Saturated Fat: g
Trans Fat: 0g
Carbohydrates: g
Fiber: g
Sodium: mg
Protein: g

Fried Hot Dogs

Preparation time:3 minutes
Cooking time: 7 minutes
Serving 2
3 Ingredients
2 hot dogs
2 hot dog buns
2 tablespoons grated cheese
Directions
1. Preheat Instant Pot Duo Crisp Air Fryer to 390°F.
2. Place two hot dogs into the air fryer basket.
3. Close the Air Fryer lid and cook for about 5 minutes.
4. Remove the hot dog from the air fryer.
5. Place the hot dog on a bun, add cheese if desired.
6. Place dressed hot dog into the Instant Pot Duo Crisp Air Fryer and cook for an additional 2 minutes.
Nutrition: Calories 843, Total Fat 13g, Total Carbs 29g, Protein 12g

---

Sweet Potato Chips

Preparation time:10 minutes
Cooking time: 50 minutes
Serving 2
4 Ingredients
2 medium-sized Sweet Potatoes thinly sliced
¼ cup of Olive Oil
1 teaspoon of ground Cinnamon optional
Salt and Pepper to taste
Directions
1. Thinly slice the sweet potatoes. Use a mandolin or a food processor.
2. Soak the sweet potato slices in the cold water for thirty minutes.
3. Drain and pat dry the slices thoroughly. Repeat it multiple times till completely dry. This is an important step to ensure crispy chips.
4. Toss the sweet potato slices with salt, olive oil, pepper, and cinnamon (if using), ensuring every slice is coated with the oil.
5. Place the slices into the Instant Pot Duo Crisp Air Fryer Basket.
6. Press the start button to air fry the sweet potatoes at 390°F for twenty minutes, giving the basket a shake every seven to eight minutes for even cooking. If it is still not crisp, air fry for an additional 5 minutes.
7. Serve it hot with ketchup.
Nutrition: Calories 327, Total Fat 25.2g, Total Carbs 23g, Protein 2g

Cauliflower Fritters

Preparation time: 5-10 Minutes
Cooking Time: 8 Minutes
Serving: 6-8
Ingredients: 1/3 cup shredded mozzarella cheese
1/3 cup shredded sharp cheddar cheese
½ cup chopped parsley
1 cup Italian breadcrumbs
3 chopped scallions
1 head of cauliflower, cut into florets
1 egg
2 minced garlic cloves
Directions:
Blend the florets into a blender to make the rice like structure. Add in a bowl. Mix in the pepper, salt, egg, cheeses, breadcrumbs, garlic, and scallions. Prepare 15 patties from the mixture. Coat them with some cooking spray.
Place Instant Pot Air Fryer Crisp over kitchen platform. Press Air Fry, set the temperature to 400°F and set the timer to 5 minutes to preheat. Press "Start" and allow it to preheat for 5 minutes.
In the inner pot, place the Air Fryer basket. In the basket, add the patties.
Close the Crisp Lid and press the "Air Fry" setting. Set temperature to 390°F and set the timer to 8 minutes. Press "Start."
Halfway down, open the Crisp Lid, shake the basket and close the lid to continue cooking for the remaining time.
Open the Crisp Lid after cooking time is over. Serve warm.
Nutrition: Calories: 235
Fat: 19g
Saturated Fat: 8g
Trans Fat: 0g
Carbohydrates: 31g
Fiber: 5g
Sodium: 542mg
Protein: 6g

Buffalo Chicken Strips

Preparation time: 10 minutes
Cooking Time: 8 minutes
Serving: 4
Ingredients:
1/2 cup Greek yogurt
1/4 cup egg
1 ½ tablespoon hot sauce
1 cup panko breadcrumbs
1 tablespoon sweet paprika
1 tablespoon garlic pepper seasoning
1 tablespoon cayenne pepper
1-pound chicken breasts, cut into strips
Directions:
Mix Greek yogurt with hot sauce and egg in a bowl.
Whisk breadcrumbs with garlic powder, cayenne pepper, and paprika in another bowl.
First, dip the chicken strips in the yogurt sauce then coat them with the crumb's mixture.

Place the coated strips in the Air Fryer Basket and spray them with cooking oil.
Set the Air Fryer Basket inside the Instant Pot Duo.
Put on the Air Fryer lid and seal it.
Hit the "Air fry Button" and select 16 minutes of cooking time, then press "Start."
Flip the chicken strips after 8 minutes of cooking then resume Air fearing.
Once the Instant Pot Duo beeps, remove its lid.
Serve.
Nutrition:
Calories 368
Total Fat 11.8g
Saturated Fat 3.2g
Cholesterol 157mg
Sodium 413mg
Total Carbohydrate 23.5g
Dietary Fiber 2.5g
Total Sugars 3.1g
Protein 40.4g

Conclusion

The new instant pot air fryer lid is one of the versatile cooking appliances available now in the market. Using this lid, you can easily convert your instant pot into the air fryer. You never need to purchase another air fryer which will help to reduce your cost and saves your money.

With those many recipes and a comprehensive guideline about the Instant Pot Duo Crisp, now you know how to put to its best use and enjoy a range of flavorsome crispy meals in no time. this ten in one multipurpose kitchen miracle has brought much-wanted peace and comfort to the lives of the homemakers who can now cook a healthy and delicious meal for their family, in no time. The different segment of this book provides a step by step method to cook a variety of meals ranging from breakfast, poultry, meat, vegetarian, snacks and much more. Get this latest hit of the Instant Pot series and bring convenience to your kitchen floor now!

This book is dedicated to all beginners that aim to master cooking at home. This book includes easy to prepare recipes for all meal types to effortlessly prepared using automatic cooking functions; that way, each beginner can effortlessly prepare the recipes without any challenges. I ascertain that the introduction about Instant Pot Air Fryer Crisp will help all the readers to know everything about this new cooking appliance.

Enjoy your time cooking with Instant Pot Air Fryer Crisp!

Made in the USA
Monee, IL
29 June 2021